RUNNING
WITH
WOLVES

A Woman's Memoir of Sex, Scandal and Seduction

GAIL THACKRAY

Printed in the United States of America

Thackray, Gail

Running with wolves: A Woman's Memoir of Sex, Scandal and Seduction / by Gail Thackray

ISBN-13: 978-1-948358-07-1

Layout and design by Teagarden Designs

Published by Indian Springs Publishing

More information about the book and Gail Thackray, as well as press or speaking engagement inquiries:

www.RunningWithWolvesBook.com

Contents

1. It's a Mad, Mad World 6

2. Unlikely Pinup Model 14

3. Those Sex Crazed Americans 22

4. Money in the Trash 27

5. Big Apple Sex Slave 39

6. Sex, Drugs & The Playboy Mansion 46

7. Penis Pump Tester 54

8. Guccione and Owning it All 60

9. Date with a Prince 72

10. Shotgun Wedding 79

11. Dirty Little 900 Secret 85

12. Some Men are Just Weird 91

13. Meeting the Phone Sex "Investors" 97

14. Shooting Sexy Grans 107

15. Milk Money 118

16. Women with Agendas 126

17. A Walk on the Sleazy Side 134

18. Hollywood Casting Couch 137

19. The Phone Sex Shakedown 142

20. Creating Barely Legal 149

21. My Exciting Sex Life 158

22. Stupid! Stupid! Stupid! List 174

23. 50 Ways to Leave Your Lover 178

24. Bait at the Swing Club & the FTC 184

25. The Gold Rush 194

26. Teaching Hollywood the Web 202

27. Scarlet Letters 207

28. An American Succexxx Story 218

29. Panama–Players & Hookers 223

30. An Insane Valuation 230

31. Costa Rica Casino Money 234

32. A Very Big Banking "Error" 240

33. Time to Sell 248

34. Yahoo Clubs They Didn't Want! 255

35. Flirting with Investment 258

36. The Suing Machine 265

37. Celebrity Sex Tape 271

38. Joining Flynt & Dishwasher Dildo 276

39. Celebrity Sleuth 283

40. Larry Flynt's Ace in the Hole 288

41. Royally Screwed 296

42. Larry Gets His Comeuppance 305

43. Fall of an Empire 311

44. Smoking Hot 319

Acknowledgments 334

About the Author 335

I was going to say, some of the names in
this book have been changed to protect the
innocent. Then I thought, *fuck it!*

Let's make one thing clear; I'm not a porn star,
I never was. At that, I drew the line. The other lines,
well…. Let's just say they were a little blurred.

CHAPTER ONE

It's a Mad, Mad World

THE SETTING SUN is kissing the infamous Miami Beach skyline, turning everything under its gaze the color of the Tequila Sunrises that is flowing like water from some Spanish fountain at Happy Hour. Actually, every hour has been Happy Hour for the last few days, since this rowdy group of hyped up testosterone-crazed former geeks, rolled into town for the year 2000 "Expo."

I turned heads as I strutted purposely through the luxurious, fancy pool area of this quaint but exclusive hotel making my way up to one of the hotel suites where I have an extremely important meeting to get to.

A few days ago, this same pack would have appeared like a rich boy gathering of some nerdosaur engineering Frat at a South Beach hotel for Spring Break. But we were now three days in and these over the top "businessmen" turned shit-faced hooligans are having the time of their lives, a huge testament to the industry leaders like myself, creating and selling "The Dream."

More booze and coke than one should consume in a lifetime, all lavishly provided on the house. Plus, a copious number of fake tits, tight assed, skinny blondes and the plainer but pretty local-hires, all throwing themselves at these young, not entirely unattractive, up and coming millionaires. "Promo models," complimentary of some company like mine, trying to capture their attention.

As I attempted to cross to the lobby, I stood out as one of the few girls there. If they had not known me, one might have presumed I was one of the young promo girls dressed up to look like a businesswoman, but they did know me. As I weaved and shimmied my way through the undulating pool crowd, brushing against all these hot sweaty bodies, most of the guys recognized me. I recognized many of them too, but those I didn't, had probably crossed my path as part of an indiscreet name on the upper right corner box on an invoice. Still I didn't have time to socialize right now.

I stutter-stepped, twirled, high-fived and air kissed my way across as fast as I could in my strappy heels, turning heads in my sexy sleek dress, off the shoulder but still conservative enough to stand out as business attire. These men didn't look at me as a sex symbol though. I was well respected, even idolized and as I moved through the crowd trying to make my way to the lobby, I got "Hey Gail!", "What's up Gail?", "Can we talk about that deal, Gail?" They didn't know me as an English pin-up, Page Three model or a B movie scream queen, they knew me as the owner of "Falcon Foto" and the girl who had made them millions. They knew me as one of the forerunners of the

ADULT INTERNET BUSINESS!!!

Escaping the controlled orgiastic mayhem of the pool, which looked more and more like one of Wilhelm Reich's wet dreams by the minute, I now made my way through the lobby, packed with a bunch of young Brooks Brothers button down, Harvard types and strippers in clear heels and super high bootie shorts, so tight you could see what they ate for lunch. In booths around the lobby, pockets of men were striking deals, oblivious to the hi-def screens playing sucking-n-fucking orgy scenes behind them. It's just another day doing business in this crazy, fast paced world of the Adult Internet.

I nodded to a few of the players in the lobby booths. I didn't have time to stop. I had to get up to the penthouse suite. I had an exciting meeting with Calvin, the owner of "Fast Money," the marketing arm to his massively successful adult Internet sites and someone everyone wanted to make deals with. Still, in this kind of an environment, I knew "meetings" could change on the fly and I was determined to catch him before he got distracted with something else.

Hotel staff stood in full uniform behind the check-in counter diverting their eyes and pretending politely not to notice that their hotel lobby had been transformed into Hieronymus Bosch's Sixth Level of Hell. I smiled to myself as I was sure the hotel staff greatly underestimated these smacked-out party animals. These guys were the bomb! These boys were on the cutting edge of the technology wave that would change the world we lived in forever! These boys were reshaping and creating the world of business and pleasure. The very breath of our future global existence. No one knew just how hot shit they really were, not even them! It was hard to imagine looking at them now in this drunken stupor, but these guys were literally reprogramming the world and our total future existence was going to be driven by their talent, imagination and expertise. We were at the helm of the HMS BIG BUX, riding the crest of an enormous, euphoric tidal wave. And the meeting I was going to, was one of those that could steer the course of history.

Just as I was about to get through the lobby, one of the Brooks Bros. caught me. It was Greg, who owned a well-respected financial transaction processing company involved in international banking, with a couple of his executive minions.

"Gail, can we get together later for a drink. Love to talk to you about an exciting new processing tool we have. We'd love to handle your high-risk traffic. We've added banks out of Caymans and getting processing rates less than four percent, international!!!"

"Sounds interesting. We can always use extra banks." I made an empty promise to stop by the party he was sponsoring later, with little intention to actually do so, and made a mental note to put him on the bottom of the "If I Get to It" list. My attention was solely focused on the meeting ahead.

Finally arriving at the second floor, I noticed some chick in a dollar bill patterned cheerleading skirt with the logo "Fast Money" puking in a silver champagne bucket outside number 205 and figured I'd arrived at the VIP hospitality suite. Hospitality includes all you can eat, drink and partake in—and food and wine were not the only things on the menu. I'm looking for the owner of this particular offering, "Mr. Fast Money".

I was greeted by four hot chicks in dental-floss thong bikinis, with just enough space in the Bermuda Triangle for the words *Fast Money,* and one dark, muscled, bald-headed steely-eyed bouncer, who scowled down at me.

Brandon shouted from the balcony, through the door, "Hey Gail!" He waived off the bouncer and beckoned me in. The girls immediately offered their hospitality, touting trays of Bollinger champagne, twenty-year-old single malt Glenfiddich whiskey and Cuban cigars they swore were rolled on the thighs of luscious Cuban dancers. There appeared to be hors d'oeuvres as well, but I only noticed the ones being hand-fed by a voluptuous topless bunny grinding on the lap of Ted, the owner of Traffic Buxxx.

The speakers were blaring loud, heart-attack-inducing rap music to which a rather flexible exotic dancer was gyrating upside down on a makeshift stripper pole in the center of the room. In a move worthy of Nadia Comaneci, she rolled down right side up, began to wildly twerk her magnificent muscled ass, as she attempted to squirt a ping-pong ball strategically placed between her legs, into the mouths of a small group of intently focused geeks.

Over the music were even louder roars of goading and cheering coming from the balcony where party masters were egging on the eager crowd around the pool below. Hanging on either side of the balcony, were two guys stripped down to only their underpants. Each had been hoisted up high by their briefs, and strapped to a nicer quality hotel suite chair, which was perched precariously over the balcony's edge.

"Let's hear it for *Fast Money*," shouted Brandon to the crowd below. Brandon was the crazy half of the Fast Money partnership in charge of promos, partying and general debauchery. He was the poster boy for the obscenely rich, indulgent bad-boy image that Fast Money promised its subscribers.

"YAY Gail!!!" Brandon yelled, "Calvin wants to talk to you. It's some hot shit! BAAAA-BEEEE!" Brandon was a ton of fun and actually brilliant when he was sober for five minutes, though that was a rare occurrence. Brandon had the attention span of a newly born litter of cocker spaniel puppies and his attention was now focused intently back to the games.

"*Mad Buxxx*! *Mad Buxxx*!" chanted Brandon's equally-blasted game competitor, with his Atomic Wedgie-man in his makeshift sling-shot, ready to launch.

"I have a grand on *Mad Buxxx*! Do I hear more?"

"Ready, Set, Gooooooo!"

The unmistakable sound of a giant elastic snap on two bare butts echoed and the guys were catapulted off the balcony.

The half-naked guys were still strapped to their chairs with their little dangling legs running airborne in space, their underpants flapping like tiny parachutes, silhouetted against the crystal-clear azure sky for some crazy amount of time before finally making a huge splash in the pool below. The crowd went nuts as the atomic-wedgie slingshot astronauts and pieces of hotel furniture floated to the surface of the pool. Brandon was leading a victory cheer from the balcony to the screaming delight below.

Moments later there was a ruckus going on at the suite's front door. The mountain of a bouncer had a poor hotel security guy crushed in his rippling python–like arms. He had come up with a front desk rep in a futile attempt to prevent further damage.

"Sir!" said the hotel suit in a sing-song Indian accent. "You must stop!"

Brandon made a slight twitch of his head, and the bouncer relaxed his grip, and the security man fell backward gasping for air. "Don't worry man. Put it on the room," Brandon said dismissively.

Then turning from the hotel reps as if they had simply ceased to exist, he went back out to the balcony and screamed to the crowd below, "Games are sponsored by *Fast Money*!!!" he shouts, with gladiator like hubris. The crowd roared in response, chanting; "FAST MONEY! FAST MONEY! FAST MONEY!"

Defeated, the Indian hotel rep lets out a puff of air as he leaves.

Finally, I eye Calvin, the other half of Fast Money, a much more behind-the-scenes, no-nonsense, businessman. Calvin is an older, mature guy, probably approaching thirty-five. He's in the master bedroom area of the suite and he appears to be finishing a "meeting." He motions me in and a sly, knowing grin spreads across his face.

The room looks more like Caligula's birthday party. Sucking, humping, writhing naked bodies are draped over furniture, sprawled across the king bed. Calvin's shy, brainy assistant Daniel is slouched in an armchair wearing a robe with a really hot blonde with huge fake tits, straddling him and riding him hard enough that his glasses are hanging off the side of his face.

Next to the bed is a Jacuzzi tub with a bunch of arms and legs sticking out of a mass of foam, laughter, and Calvin's holding court in the center of the room. He is a brilliant entrepreneur. Well known as one of the founding fathers of our industry. Always has a million things going at once but if he says he's going to do something, it's gonna get done, and it's gonna go big.

But now he has something really exciting. He has some hot new technology his team of brains are working on to track IP addresses through all their various activities. Meaning you can tell what country a guy is logging in from and exactly what he is viewing at any particular moment and this comes with multiple opportunities to bill his credit card. I want in. Calvin has great respect for me and for what I can do. Now if I can only persuade him that I'm going to be an important link in his chain. And it's not just about the money for me. This deal would give me the prestige and respect I longed for.

Calvin's other meeting gets up and leaves. He gestures for me to join him on the bench at the foot of the bed.

There's a couple on the other end of the bed and the guy is banging the shit out of her so the bed is moving back and forth, and the motion is very distracting. Still it's hard to get an audience with Calvin and I've finally got one, so I focus. Well, I almost had his attention! Suddenly he's on the phone giving me the sign language of, *I'll be off in a second.*

Just a few inches away are naked bodies, I recognize one as Sammy. Sammy's married. I've met his wife at a couple of posh dos Clearly, he didn't bring her on this one. He's knelt up on the bed dangling his testicles over some chick that is laid on her back licking his ball sack. Another girl is doggie style in front of him, her head bobbing up and down as she goes to town on him.

Calvin's completely oblivious to the scenes around him. He hangs up the phone, then a second later he gets some kind of notification that he quickly checks.

"Who the fuck put twenty grand on room service?!!!" he screams, looking over at Daniel.

"Dunno," Daniel shrugs, he's having a hard time caring about the Drugs, Girls & Booze Budget right at this moment; he's in the middle of getting laid.

Calvin takes a deep "oh-fuck-it" sigh. It's the cost of doing business. Calvin turns back to me, as I fidget impatiently. I finally have his attention.

"Calvin. Tell me about this tracking you've got."

"These invisible cookies are amazing," he shares in an excited whisper. "We can see exactly what the guy is looking at."

"Real-time?!"

Calvin nods like he just found the map to the Holy Grail.

"Calvin, this is what we've been talking about. If we can change content real-time, we can change the content the guy sees on the fly."

"Yeah and it's seamless; the customer has no idea," Calvin can't help his excitement.

"Meaning we can program it, so the customer sees an experience that's right for him!" I exclaim.

"Exactly!"

The wheels are turning in my mind as I see the entire experience before me. All those years of experience, learning about men, coming together, now technically possible.

"Calvin, this is amazing. It's no longer some pop-up trap the guy can't get out of that he hates. The guy's gonna stay because he gets exactly what he wants and LOVES IT!"

Our intimate meeting is suddenly interrupted, "Aweeeee God, Fuuuuuuuck, Yeeees!" screams Sammy in an orgasmic cry, inches away from me. And no sooner do I hear that, then a warm wet splash hits my bare shoulder.

"Oh shit! Sorry Gail," says Sammy with a boyish grin.

Then turning to the girl, he reprimands her, "Look you made a mess. Now lick it off."

Calvin doesn't miss a beat and hands me what looks to be a hand towel laying on the bed. As I go to use it, I realize it's actually Sammy's sweaty undies.

Nevertheless, I am not going to let some stray flying cum ruin my chance of an amazing deal with Calvin. I've now got Calvin's focus. So, I pretend not to be fazed and continue, "Let me build specific pods of content. If we channel the guy into the experience they want they're gonna be hooked. You have the eyeballs, I have more content than anyone, and I know what will work!"

"It's a big risk to send you my prime traffic," Calvin considers carefully.

"Let's do some test sites," I suggest. "If I know what the guys want, and I get it right, I bet I can double or triple your retention rates."

Now I've got his attention.

"Ok, let's give it a shot. Do some joint test sites, fifty-fifty."

He holds out his hand and we shake.

As I turn to leave, I try to hold back my huge excitement and restrain myself from jumping for joy.

I've just been given the GREEN LIGHT ON A MULTI-MILLION DOLLAR DEAL!!!

And a course that could change the future of the Internet and how we'll view things on the web.

CHAPTER TWO

Unlikely Pinup Model

I WAS RAISED in Yorkshire, England, believing I was pretty ordinary and run-of-the-mill in the looks department, riddled with doubt and lacking self-confidence. A quiet desperation that is ingrained in the British from an early age.

Dad died suddenly of a heart attack when I was seven, so my brother and I were raised single-handedly by my mom. Like many girls who, for whatever reason, lack that paternal connection, it left an unconscious gaping hole, desperate to be filled by male attention and that life-long helpless quest to replace it with the respect and love from men who would invariably fall short of the impossible task.

Mom was busy with more practical matters and left me to get on with it most of the time, adding to my independent nature to think out of the box and my necessary life skills to fend for myself. I didn't know at this tender age, but my entrepreneurial nature was being formed.

Some girls grew up relying on their looks and didn't need a career, as they were destined to become someone's trophy wife. That was not an option for me with my ordinary appearance, and that was the epitome of the female species in my eyes. I defied British sensibility, which ensured the old-fashioned theory that boys were the dominant gender. Even at that age, it was important that I be equal to my male peers. And by equal that meant you had to be better. My brother, love him dearly, was my first sparring partner. Armed with the typical slightly demeaning British sense of humor and brotherly digs, he confirmed my belief that I was utterly lacking in the attractive department. He called me "Goose Pimple Gail," on account of the two little goose bumps on my otherwise flat chest. Lacking in self-confidence, I resorted to locking his friends in the bedroom forcing them to kiss me. I'd lure them in, barricade the door and pin them down, pressing my lips against theirs.

I suppose, I must have been sexual most of my life. I can't remember when I first learned to masturbate. I just remember my grandma catching me when I was very young and angrily warning me, "If you do that, it will drop off!"

What will drop off? I wondered for years; as to what part of me would just suddenly fall off, that is until puberty hit. My vaginal lips started to protrude and scared to death, bent over between my legs, I tried in vain to stick my vulva lips down with Scotch Tape. My two little goose bumps had finally started to swell into full grown breasts, something I didn't understand would later be a mesmerizer of most all men.

I attended a stereotypical British all-girls' high school, complete with traditional school uniform with matching blazer and beret. It included occasional panty checks to make sure we wore the regulation full bottom navy blue panties and bare bottom canings by the head mistress if you stepped out of line. The Physics' teacher was a little less directly authoritarian. If you were disobedient in his class, you simply had to go in the dog cage under his desk where he made you get on all fours and bark like a dog. At the time, it never occurred to me that this might be somewhat sexual. But perhaps this was the first time I formed the opinion that *Some men are just weird.*

Still, I thought, if good looks were not in my future I'd have to work much harder at life. I had known from an early age that I was going to be a veterinarian and had been working at a vet's, getting hands on experience since I was fourteen. I proved I was willing to get out there in my knee-high rubber Wellies, stick my arm up a cow's butt, wrangle a couple of bulls and get chased around the barn by some toothless, horny, old farmer trying to grope me—and that was my first day out! My passion, my drive, was animals and that was going to be my life's path.

By seventeen, I was in college. Being a Math and Chemistry geek, my classmates had done a one-eighty to almost all male. I don't think I realized quite yet, that I had grown into an attractive blond with a rack to be reckoned with. I was still sparring with the guys over a good Math equation, hoping to impress them with my brainy side, when they were probably just lusting over my full cleavage. And it wasn't until shortly after when I stumbled into modeling that I began to discover my feminine allure.

15

Actually, I never would have dreamt of being a model, I just fell into it by mistake. I already had a couple of jobs on the side but was always open to an extra one as I pored through the ads of a local newspaper. There seemed to be lots of ads for vacuum cleaner salespeople. I was drawn to an ad "Earn one hundred pounds an hour." Intrigued I arranged an interview after school and before my other job.

I arrived at a small store front office with lots of intimidating pictures of attractive girls in the window. I didn't detect any sign of vacuums. An overly well-dressed man in a shiny silver suit, slippery snake-skin shoes and greased jet-black hair, opened the door for me.

"I came about the ad in the newspaper," I announced, as I shoved the ad forward, crumpled up in my outstretched little hand, but as I scanned the walls, my arm sank down as I quickly felt very silly as it became apparent this was a modeling agency.

"Oh, no, sorry!" I apologized, "I thought it was for vacuum sales, not modeling. Sorry obviously I'm not a model." I laughed, stuffing the lying little ad back into my coat and turning to leave.

"Come on in, Love," he greeted me, "Who eva gave ya that idea luv? You're beautiful. You'll be a perfect model!" he said convincingly.

I was a little confused and blushed, fully expecting him to be making me the butt of some joke.

I cocked my head and narrowed my gaze. "I thought I was too short?" I said suspiciously.

"Nah luv," he assured me, "Darling, little tiny thing like you! They will love you."

He didn't want any money from me and it sounded semi-legit, so I decided to give it a go.

I left feeling undeservingly special. *He says I look like the model type,* I thought to myself and smiled, *Wow, did I fool him!*

Surprisingly, I found there was quite a demand for petite models that made cars and RVs look much bigger than they really were. Small local ads to be sure but hey, I was getting paid! For people to take pictures of ME! And it was dead easy! I felt empowered that I could actually be labeled a "model."

Unfortunately, the modeling agency didn't last very long. It burned to the ground. Literally. I showed up one day and it was a smoking pile of rubble. The guy in the business next door said it was "Jewish Lightning," by which he meant it was burned down for the insurance money and my agent was conveniently nowhere to be found. I felt defeated. I was a wallflower again.

Still, I had gotten my start and I had kept everyone's business cards. I followed up with all the people I had met. I may not be that attractive, but I'm friendly and hardworking, and that could make up for a great deal.

This led me to a back alley sleazy amateur photo studio where I was hired as a model for the amateurs learning photography class. The "Out of Focus Wonderland," I called it. Eventually, it led me to London and the infamous mad photographer for *The Sun* Newspaper, the British Andy Warhol, decidedly cool and creative with every bit of swag and charm that would make a girl feel more special than any other. "Look at you! Natural beauty! Absolutely Gorgeous darling!" he would say.

Now if you are from the UK you'll probably know where I am going here. You see, on the third page of *The Sun* every day is the picture of a busty girl showing off her natural bare boobies. Not only *The Sun* but every major newspaper, with the exception of a couple of real snobby ones like *The London Times*. It would be like the *Los Angeles Times* having a girl on the third page flashing her naked breasts. Completely normal to the Brits. These "Page Three Girls" become mini-celebrities in England. They represented the newspaper, making signing appearances all over the country. And these girls can be as young as sixteen and often are! So, you guessed it, I became a Page Three Girl! Eat your heart out my brother's wanker friends who I locked in the bedroom and had to lie on top of and force to kiss me.

Running all over to signing events where guys would stand for hours just to get my autograph? 'Lil old me! Wow! This was crazy! I was so flattered that they would line up to meet me! Most of them would be so nervous that they'd spend an hour waiting to talk to me and when they finally got in front of me they were lost for words. *Why are they nervous meeting me?*

I'd picked up a couple of other advertising roles, that of "Miss Tetley's Beer", "British Gas Girl" and a few other titles that came with regular modeling gigs, billboards and swimsuit shots on tropical beaches—Jamaica, Barbados, Spain, Ibiza. The money was good, and this gave me a great feeling of independence, but I have to admit, there was a big part of me that just wanted to be called beautiful.

I didn't think I was pretty enough to be a "top model," and was still in disbelief that anyone was interested in me at all, so I was very grateful and tried to make up for it by always working hard and never complaining, unlike the drop-dead gorgeous ones who were allowed to be prima donnas. I was very appreciative of any jobs I got, even the ones that had sounded much more glamourous than they'd turned out to be. Which is how I'd ended up doing a few full-nude shoots that I wasn't proud of. I'd been sort of misled into what sounded like some prestigious shoot and a big pay day, only to find out the items of "fashion" were getting less and less. I thought afterwards, they were horribly embarrassing, but I figured no one would ever see those. They were pretty tame by today's standard, but still, I cringed at the thought of anyone I knew seeing them. There was no such thing as the Internet and so little chance of any of my school friends ever finding out. Thank God, I was getting teased enough by the boys over Page Three!

Luckily, college was a cakewalk for me. Science was my forte and I was able to breeze in and out with my modelling jobs, still getting straight A's. Or so I thought. My veterinary dreams came to a crushing halt when the principle read my college results out in front of the whole school. I was being honored with a double scholarship to Cambridge University to study medicine. Tears streaming down my face, I was devastated. No one could understand. I hadn't quite made it to vet school. As a boy I would have passed with flying colors, but in the UK it was much harder for a female to qualify as a vet. I was crushed, my self-worth was in the toilet and I cried for weeks. I was signed up to one of the most prestigious colleges, for the prestigious career of a physician; life sucked.

Still, I had to be the only Page Three Girl who was ever enrolled at Cambridge, and knowing that serious studying might infringe on my time modeling, I decided over the summer I better take every opportunity, especially to travel to tropical islands. I thought: *It's a fluke they're even asking me. I'd better hurry and squeeze those in before medical school.* I had the rare opportunity to travel the world on someone else's dime, and so I did. I took every calendar, every travel brochure. I was the girl on the beach with the shiny oiled buns.

Back home, I'd totally forgotten my agent had months ago signed me up for a charity publicity parachuting jump. I couldn't back out of it, he'd made the most of it with the press and our pictures in all the newspapers. The day had come, and a group of models were shipped off to an Army base in North Yorkshire. We spent the entire weekend in army training boot camp.

"DROP, TUCK AND ROLL," the Sergeant bellowed, pushing one of the girls firmly off the edge of a six-foot ramp.

This is no joke, this is hard core! I thought, quite surprised by the army drill. *What happened to a bunch of girls doing some posing for the newspaper?* No, this was the real deal. The next morning, we would all be forced to jump out of a perfectly good airplane and, excuse my French this once, I was scared shitless.

I was quite relieved to wake up to a typical miserable, dark, cloudy English day, presuming we would be weather grounded. We were not to be so lucky; we were all going to jump through these thick black pregnant rain clouds anyway. The first group left. As we were waiting to board the plane the first girls were descending, plummeting through the jet-black, licorice clouds. We watched in horror as one of our peers, with a blood-curdling scream, came in for a crash landing on the roof of the hanger.

"That's where not to land," the Sergeant remarked nonchalantly. Apparently, she broke her leg and the emergency sirens grew louder as we boarded the next plane.

I don't think there's been a moment in my life where I was as utterly, totally and completely terrified as that ride up. My stomach felt like it was in my throat and my heart was pounding out of my chest. I didn't know if I was going to puke or it was going to come out the other end. Ten minutes of sheer shitting my pants.

On the ride up the Sergeant did nothing to ease our nerves, "When I say 'IN POSITION' you have THREE SECONDS to get in the door!"

He told us how in the last group one of the girls refused to jump so the pilot simply tipped the plane upside down 'til gravity released her grip and sucked her out of the door. After hearing that, I didn't wait for my cue in fear of being pushed, I flung myself out the plane head first.

Now, writing all this in hindsight, I take it back; the ride up in the plane wasn't that bad; the next five seconds of free fall was the moment in my life that I was the most completely terrified! You know, that moment falling at a terrifying speed with your stomach in your mouth. Suspended by nothingness, hurdling at full velocity to the ground below. Bracing for that massive jolt that would snap your neck back in two, but which also meant your life was saved. Bang! BLAM! HUUHHNNN! Whiplash. My parachute opens! My life is SAVED!

It was an old round parachute and I managed to land this big archaic thing just as we had been trained; smack hard into the ground at full speed, tuck and roll, bounce a few times, get scraped across the ground by a full force wind and pray like hell you don't break anything before coming to a crashing halt. It was a miracle I survived!

So, excited was I first that I was alive and second that I'd done something so brave. I was hooked. I wanted to do it again. And again, and again…

My skydiving daredevil streak caught the attention of the advertising agency for Vladivar Vodka and soon landed me the contract to be "Fiona Vladivar," with all kinds of crazy publicity stunts. We signed a contract for a twelve-month calendar. I had to agree that I would likely get arrested in doing most of these stunts (that was the goal) and I was not allowed to give my real name, rather the name *Fiona Vladivar*. Each stunt was a play on British culture; ride into the Ascot races on horseback wearing the traditional hat and not much else, skydive into Prince Andrew's wedding topless, appear during the Oxford Cambridge boat races being rowed in; well, you get the theme.

The first ad I did for them was a simple billboard, rather tame in comparison. Me on a jet as an airline stewardess, my uniform clearly ruffled, lots of cleavage showing and looking quite tipsy. A bottle of Vladivar Vodka next to me and a caption that read something like, "Join the mile-high club with Vladivar Vodka."

Apparently back in those days no one paid much attention to trademarks and being sued. Not in England, anyway. The wardrobe designer had put me in a Pan Am uniform. Well, when the advert appeared, all hell broke loose. The women of Pan Am were up in arms. The Vladivar ad was on billboards all over England. How could a Pan Am stewardess be portrayed in such a light and who was this model that would do this? — *Fiona Vladivar*! Still it was out of control and the ad agency was being sued. Everyone else was guessing who Fiona Vladivar was. Well Fiona Vladivar was now hiding out, as women wrote in calling me "a slut," for having agreed to pose for such smut. They certainly did make me feel like a low-life though no one knew who I was. Reading the paper; people were saying they knew I lived in this town or that town, which I didn't. It was much more publicity than Vladivar had bargained for. I needed to lay low for a while.

The same ad agency also represented Marlboro Cigarettes, which is perhaps how I was lucky enough to land the role of The Marlboro Cigarette Girl, which took me out of the country and away from the British press. I was flown on an exciting trip around the world, shooting crazy shots, like in remote jungles hanging by a thin rope over a two-hundred-foot-high waterfall and all kinds of other exciting stuff.

And it was Marlboro that brought me to Hollywood, with all its glitz and glory, the land of money, fame, and of course sex, where my adventure really begins.

CHAPTER THREE

Those Sex Crazed Americans

IT WAS AROUND 1984 and I was a fresh faced eighteen year old, arriving in California. I instantly met American agents and casting directors who put me in all kinds of TV commercials and little acting roles. I had a tiny role on *Baywatch* as the girlfriend of one of the lifeguards. Shooting out on the Pacific Ocean, running along the pristine Malibu beaches (breasts bouncing up and down in slow motion), being fawned over and doted on, getting paid the big bucks. I thought I had really hit the big time. America is fantastic! That day on *Baywatch*, laying on the film boat, soaking in the sun, I thought, *Wow this is the life. The weather's nice here. I think I'll stay a while.*

I made the fateful phone call to my mom back home, "Hi, Mom? Think I'm putting off college 'til next Fall. Take a year out."

And I did.

And that was many Falls ago....

The local natives proved to be very strange. Even on the plane over, the guy sitting next to me was staring into my eyes when he boldly declared, "You have the most beautiful eyes!"

I looked at him suspiciously, "Are you pulling my leg?"

He was confused, "No, you have incredible eyes."

You see, men in England would rather stick a needle in their eye than stoop to give a compliment. Or if they did, it would come in the form of a sarcastic negative. The best you might hope for would be something like, "Hey, I wouldn't kick you out of bed!" It took me a while to realize that Americans would give direct compliments and the *beautiful eyes* comment I would have to get used to for the rest of my life and believe me, I love it and it never gets old!

Then there were the usual language barriers like explaining that *I'm really pissed* meant that I wasn't upset, rather I was sloshed and having a good time. And *cock-up* meant I'd messed up, not caused someone an erection or anything. Or the look of horror on my face when a guy said; "My wife has an awesome *fanny*, I just love to grab it." Someone had to explain to me that *fanny* actually means *butt* in the US, an alternative to the UK version, where it is a really classless word for pussy!

Then I met Clive, a sliver of home in the new world. An older lady I knew in England made me promise to look up her son, Clive, who was a photographer in Los Angeles. He'd been in the music biz, having been Cat Stevens' manager until Cat Stevens became a Muslim and donated all his royalties, along with Clive's percentage, to a mosque.

"What a tosser!" was Clive's take on it. So, Clive still had his big toe in the music industry, but his main gig was as a photographer for some nudie magazine.

Clive was suave, bright, funny, dashingly handsome, very English and utterly charming, and it didn't hurt that he seemed to know everyone. On our first real meeting, we were going out for lunch, but he had to first interview a new girl for a photo shoot who was coming over with her husband.

"Why don't you hang out by the pool and sunbathe. And if you could talk to her that would really help, she's never done any modeling and she says she's really shy. Maybe you can show her your portfolio book with your calendar pics, talk to her and make her feel at ease."

So, a little later the husband and wife show up. She's a cute, tight little number wearing a Day-Glo fluorescent spandex mini-dress, and he's tanned and bare chested, with mega muscles, looking like he lives and breathes Gold's Gym. As instructed, I get out my portfolio. They oo-ed and aww-ed as I chatted and made small talk about what was happening around the shoot that particular day. I think I did a good job making both of them feel at ease, as it seemed it was the husband who needed to be convinced that this was right for her. They were both impressed with my calendar pics and I told them I'd done a couple of naked shoots myself in England. Feeling a little more confident, the wife went off to the studio, which was a little room right off the pool, while I am left with the husband who was not really a great conversationalist, rather far more brawn than brain.

I go back to sunbathing and ignore him, but he keeps chatting. He's very impressed with the photos, a little too impressed.

"So, you feel very comfortable being photographed on a beach in a bikini? They are very sexy pictures, you are very beautiful. You must feel very at ease with your body…" he blathers on while running his eyes over my body.

I can sense his shining muscular body pumping up with excitement as he leaned in close enough I could feel his breath in short puffs on my skin. I could tell his sexual energy was rising and at this point it is getting a little uncomfortable and excused myself to get a glass of water in the kitchen. But he jumps up, hot on my tail.

Breathing down my neck, he is in full pursuit. Then in one fell swoop he grabs me and launches my petite frame above his shoulders landing me on top of the kitchen counter. I was now pinned over the stove by this hunk, my thighs spread open and his huge muscles wrapped around me squeezing me in a death grip. I can't move, as his tentacles crush me into him, his face is rubbed up against mine, the stubble of his beard grating my cheeks, he desperately tries to make out with me. Not sure if he was thinking rape is assault with intent to please? Or battery with a friendly weapon? Actually, he probably didn't think much with his bigger head. His hard cock was now protruding through his pants and pushed firmly against my inner thigh. He's frantically pulling at my bikini, his hot breath on me, telling me how sexy I am. I'm outraged, but far more concerned about his wife and Clive coming out and getting the wrong impression. His souped-up testosterone level, was out of control and he wouldn't listen to my pleas for him to let go.

I tried to pry him off. "Stop! Your wife could come out any minute! You…. need to… get off….me!"

But he's not in the least put off and starts in with short, sharp staccato kisses on my neck. "Oh, my wife wants to do you too! She loves girls and she thinks you're soooo hot!"

Desperate, I boxed his ears as hard as I could, which hit the switch in his brain and turned him off. He pulled back with this hurt look as his eyes turned red.

"OWWW!" he howled at last like the dog he was, holding his head in both hands. I jumped down off the stove, rearranged what little clothing I had on and, right on cue, out comes Clive, all flushed and red-faced and the wife in the same state of disarray that I was.

As it turns out, the wife had cornered Clive, about jumped on him with that Doctor Octopus make out move the husband had just tried on me.

Once everyone regained their composure, and the hunk took a handful of aspirin, the couple, quite unabashedly tried to persuade us to go out for drinks at some Beverly Hill bar called the Polo Lounge to "get to know each other" and "you know…."

Clive, the epitome of English charm, quickly made some excuse. This husband and wife wanted to do the both of us, right there! We were both in shock at being mauled by these animals, which brought on the genetic English reaction to all situations such as these: hysterical laughter.

Mind you, I was still very new to America and this was my first introduction to what I believed were Mr. and Mrs. Joe "Regular Americans." I was shocked and intimidated, yet, I told myself I'd better suck it up, stop being so prudish and get used to this. This is America!

Clive and I started dating. I was head over heels and it was nice to have a fellow Brit I felt I could relate to and not one of those sex-crazed, wife-swapping Americans. I was about eighteen and Clive a fair bit older than I was, but he was charming, and his sense of humor wooed me. He was also entrenched in the whole Hollywood scene. It was the eighties; there were limos with rock stars, parties with mounds of cocaine, ludes and pyramid-party-get-rich-quick schemes. I was a wannabe actress with a rock-star, photographer boyfriend. I had certainly arrived in Hollywood and before you knew it, this crazy lifestyle was starting to become the norm.

I joined the local skydiving center and my skydiving seemed to be a great attraction for Hollywood. Then I did a bit role in *Road House* as a girl in the bar with Patrick Swayze, who I thought was just the sweetest person I'd ever met, staying long after on the set for hours to sign autographs.

I got him into skydiving, and the classic film *Point Break* with Keanu Reeves followed.

By now I had achieved an "Expert License" in skydiving, which meant I had five hundred jumps and could hit a five-meter disc from twelve thousand feet. More importantly it meant I could be insured for skydiving stunts in movies. I was apparently the only girl in the Screen Actors Guild holding this and it meant I was the go-to girl for all these kinds of roles. Even more useful, since no other American citizen was doing this, I was able to get a temporary work permit to stay awhile. A pass to Hollywood with all its glamour, intrigue and the deep dark sexy side I was about to discover.

CHAPTER FOUR

Money in the Trash

MAKING IT ON my own in Hollywood wasn't easy, living on the outskirts of Beverly Hills and paying for acting classes and the like, out of the few acting jobs I was getting, was tough. I was struggling pretty hard but wouldn't admit it. Going back to the UK would be giving up, so I was determined to figure it out somehow. Clive was comfortable but not loaded by any stretch, and I didn't want any man supporting me anyway. I had plenty of men that had offered to "take-care" of me financially but I still had the naïve belief that such a thing would mean I'd failed miserably as I needed to prove something to myself and make it on my own.

Meanwhile, a means to provide for myself was to come about in a most serendipitous way. I came over to Clive's studio, to help with some spring cleaning. Clearing out his old inventory, he was tossing worthless stuff in the trash. I noticed several chrome images atop a pile in one of the silver trash cans. I picked up a couple of photos to see they were nude pics of several different girls. Hmmm…quite attractive.

"What have you thrown these away for?" I asked.

"Oh, the lighting's not very good or I wasn't happy with them for some reason, so I threw them out."

"You think someone would want them? Do you have a model release?" I inquired, after all that British side of me hated to waste anything in life.

"Yeah, I have releases, but they aren't very good, hence, they're in the trash!" he said, confused at my fascination. "No one would be interested …" He hadn't finished his sentence and I was already re–sleeving them into brand new sparkling plastic photo sheets. Once dusted off and nicely cleaned up they looked quite presentable. He just shook his head like I was some crazy bag woman picking through his trash.

Later that day, I made a point to swing by a local newsstand. There was a copious selection of nudie mags and I opened a few scanning the inside.

I must have been the only young girl carefully browsing through the girlie magazine section that day. Men at the newsstand stopped mid-browse, more interested in watching me and my expressions as I glanced at the same sexy pages they were looking at, but I was looking at the fine print for the editorial submission information. I copied down a few addresses that looked like potentials and found that most of the publishers were in New York.

Back at the studio, I placed the photo sleeves in nice looking folders and wrote a professional cover letter.

Dear Mr. Editor

Blah-De-blah... Naked-pictures... Yadda-yadda... please buy my stuff. Blabity blabity.... [BIG SMILE]

Your obedient servant, Gail.

I mailed them off to the small print addresses in New York where I hoped these professional publishing companies would receive them for review.

Then I went about my acting business, going to my classes and setting up scene practices with my partners, making appointments for auditions, and put the nudy photos out of my mind. I was stunned when I received a phone call about a week later. It totally caught me off guard. It was an editor from one of these mags I'd sent the images to.

"Oh yes! Thank you. We are interested in some of these sets and we were considering...hmm...let me see now...ah, Julie...Oh my. Brandi, Sophia is very nice...." He was reading off a list of whatever I had named the girls, picking out the photo sets that were clearly the best.

"We can offer you fifteen hundred per set."

Without thinking, I took a shot at the moon, thinking *I bid high, he bids low, we come to something in the middle,* and I blurted, "I was hoping for twenty-five hundred each?"

There was a long pause. I was sure I had blown it. But then I oozed into the silence, "but if you take them ALL you can have them for the bargain basement price of.... two grand each."

Then to my utter gob smacked amazement, he said, "It's a deal."

Luckily, he couldn't see my reaction, on the other end of the phone, my jaw was wide open. He was going to pay me two thousand dollars for each of these sets! Did I really just get THIRTY THOUSAND UNITED STATES DOLLARS for digging through my boyfriend's trash?

Still, I had no idea at that moment the seed I had planted.

I was thrilled to give Clive the good news, "Yes, I sold ALL of them! And when the check comes, we'll split it."

"Wow, babe, that's fantastic." Clive was in total shock and I relished in his admiration of me. Next step was to raid Clive's cabinets for any more "crap" images I could find. Clive looked on laughingly as I rummaged his bottom cabinet drawer.

"You're not going to find anything worthwhile in there. Total waste of time."

I held a sheet of images up to the light for a better look and Clive shook his head, "Oh, not her, she was a big mistake, her nose is the size of Texas."

"No, she's really pretty, what are you talking about?! I just have to edit the pics to show the best shots," I said, adding her to the pile of other layouts I intended to spruce up.

Clive laughed and shuck his head, but there was no harm in letting me try. I contacted other publishers with these "new" layouts and to Clive's amazement, I sold these just as easily.

It gave me great pleasure to tell him all his "unsellable" photos just got top dollar.

"Come here my little sales rep!" he gushed, swinging me into an embrace. This made me happier than anything. I had found quite a little gold mine and it was quickly turning into a nice little side-line business.

Then I made a suggestion, "I've gone through all your old material now, but what if you were to shoot some specifically for us? I mean when you're shooting a layout of a model for someone, why not shoot an extra one for us? I can do the makeup and styling."

Clive had encouraged me to complete a professional makeup course, so I could be useful to travel with him on his photo shoots, doing makeup and generally prepping the models. Many times, he was commissioned to shoot in Cabo, Mexico. Not a bad place to hang out and work on my tan. And whenever Clive was on location for his main client, I could sweet talk the model into doing an extra shoot for us.

Clive was one of the best photographers in the biz and I got a university education about the poses, the shots and the lighting.

I'd spend hours pampering the girls, doing their makeup, primping their hair and nails, dressing and undressing them. Quality time where I'd really get to know them and since I was about the same age as most they'd confide in me like a friend.

Jenny sits in a skimpy tank top on the porch of our fantastic beach rental. As I finish her makeup, she tells me her story, "I came out to LA from Arizona with my boyfriend, but we broke up. I met Jimmy at this party, he's a lot older but he said he'd help me out. That's how I got the apartment; Jimmy pays for it. So, it's sort of an arrangement. He comes over on the weekends. I have to pretend I'm sleeping, and he climbs into bed with me and likes to rub his cock on my panties 'til I pretend to wake up." Jenny squeals in delight at how silly it is but with a twinkle that makes me think she likes it, "Honestly though, he reminds me a bit of my stepdad, he used to do that to me."

"Do you have a real boyfriend?" I inquired putting just a little tinge of shadow on her eye lids.

"Oh, yeah! I met this actor Tim, he's so gorgeous!!! Biggest cock you've ever seen!!! Jimmy doesn't know though, he'd kill me."

I stand back to admire my makeup and she continues, "I want to get into Hollywood. You've done acting right? That's so cool."

I nod, smiling and taking it all in, "Ok, I'm just going to do a little lip gloss and keep you really natural looking," I say, finishing her sensual lips.

"I wish I could get my hair to look like yours. You're so lucky, you have amazing hair," Jenny says, admiring me. "I saw some of the pics in your portfolio, that you did here, they were freaking awesome! But you've done real modelling. Like in Europe, right? I don't know if I could look like that."

"Yeah, Clive's an amazing photographer, he'll make you look fantastic. He did a bunch of nudes of me here too and they are really artistic."

"I usually wear my hair blow dried," Jenny suggests, as I start to arrange her sun-kissed golden locks.

"We're going to do the beach wet-hair look today, it's so sexy on you and the sun is just perfect right now. You'll look very natural."

A little later, we're down at the beach, Jen dressed in just a scrap of a top that adds a little color to the shot but doesn't leave anything to the imagination. Clive is catching the most perfect pics right before sunset as I bounce the light shimmering on the back of her hair using a mirror.

"Gail, get the corner of the other mirror to reflect the light right into her pussy," Clive directs me as he looks through his lens, and I adjust the smaller mirror in the sand, "That's it! Perfect!"

He puts his camera down for a second and looks over to me, "A little more baby oil and wet her down again."

That's my cue to run in with the oil and spray the grateful frying model with cold water to tighten up those pert nipples and give those little beads of sweat on her naked body.

"That feels so good, thank you," Jenny says looking up at me with her big brown eyes.

I go to take my position, when Clive makes a suggestion to me, "Gail, she's a little stiff, why don't you show her some of the poses."

I leave my mirror holding post and stand behind the camera next to Clive.

"Ok, darling, like this," I say striking a sexy pose and continuing to direct her, "Wow Jen, that's awesome. Pout your lips. Now arch your back more and really stick out your butt like this. Perfect! And touch your nipple." I show her by caressing my own breasts, and she follows me. "Wow, beautiful darling. Love it. Now give me that look…" I'm in my bikini doing a sensual show for her from behind the camera. Now Jenny is getting totally into it, looking much more relaxed and sensual and Clive is snapping away in delight.

Later at dinner, I take the opportunity to approach Jenny, "You looked amazing today. I was wondering if you would be interested in doing a second shoot while you're here?"

"Yes, would love that," Jenny replied.

I was Clive's Secret Weapon, helping him with his shoots and in return I got fantastic new layouts for me to sell. A nice little business was blossoming.

Clive and I had taken our relationship to the next level and I moved in with him.

His quiet little home on the outskirts of Beverly Hills transformed late night to a full-on party house. After all it was Los Angeles in the eighties; wild parties out on the town, winding up as all-nighters back at our place, were the norm. Unfortunately, this era brought a flow of cocaine, which had also taken a hold of him.

The Roxy, The Rainbow, the Hollywood Rocker scene, the Beverly Hills Mansion Parties and Pyramid Gambling schemes, it was insane and out of control. Don't get me wrong, it was crazy fun if you didn't get pulled in too deep by the toxic red tide. Celebrities, rock stars and porn stars, they were all whirled into the mix. Yes, I could drink and party with the best of them, it was the eighties, so I tried everything at least a few times and sure I did coke with him if it was a party night. At the time, I didn't think it did much, just like a few heavy shots of coffee. Though you'd sit looking at scribbles on a beer mat for hours, believing you'd come up with some blinding revolution that was going to change the world, only to find in the morning it was just a beer mat and you can't understand what was so great and why you have a really, really, bad headache. Luckily, I didn't have an addictive personality. Doing it a few times, I thought it wasn't really worth it and it only slowed me down.

Clive on the other hand, my poor lost love, God bless him, was now hooked. His fantasy and reality had merged into the same thing, and it had become difficult for me to decipher the difference, and he was starting to be impossible to live with. Many of the fantastical tall tales he'd told that had so impressed me and gotten me into bed with him in the first place, I now started to realize were actually fairy tales based on the castles in the air of his drug-fueled fantasies.

Living with Clive between never knowing if what came out of his mouth was truth or fantasy and the climbing the walls like a cat on fire cocaine uppers and the sloth like splat of the valium downers had become an emotional rollercoaster that I had just run out of tickets for. The man I had fallen in love with was sometimes a wonderful, charming, gentleman and the rest of the time an abusive, narcissistic dick.

It was an absurd life, the glitz, the glamour, the naked chicks, drugs and Hollywood, but I had been sucked into believing this was a pretty normal American existence and I needed to wake up from my sheltered English upbringing.

I didn't understand the effects the drugs were having on him and being too much in the situation, I felt most of the time like, due to my massive inferiority complex and the twisted reality he'd convinced me of, it must have been me that was inadequate in some way. And yet, I loved him. I felt trapped. That there was no way I could leave him and make it on my own, so it was better just to stay and deal with it.

The train wreck of a coke dealer didn't seem to put him off his habit any. His supplier was supposedly a doctor and the brother of Marvin Gaye, but again, fantasy and reality could have been more a mergence of drug induced illusions.

Dr. Gaye, MD, "The Dealer," was familiar enough to let himself in the house, "Hi Gail," he said, passing by me to go directly to the kitchen faucet to clean out the crap in his nose, grunting and snorting under the running water, as he irrigates his nostrils.

"Hey Clive, found out what the nose problem is. Turns out it's nose worms!"

"What you mean like real worms?" Clive looked at me slightly disturbed.

"Yeah! You can see the fucking little things under the microscope. Tracks of them. Irritating bastards."

"Gail do you have any of that Bactrim left I prescribed you when you had that stomach problem? I'll take that. It ought to kill 'em off. It's not a big deal but it was probably that last batch of Coke I got."

But the nose worms weren't enough to put Clive off his coke habit. Not even a few weeks later when his dealer turned up dead in an alley. Dr. Gaye's toothpick drugged-out girlfriend continued his distribution biz and Clive was still good to go.

Often after a Hollywood night out, I'd retire early to bed while Clive continued partying until well into the next day. Like one night, half asleep, half naked, I wandered from the bedroom to the bathroom at maybe three am, only to find a whole room of porn stars and a coffee table that looked like someone had emptied a one-pound bag of confectioner's sugar in the middle.

"Hey Gail, come on, have a line," Amber said.

"You're looking hot Gail. Hey, come over here and play with us," Ginger said flickering her tongue in a very suggestive manner to show me how flexible it might be.

I looked around at these five women, all porn movie superstars you'd surely recognize, ninety-five percent naked, just hanging out, snorting and smoking. I was slightly tempted to have a new girly experience, as after all these were the perfect little Golden Girls that had been the fantasy of almost every man in America!

"Let us corrupt this innocent little thing," one of them said, making a move towards me.

"Come on honey," Clive grinned. I knew it was his fantasy and I wanted to please him and look "cool." And, I must admit I was a bit intrigued. I'd fantasized about trying a lesbo experience. I mean, I had dabbled with my girlfriend when we were pre-pubescent; blindfolding each other and playing the "guess the object I'm rubbing down your panties" game. I had gotten to know a couple of girls "really well" in my modelling days in England, but never completed the fantasy.

Anyway, here I was. Part of me was secretly excited to try the real thing. But then having a first experience in anything getting tag teamed by these super-pro-porn sex experts, Amber Lynn and Ginger Lynn, scared the shit out of me!

I didn't stick around to be corrupted. Nor partake in their all-night drug binge where they'd planned some incredible scheme, nor their crash the next day where they had no idea what they were talking about and had gone sub verbal from the night before, sounding like Pentecostals speaking in tongues. But they were certainly not slain by the Spirit of the Holy Ghost, and this had become a normal scene at the Chateau De Clive.

Meanwhile I was trying to pursue my dream to be a "real actress," which Clive said he'd help me with. In reality, he was the exact opposite of anything that resembled supportive of my Hollywood acting career.

I'd just been sent on an audition for the co-starring role in the movie *Summer School.* I was so clueless, ruddy, shiny and new; I had never done a real serious leading role with dialog, and barely read off a script before.

"Just read the lines on the page, like you're talking them," the director said to me, smiling and calm. I just stared utterly puzzled at the pages, took a breath and burbled out what could have been heard as Mandarin or interpreted as a minor stroke. Beginner's luck or what, I am not sure, the producers saw something in me and offered me the co-starring role. I was over the moon, ecstatic with joy at my first big break on my first toss o' the ring!

I rushed home to Clive, my heart in my throat, barely able to contain myself as I burst through the front door like a summer tornado. "You're not going to believe this! I just got the co-starring role in a huge movie!!!"

Expecting my boyfriend to be jumping up and down celebrating with me, he was decidedly more reserved. It was three in the afternoon and he was making his breakfast of super-caffeinated high-test leaded black coffee, "healthy" vitamins and a spongy green juice drink to counteract the drugs he'd needed to sleep the night before, to put him down from the coke he'd overindulged in.

"How? When? What are you talking about?" he said sluggishly.

"It starts next month, it shoots in Greece for six weeks. We'll start rehearsals next week!!!" I said in a flutter of excitement.

"What! You're not a real actress. You're not going to be able to do that! You'll make a complete fool out of yourself," he responded, almost irritated with me.

"They read me, and they loved me."

"It must have been a complete fluke. You haven't even had any real training. You're going to look like an idiot," he said staunchly, his face growing redder by the second. He's now frantically looking through the cutlery drawer for something, "Have you see a bag of coke? I had a half bag of coke, was here last night." I shook my head.

"But they knew all that!" I said, crestfallen, with water welling up in my eyes, mascara starting to smear down my cheeks. "They're willing to… work with me," I protested.

"Did the producer come on to you or something?"

This was obviously his real underlying fear, that I'd become a movie star and not need him anymore, or that some movie producer was going to want to make me his girlfriend and then turn me into a movie star…. Which I did learn later was quite true as to the workings of Hollywood. Still, surprisingly enough, this offer was completely straight up and one of the few roles where the casting couch had not even been implied.

"No, nothing like that."

He didn't look convinced, but he tried to change his tone to be more sympathetic, "Look, Love, they made a mistake. Once you get on the set and you can't act, they're going to be so mad at you. Honey, you need to tell them you can't do it."

"I'll get an acting coach to work with me on the scenes…"

Now he's pissed off. "We've got photo shoots to do. We're making money doing photo shoots!"

"We don't have anything new booked right now. I've still got a ton in the can and it won't make any difference if I take off for a few weeks."

"FINE!!! If that's how serious you are about making money with photos, then give me all my photo sets back. Pack your shit and get out tonight. We're done!!!" He stomped his feet like a spoiled child. "And when those checks come in, don't expect any part of them."

"But what do you mean? Why does it have anything to do with our photo business? And we haven't been paid yet from any of those sets that I SOLD. That's not fair, I worked really hard for that."

"Well, it's your choice. It's not my fault, you're making the decision; the photo sets or this stupid acting thing."

I burst into tears, sobbing defeated. The ultimatum was on the table. Take this acting job and lose all the money I'd earned from the photo sets and a great business partnership, not to mention the man I loved. And what if I give all that up to do this acting job and he's right and I make a complete fool of myself?

"I don't even know what to say to them. I already agreed to do it," I said, as a last-ditch effort before defeating.

"You don't have to tell them the truth. Just tell them you've talked to your manager and you want triple the money. That will do it."

I felt terrible. But the choice was clear, so I did just what Clive demanded of me. To both of our surprise they agreed to my higher price. Still it was him or the role and his foot wasn't budging.

He had just crushed what miserly amount of self-confidence I had, that had managed to get my tippy-toe in Show Biz. Putting my hands to my face, sobbing. I thought I needed him emotionally and he knew more about this than me.

Clive offered a condolence, "Look if you really want to be an actress, take some serious acting classes and then try out for some roles. There will be lots more like those and you'll be more prepared. I really am being supportive; I just want you to look your best."

It was an empty promise, *but at least I had been given the green light to pursue my acting and he'd support me in the future, right?* As the months went by I threw myself into acting classes, got myself a good acting agent and started going out regularly on auditions. I started booking jobs, but they were small roles and more often than not, I was cast in the sexy babe role. I began to realize just how much I'd blown it, by turning down such an opportunity, and I resented him, yet I didn't have the guts to leave him. My rebellion was stirring, and I had one eye open for the real love of my life. A gap was definitely growing between us.

My acting was no longer something I shared with him, rather it was something I kept to myself, especially when I was cast in a steamy scene with some handsome Hollywood actor. On the other-hand I was more than suspicious about the odd model Clive would have a specific interest in shooting when I happened to be away.

My relationship with Clive clearly had some ups and downs and I had a whole other Hollywood life without him.

I decided perhaps I shouldn't hang everything on Clive as my one photographer and decided to call some photographers I had modelled for in England. These were mainstream, advertising chaps but most of them shot calendar material as well. "How about shooting some of this nudie girly stuff for America? No one will know it's you! You can even use a different name!"

"Of course, love, absolutely, are you kidding! Get paid to shoot beautiful nude girls!" They were on, and these were excellent photographers, so I started to get some shoots out of Europe that were the best quality work. I had photographers from the top ad agencies, normally charging top dollar, doing little girly shoots on the side in exotic locations, "just for shits and grins!" Plus, they'd get mainstream advertising models to go nude for American mags where "no one would ever see it." So, I started to get amazing models and fabulous photos coming out of London that no one back home in the UK would ever know about!

Clive of course wasn't crazy about my partnerships with other photographers, but he couldn't find much of an excuse to stop me. I was now collecting a lot more photo sets that I could present to the publishers and so I reasoned with him that it was actually helping us.

I noticed many of these New York publishers also had mainstream magazines as well. Everything from "Home and Garden" type publications, to culture, cooking, history, you name it. Now this was something I could really get into. I knew great photographers who shot this kind of work and this was really the art I liked. So, I started collecting fantastic photographers in London, offering to be their agent and opening up a whole new market for them. Incredibly beautiful landscapes, horticulture photographers and photos of historical castles. Equally there were great photographers in Los Angeles and I started repping photographers in America and selling their work back to magazines in London.

The beautiful, creative, real art photos were my favorite, but unfortunately the girly stuff always brought in more money. Acting was still my main pursuit, but my little side business was starting to flourish. Without even much real thought, I called it *Agency International.* Had a real bland, spy-type ring to it, like *Universal Exports,* the fake company that James Bond always worked for. Without thinking about it or planning it at all, I was, for better or worse, officially in the Sex Biz!

CHAPTER FIVE

Big Apple Sex Slave

WOLF WHISTLES CHASED me down Broadway and my ego was lit up by the attention. I was a mature nineteen-year-old, wearing a crisp, burgundy, sexy suit and heels and pulling along a suitcase full of images for my first business meetings in New York City.

First on my list was editor Stan. Arriving at this sprawling Manhattan publishing company, Stan met me in the reception. A small balding chubby man, dressed in a business suit, that was a little warn and ill fitting. He had a very inviting round face with a huge grin. "Lovely to meet you Gail. Thank you so much for coming all the way out from Los Angeles," he said nervously twitching as if he had never had a visitor before, especially not a female one.

As we entered, we passed by the publisher's executive offices where we bumped into the head honcho.

"Mr. Simpson, this is Gail. She's the rep I was telling you about with the great material out of Europe."

Mr. Simpson was a very well put together, older gentleman with graying hair and he looked surprised at my appearance. "Welcome to our little publishing house. VERY nice to meet you," he smiled sweetly. "So, you came all the way out here to visit us? Perhaps I can take you to dinner while you're in town?" he asked hopeful.

"Would love to. That would be great."

"Wonderful! Stan, please take good care of our visitor and show her around."

Stan took great pleasure in showing me off around the office to all the other staff, like I was some rare find. Like most magazine companies, there was an executive area and production rooms, and the editorial staff had either a very small office or a perhaps only a cubicle in the large open area. Each editor seemed to be assigned as the head to one or two magazines and even though they didn't seem to have much authority in the company, I learned that these guys were mostly given free range as to what photos to purchase, so these were my guys!

Back in Stan's little corner cubicle, he started to look through my photo sets as we chatted.

"So, do the other reps not come to New York that often?" I inquired.

"No, we just talk on the phone. I met a photographer John once, he came out. But, no, normally we just talk on the phone."

"So, do you meet the models?" I said, looking at the pages of naked girls from his magazine in various stages of production all scattered around.

He blushed, "No never met any of the girls. Except once, I got to go to the Video Awards. That was great! I got an autograph from Ginger Lynn!" he said proudly pointing at the magazine clipping posted on his cubicle wall with a lipstick stain and his name scribbled and 'with love, Ginger' below.

Stan was making a large pile of photo layouts he was interested in, when he hesitated as if he was not sure about this one particular layout and I quickly picked up the reins, "I love this layout. I think that girl is just stunning and I'm sure it's not often you get beach sets from Europe."

"Yes, you're right," he agreed, adding it to his "buy" selections.

"Stan, would you have time for lunch today? I thought we could get a bite to eat."

"Oh, wow," he said, shocked and delighted, "That would be wonderful!"

I quickly realized, selling photos was going to be so easy....

Although men were the norm, there were a couple of women editors I was excited to meet. Next on my list was Yvonne.

A few blocks south, I arrived at Yvonne's office reception. "Hi, I'm here for Yvonne."

Suddenly a door opened, and the strangest sight appeared. A very tall lady in pumps, stockings and a mini skirt carrying a small little man on her back, jogged across reception. The man bounced like a little backpack on her back screeching the most bizarre erotic noises.

"That's Yvonne," the receptionist said like nothing was out of the ordinary.

Yvonne promptly dropped the little man, who quickly scurried off through the opposite door.

"Hi, you must be Gail?" Yvonne said as I tried not to look too shocked. "That was one of my art guys, gets a piggy back ride as a special treat, once in a while. It gets him off. How are you? How was your trip in."

"Err... great thanks."

Yvonne led me back to her office as if nothing was amiss. She was a smartly dressed, in-charge sort of businesswoman who towered over me. Six feet, three inches with bare feet, but she didn't have bare feet, she had perfectly crisp shiny six inchers on and silk stockings that seemed to go all the way up to her chest. Certainly, all the way up to my chest. She was intimidating, but right off the bat she took a shine to me. "You are much younger than I expected," she remarked. "It's very admirable to see someone of your age, especially a woman, doing what you're doing."

Have a seat. "Let's see what you've got." She said pointing to my suitcase and I quickly got out all the layouts for her to look through.

She seemed to know exactly what she was looking for as she wasted no time examining the images.

"Love the lighting, fantastic model! And love the pics in the street! Wow, these Europeans really capture the essence," she said holding a sheet of chromes to the light of the window, her expert eye focused through a small magnifier.

I explained a little more, "Yes, this photographer has a well-known advertising studio. His work is amazing. He's a good friend, so I was able to get him to shoot some nude layouts."

"His photography is top notch. Needs to angle better to accentuate the legs more. He needs to get lower to create the length of the leg. The shadows are perfect but if he'd just lined up the stocking seams."

"I can work with him on the poses and angles," I offered.

"We need to get you some real antique stockings though. Not the stretch fake ones. Glossy, my readers love GLOSSY. I'll give you some places to get the correct denier and sheen. Still, there's some excellent shots here. I'll take this one." She moved the folder of "Judy, Stockings London Bridge" to the increasing "Yes" pile.

OMG Yes!!! I tried to hide how thrilled I was at the amount she was going to buy.

As she carefully went through each set, my eyes browsed her office. You couldn't miss the bookshelf of carefully organized six-inch heels; red ones, black ones, polka dot ones, ones with diamonds, ones with spikes, all spanking brand new with not a scuffmark in site.

"Readers send them to me," she said deservingly. "They send me fine stockings, silk fishnets, just the best hose and I acknowledge them if they're good."

Then, I noticed the collection of "things" in jars on her desk. You know, pickled spiders, a preserved baby chicken and other oddities. She must have seen my eyes focused on her special jar. Something that looked like an alien baby.

"That's an alien baby!" she said proudly.

Oh....? I thought to myself.

Yvonne continued: "The other day some guy asked me if it was a real alien. Hah! I laughed. I said; 'Yes it came from Queens."

I was glad I hadn't asked.

She continued greatly amused, "Then he thought it was a real alien from Queens! Men!"

I was completely baffled and feeling rather stupid. I must have looked confused and she referenced that they sell a bunch of plastic crap like that in Queens. I was let off the hook, on account of being British. I was trying to appear mature and knowledgeable in the realms of sex and whatever else was going on around here, but inside I was feeling downright dumb about a lot of this.

Luckily the moment was saved by an interruption from a young, good looking guy, with a thick head of curly blonde hair, who came in with some mail for her. Yvonne pulled out a twenty-dollar bill and handed it to him, "Can you run to the corner and get me some tampons."

As he left, I must have blushed for her and she looked at me quizzically. I explained myself in a whisper, "You send your male assistant out for tampons? I'd be too embarrassed."

At that he popped his head back in and unfortunately heard me and I was even more embarrassed.

"Yeah, he doesn't mind, do you *Panty Boy*?"

He groaned with a smile, like it was all part of working around here.

"You can borrow him for the rest of your time in New York," she remarked flippantly.

"You'll be Gail's slave for the rest of the week. Driving her around and whatever else she needs. Okay?" she ordered him.

"Sure," he answered beaming at me and I was a little taken aback but not complaining.

I wondered if men ever filed sexual harassment suits against female employers, but knowing her office, it was probably something they happily signed up for.

We went across the road for a quick coffee and I got to see a day-in-the-life of the New York businesswoman. She was awesome, a little intimidating yes, but awesome. And I'd found a new contact and friend.

Back at the office we were finishing up, counting up the number of layouts she was considering, and I was trying to hold back on the victory dance and restraining from showing just how completely thrilled I was, when she said, "Would you be up for going to a club tonight?"

"Yeah sounds great," I responded, honestly rather excited.

"It's a very cool club, downtown, exclusive," she said in an excited whisper.

"Great!" I replied.

But there was more…

She continued, "You know how it is after work when you are all pent up, you just wanna go home and beat the shit out of someone?"

Err…well no, I didn't really but I didn't want to look stupid, so I nodded slightly hoping she'd explain.

"Well this is a great place because these guys love to have the shit kicked out of them. So, we just go and get it all out. They line up and love it."

I was completely bewildered at this thing she thought was normal, but there was even more…

"*Brian the Pony* should be there tonight. He's great."

I was trying to look nonchalant like I knew what she was talking about but inside I was clueless. At this point I must have really looked puzzled.

"You ride him. He has a saddle all strapped on. He gives you the spurs and whip and you can ride him around."

Now I was even more confused, but I left it at that. I knew I had a pile of layouts being considered and going to the Pony Club might endear me to her and be the incentive for her to buy the lot. I semi-committed to go in the hopes of making a deal.

She smiled at my acceptance, "I can go twenty-two hundred on these and I'll pass on the maybes," Yvonne said, pointing at the fifteen or so sets in the "buy" pile and handing back her "maybe" pile.

"Well, I really wanted twenty-five hundred each, especially since a lot of them are out of Europe, but I'll agree to twenty-two if you take the "maybe" pile as well."

"Oh, you're good!" she said, smiling at me, and after a second of consideration she said, "It's a deal."

OMG, wow, I can't believe I sold the lot! I thought.

I left the office, making sure I was fully around the corner before I did a huge victory dance!!!

I figured I'd come up with an excuse later that evening to gracefully bow out of the *S & M–beat up guys–pony club,* which thankfully I did.

As promised, Panty Boy drove me around for the rest of the week. I am sure he was available for anything else I asked, but that and doing the odd deli run were all I asked.

This was the first of my many trips to New York and over the years, I got to know Yvonne quite well, and every visit was always entertaining. The Pony club was offered a few times and eventually, to make a sale I did end up agreeing to go to a very special New York restaurant. On the menu was fancy French food, drinks but also Public Humiliation.

While enjoying fine dining, the soft background music was suddenly interrupted by a waiter with a loud bell, "Attention everyone! Table Two just ordered Humiliation and Ten Lashings."

Everyone, paused their dinning and with delight, looked to Table Two where a man standing on his chair, was bent over and having his butt paddled by his two sexily dressed lady friends.

Yvonne's shoe collection, men sending stockings to her and the afterwork lashings were only the tip of the iceberg that Yvonne introduced my innocent little mind to.

Still, I was new in the biz and if I thought these exploits were pretty eye opening, I had no idea what was coming.

CHAPTER SIX

Sex, Drugs & The Playboy Mansion

I STILL CONSIDERED acting my main and respectable profession and the photo biz a little sideline I'd secretly gone off on. I certainly spent more of my days trying desperately to be an actress, going on auditions, in acting classes and occasionally actually shooting. My photo business, which was taking off in the background, really didn't require much time. Hollywood however, required hours of dedication. Trying unsuccessfully to get rid of my damnable British accent was a bit of a chore. Still, I was working pretty regularly now; I'd get lots of tiny roles on shows you'd recognize and lots of big roles on movies where no one was listening to my accent. I was, for sure, typecast as the sexy girl.

Meanwhile, I fancied myself as a more serious actress and spent hours learning lines and appearing in respectable theatre productions around Los Angeles. I had the acting bug and like most other young Hollywood starlets, my inadequate self was desperately chasing the dream to be admired on the silver screen. The silver screen was more interested in my hot bod.

Clive wasn't happy about it and I can't blame him. He had good reason to be jealous. It was hard not to feel anything when the role involved throwing yourself passionately into your work. Some Brad Pit look-a-like, sweeping you off your feet both on and off camera was hard to resist. And I had certainly succumbed to the temptation to make out a little, more than once. Still, I learned pretty quick, Hollywood leading men were all about themselves. Overly good-looking men would lead to no more than a quick fling and a lot of heartache.

So, Clive knew nothing about that and I knew very little about what he was getting up to behind the scenes. Our relationship was held together by a teeny-tiny thread.

Modeling he was ok with, as long as it was local, where he could feel he was somewhat in control of me. I had the usual Hollywood commercial print agent who kept me busy with ad gigs. I had a reputation unlike many other LA models as pleasant to work with, happy, hardworking and on time; this went a long way. I could strap down my boobs and without makeup pass for a tweenie, selling products for the most mainstream of teen products out there. Or I could show off my DDs and get cast for a whole different look. It was probably more for that look that Playboy picked me up for their modeling agency and worked me continuously. Surprisingly Playboy had a pretty mainstream agency. They did everything from real TV commercials and regular ad campaigns, to all that their brand name was famous for.

In particular, this meant many evenings at the Playboy mansion and many parties donning the well-known black and white corset dress with matching Bunny Ears and most importantly loads of cleavage. There was a status to being part of the Playboy stable of models and this made me feel special, sexy and sophisticated, even if I didn't one hundred percent believe I deserved it.

They occasionally used me as the stand-in girl for some of the celebrities that posed for Playboy. For instance, the Mariel Hemingway shoot. They'd dress me in the outfit, do my hair and makeup and do an entire mock photo shoot to get the light perfect for Mariel. The photographers always asked me if I'd pose for the magazine myself, but I didn't dare try out. I would have absolutely loved to, but Playboy was very strict about their centerfolds and basically owned you from there on. I knew it would be a huge scandal if I came out as a Playboy Centerfold and I was the one selling the photos to his competition. I decided it was better to fly under the radar. I was already riding a fine line as it was and stuck to the Mansion appearances and the advertising gigs.

There was a stark difference between the girls like me who were hired specifically from the agency for event evenings, or even regular Playmates, to those living at the Mansion who were his "girlfriends." These were staples at the Mansion vying for Hef's affection to be the chosen one (or ones) in his favor and possibly land Playmate of the Year. Most of them had an air of aloofness and didn't seem to interact with anyone until Hef came around, when they could be seen jostling for position and attracting as much attention to themselves as possible.

I was surprised to find Mr. Hugh M. Hefner to be a very sweet, charming, more reserved gentleman than one would expect, and I thought him suave and sophisticated. He exuded power and influence with a soft tender side that could make any girl feel the most special in the world. I loved working at the mansion feeling admired and mingling with Hollywood elite. And the contacts were great for my acting career.

One evening, I was hired as a hostess for the after party for a special movie screening night and I was probably one of the few girls who opted to arrive early to actually watch the movie. I found Hef pre-party quietly sitting in his study making handwritten notes he was about to share with the guests about the classic movie being shown tonight.

"Hey Gail, how was your trip to London?"

"It was great, thanks. I'm surprised you remembered."

"I love England at this time of the year. Did you check out that restaurant I told you about?"

It always stunned me that Hef would remember the smallest detail we had talked about before and be polite enough to follow up. I almost wondered if he made handwritten notes about conversations as diligently as he did about the classic movie screenings.

"Did you see the family in Yorkshire?"

"Yes," I smiled and relayed all the highlights of my trip. That is all without mentioning the real reason I had gone to England-to get photo sets to sell. We had much to share about, except the elephant in the closet; that in a way, I was secretly becoming his direct competition. That I was providing sexy images to every men's magazine I could find, other than his. Playboy was one of the few companies that shot their own layouts. Pics in any other publications could likely be mine. This elephant would have to secretly remain in my closet, hidden from Hef and the Playboy organization I was modelling for, just as it was hidden from my Hollywood agent and most of my contacts in mainstream Hollywood. I am not sure how Hef would have reacted; still they were certainly separated, and I kept them that way.

Cindi, a stunning, peroxide blonde haired, blue eyed goddess, suddenly popped into the study. A rare appearance to see any of Hef's "girlfriends" in his quiet place of more meaningful interaction.

"Hef, I was thinking about wearing the diamond earrings tonight?" she phrases as a question and opportunity to seductively brush her white blonde locks off her bare shoulder to reveal her three-tiered costume bling. "The ones I am waiting to wear in my Playboy Centerfold," with an obvious emphasis on "waiting."

Hef was clearly more impressed with the sequined bustier, barely holding up her heaving cleavage.

"Cindi are you coming to the screening this evening?"

"What's the movie?"

"One of the most romantic movies you will ever see in your life — *Casablanca*."

"Oh, what's that? Is it one of those black and white ones? I don't do black and white." And at that she planted a baby pink lipstick mark on his cheek, "I'll see you later for the champagne after party."

She shot me a look on the way out as if to say, "What are you guys having a conversation about?"

It was a dog eat dog world amongst the group of Hef's official girlfriends, who were juggling for a slot to impress the great Hef, or more importantly to move up their place in the hierarchy and possibly make Playmate of the Year. She had nothing to worry about; Hef and I were having "real conversations" and he wasn't luring over my body. Or at least I never noticed. Perhaps I was too naive to see it, or perhaps I was not the ultra-glammed up, fake boob, peroxide type that he seemed to enjoy. After all, he made the famous quote, "Picasso had his pink period and his blue period. I am in my blonde period right now." I presumed I was not pretty enough, not glamourous enough, or too young looking to be really taken seriously by Hef.

Later that evening, Hef had changed into the red silk pajamas and long red flowing cigar robe with the black padded waffle lapels with babes on each arm to mingle with the celebrities who had shown up expecting this of their icon. The bubbly was flowing, and the "girlfriends" were showing their best public persona.

The night was now in full swing and with a little too many champagne flutes down, I found myself in the Jacuzzi Grotto doing shots with some directors. It was not the worst place for a girl to mingle and meet Hollywood directors, especially if you didn't mind being cast as the sexy "Playmate" role in a movie, and I was taking full advantage of the opportunity.

Some of Hef's girlfriends were there, as well as some hired models from their agency like me. Cindi had changed into her gold teeny tiny string bikini showing off her perfectly curved body and joined us.

One of the guys asked her, "So do you really date him, I mean really have sex with Hef?"

"NO! It's just publicity, silly," she responded adamantly.

Later that evening and a few shots down, Traci, another model from the agency, persuaded me we should go upstairs to one of the little "private after parties." This was usually where I hung up my bunny ears and opted to retire for the evening, having finished my official "work" as a hostess. But this particular evening, I was having fun and decided *why not hang out and party a while?* The main event was thinning out and a select group from the Jacuzzi had migrated upstairs hanging out in one of the girls' rooms. We were having our own little private party with flowing booze, and as Qualudes were passed around and started kicking in, there was lots of stripping off and necking going on.

Hef and an entourage of bombshell girlfriends passed our room headed to his master suite.

"Come on, let's check out Hef's bedroom," Traci whispered naughtily.

At this point I was in total party mode and up for just about anything. We headed down the hall. "Shhh, just hang back and pretend to dance around and he won't notice us," Traci instructed me, giggling, as we entered his bedroom behind his staple of regulars. You could barely make out his four-poster bed with animal skin rugs, in the '70s-esque red dimmed lighting. There was some slow music out of Studio 54 playing in the background and we hung by the entrance pretending to be grooving out to the music.

Hef was laying on the bed and the harem of drop-dead gorgeous babes were trying desperately to entertain him, dancing around like a group of exotic dancers, each gyrating and slowly stripping in front of him, while others tried to get his attention by pretending to do some girl on girl kissing show. Cindi was up front, moving sexily to the music, now bottomless and wearing just a scrap of a pink lace bra, barely holding up her perfect voluptuous breasts. Cindi took the lead and climbed on to the bed on top of Hef. Stradling him, she seductively pulled her bra straps over her shoulders, her nipples gently being released as she cupped them forward to his waiting mouth in a way that appeared more like she was showing off her new breasts for an audition rather than she was actually turned on. Still Hef looked engrossed staring at the beautiful sight in his face. Other girls were kneeling on either side of the bed continuing their own squirming, sensual show for him. Then Hef grabbed Cindi by her tiny hour glass waist and she started to ride him rhythmically back and forth. She arched her back and mouthed an exaggerated ecstasy, posing and running her fingers through her long silky locks.

Within a few minutes Cindi rolled off as if she was completely satisfied and continued to dance sexily at the side of the bed as Hef's attention was taken by another blonde beauty queen beside him. The new girl slipped her hand under his robes and pretty soon, her tight little buns were on top. Pouting her glossy pumped up lips, she seemed to be more interested in her gorgeous image in the mirrored wall than in the love making she was performing.

Luckily Hef is still wearing his robe and the light is too dark to really see, I thought to myself, disappointed, my image of the great Hef waning slightly.

He took turns with some of the other stunning beauties for a quick in and out each. Meanwhile the other girls squirmed around naked next to them pretending to be turned on. Still the game appeared to be played well on both sides. The girls were playing Hef and Hef was obviously enjoying it.

Hef had gone through three or four girls now and Traci and I had got the gist of what was going on, and figured we better exit soon before

Hef decided to rope in a couple of newbies. We headed back to the other girl's suite.

The doorway was partly blocked with three or four intertwined naked bodies in a grope fest moaning and groaning in delight. As we squeezed though, the scene was a stark contrast to Hef's bedroom. There was an all-out fucking and sucking naked orgy going on where everyone seemed equally into it. This was way more out of control and clearly the ludes had totally kicked in. A producer I had been talking to earlier was spread out on the bed, his pants round his ankle with one stunning brunette sucking his dick and another blonde perfect-ten goddess sitting on his face.

One girl still soaking wet from the jacuzzi was laid face down passed out over a dresser, her legs spread eagle with some guy blowing through a straw sticking out between her beautiful round butt cheeks.

I had sobered up a little too much for this crowd now and I looked at my watch and it read "Two Am." I decided, I better turn in early. Traci decided she'd stay.

I saw Traci a few weeks later at an event.

"Fuck, that was an awesome night!" she said, "Can't remember a lot of it! I woke up in the morning and there were naked sleeping bodies everywhere. And…you know that actor who's on that soap…?"

"The one you had crush on that you were making out with in *The Grotto*?"

"Yes. Well I woke up next to him. I'm not sure if we did it or not! I was totally naked, but he still had his pants on. And I didn't want to ask him! Found my dress but I couldn't find my bra and panties anywhere. Anyway, I ended up going to breakfast with that producer you were talking to and he gave me a role in his new movie!"

Of course, I had relayed a slightly different version of that evening to my boyfriend Clive. I told him how wonderful the movie was and forgot to mention anything else. I had always told Clive, Hef was a perfect gentleman, which, well, he always was with me, and honestly after that one night as a voyeur, I'd stuck to the more professional goings on at the mansion.

Meanwhile Clive was working across town for the complete opposite of characters; the infamous, or more accurately, notorious Larry Flynt. If there was a mirror universe anti-matter version of Hef's erudite class, style and grace, Larry Flynt was it.

Larry had been quite the "Jack O' Lads," by all accounts. The solid gold statue on his desk of a cockerel humping a fat hen summed up his crude backwater swamp redneck personality and he was damn proud of it. Unfortunately, since he'd been shot and paralyzed, Larry's famous personality was not seen very often around the office anymore. His wife Althea was still hanging in at that time and we occasionally hung out at their mansion, sunning by the pool.

The first night I met Althea, we all went to the Roxy with Clive, Althea and a bunch of her other party animals. In the back of a stretch limo, she sprawled herself suggestively, spread her shinny slender legs revealed from her silk mini, and growled in her deep sultry voice, "Clive! Your girlfriend's sooooooo hot! I could eat her for dinner!" She smiled at me hungrily, eyeing me up and down, undressing me with her gaze, as if she was going to make good on her cannibalistic threat. She laughed with that provocative, scratchy voice, probably from the over abuse of smoking too much wacky tobaccky or more likely crack cocaine. Even in her anorexic state, she was still incredibly sexy, but she scared the bejesus out of me.

Then seductively, she leaned in, I thought to untie her strappy heels, rather she was looking for the last decent vein between her toes where she could shoot something. Access to Larry's pain killers and more money than most would see in a lifetime, meant she was on a steamroller of self-destruction.

Nights out with Althea, after parties, even the afternoons I just went over to hang with her at the pool, were always insane. Thank God, I hadn't participated in anything Althea would have had me try; as anyone could see the angel of death standing over her, her lifestyle dictating that her days were numbered. Unfortunately, it wasn't much longer 'til she passed away.

CHAPTER SEVEN

Penis Pump Tester

BY SHEER LUCK, Blue Cross Blue Shield decided to write a TV commercial involving a girl skydiving and the aerial cameraman Ted, a friend of mine from the skydiving center, put me up for the role.

"She's the only one in the Screen Actors Guild that is qualified," he boasted about me.

"Yes, you're fantastic! You're it. So, what's your rate?" the producer asked.

I looked at Ted totally clueless and he stepped in, acting as my agent, "She should get three times scale."

"Sure. We can do that," the producer agreed.

I had no idea what this meant, and I'd have been happy to get anything at all. What it really meant was that I would get three times residuals on a national commercial that would run for five years!!! I was eternally grateful for this nice little income that would help support me in my early days in Hollywood.

The execs at Playboy heard I did skydiving and asked if I'd do a different kind of skydiving segment for their Playboy channel. A day in the life of a Skydiving Playmate. It was exaggerated fantasy and much more glamorous, but it did include my real-life skydiving, albeit this time with bare boobies.

I returned the favor and got the skydiving camera gig for my friend Ted.

The script called for some non-skydiving intro, an entrance shot of me driving my real life red convertible into my luxurious home and then doing laps in my pool. My "on camera home" was to be the Playboy Mansion but when we turned up for the shoot, there was a double booking that day. Clive's house was nice but would not suffice. They needed a grandiose, over the top luxurious mansion type setting. I suggested to the director that we use Larry Flynt's house. I knew the code and I often went over to the pool to hang out. Plus, Larry's mansion was always deserted. It was lavishly decorated with imported Italian statues, bronze goddesses and dripping gold trimmed everything, so it was perfect for the shot.

Hefner would have had an absolute fit had he known we went to Flynt's house and Flynt would have had a fit if he had he known the shoot was for Playboy. But neither of them did.

When we arrived at Larry's incredible Beverly Hills Mansion, as usual there was no one around. Since Althea, Larry's love, had finally succumbed to her fate and left Larry heartbroken and alone, the house had been very strange. Not the fun bustling social gathering place it had been with her around. Larry now spent most of his time depressed and drugged up, alone in his palatial bedroom suite while the rest of the mansion was going to pot.

There was an art dealer lady who came around quite often to console Larry and take advantage of his condition and convincing him he had impeccable taste as a fine art collector. Larry's taste in art was dictated by his designs on sleeping with the art dealer, or eating her pussy, because he couldn't do much else. And in return hundreds of the finest European oils on canvas were stacked up against the walls with the price tags still on. Impressive bronzes and Picasso sculptures just scattered around, still in the bubble wrap. The house didn't look like anyone was even living there. It was more like an abandoned art gallery. The only room that was in use was his upstairs bedroom where he was pretty much confined twenty-four hours, seven days a week.

Outside the front of this grandiose mansion in the impressive circular driveway we were secretly capturing the most amazing backdrop. As I pulled up in my convertible the camera zoomed in on my license plate that read "SKYBUNY." Obviously, it was a movie license plate they had made at the Hollywood prop-house, but I thought it was fun and kept it on my car for ages after. The cops in Beverly Hills pulled me over a few times because of the "Hollywood" plate. I would explain to them what it was for, which usually led to all kinds of questions about Playboy and an autographed photo and I was on my way. So, the Beverly Hills cops knew me as Skybuny.

We were now in the pool area, me in my hot bikini doing my "routine," casual but sensual, morning laps, when the grand golden gates opened unexpectedly and in drove a huge dinged up and dirty pick-up truck I recognized as Morgan's.

The director and I looked at each other, sure we'd been caught. Morgan had pulled in the drive with some hot chick passenger. Morgan also appeared a little surprised and clearly nervous to see someone else there. Morgan was an editor who worked for Flynt who I knew fairly well. One of Larry's minions, who to say lacked confidence would be a gross understatement. Always awkwardly dressed in jeans two sizes too big for him, hoisted way up at the waist almost to his chest by a pair of his signature suspenders and a wrinkled and stained shirt he'd clearly been living in for a week. All an indication of his lack of female company to take care of him which made this sexy passenger a total mystery.

Morgan looked a little sheepish as he explained very hush hush that Larry had just had this new, miraculous operation. Larry had been paralyzed below the waist for several years, but thanks to this new surgical penis implant, he was now supposedly able to get an erection. I don't know if it was a pump that could be inflated like a blow-up pool float or something, or how exactly it worked, but he apparently should be able get something that resembled a hard on. And maybe he could even have sex with someone. Hence the hot chick was the "someone" who was there to test out the theory.

I confessed to Morgan about our illicit photo shoot and that we were there incognito as well. Morgan was sworn to secrecy not to tell anyone. In return, we were sworn to secrecy about the whole pump fucking hooker thing. Morgan went into the house with the chick to test out Larry's new operation, leaving us outside by the pool doing the Playboy video.

We finished filming with only a glance from the gardener who was taking his sweet time to ever so carefully prune the roses and some security guy who just waved an Okay and then stared at my chest for a while.

Footage in the can, we wondered how Morgan and the new appendage were getting along. It was suspiciously quiet up there and I was dying to know.

We tiptoed quietly up the grand staircase and carefully cracked open the massive carved oak door. Larry was laying out like a beached whale, half naked on his red and gold satin sheet adorned four-poster. The little chickie was dressed in red lace crotchless panties, matching bra comprised of a wisp of the lace just barely decorating her pert nipples and patent leather thigh-high boots. And there, perched near Larry's feet, was Morgan, squatting on the edge of the bed, his jeans and suspenders around his ankles, and the red goddess on her knees in front of him, her head bobbing up and down, clearly going to town on Morgan.

Morgan's face went white when he saw us. "Shh, don't wake him up," he motioned in a whisper. Terror and ecstasy flashing across his face, as he debated whether he should stop or keep going. He kept going, the expression on his face telling me to be quiet for just a second longer.

I thought, *If this sleeping bear wakes up to see his lowlife editor fucking his chick at the foot of his bed we are all going to feel his wrath.*

"Oh my God! Morgan! If Larry wakes up, he is going to have a fit!" I exclaimed frantically in an exaggerated whisper.

"Hold on, shhhhh….. awe….ahhh……" Morgan released in ecstasy as quietly as he could.

And then, as the blood started to return to his main head, he suddenly came back to reality and was trying frantically to get his pants on.

"She was here, and we were sitting around waiting for Larry to wake up. We'd been waiting ages and ages. And I thought, *She's already been paid. He wouldn't want it to go to waste.* So, I decided to just take the opportunity and do what Larry would do, if he could, and fuck her."

Luckily, Larry was in a drug induced sweet dream and we all got away with it.

The next day I went to a different location to shoot the skydiving portion with Ted the aerial cameraman. We had done a few shows and now a commercial together, but this was the first nudie one for us and Ted was not complaining. I rode up in the C130 in my bikini and parachute until it was time to jump.

As a cinematographer perfectionist, it was important for Ted to line up the sunset perfectly to give my naked breasts that glistering glow, reflecting the baby oil off my bare chest. A lesser priority was lining up the airplane to exit in order to safely land back at the airport. We were miles off course.

In preparation for the jump, I undid my bikini and threaded it through my rig, handing it to Ted who carefully zipped it in his pants' pocket.

Standing in the open doorway at twelve thousand feet, adrenaline pumping high, I fake a few sexy lines to the camera about how this just turns me on so much. Then I make a dramatic exit out of the plane, naked with Ted hot on my tail. I smiled sexily in free fall and did a few acrobatic moves trying to look erotic to the camera. It was hard to be convincingly sexy, as my breasts hit one hundred and twenty miles an hour, smacking me in the face and bobbling all over the place, just as Playboy ordered. Who ever thought breasts pounded and distorted like Jim Carrey sticking his head out of a full speed freight train, would be attractive, I don't know. Clearly fantasy was probably quite different from reality. Still it was certainly exciting and naked, so guys would watch it.

Shot in the can and out of altitude we both pull our chutes. I am instantly whisked away, yanked up to the clouds by my brightly colored rainbow parachute. I look below at the Ted who continues to fall away at high speed; a little trail of flailing white silk was a tell-tale sign his parachute was malfunctioning. My heart leapt. But all I could do was pray for him. Finally, after several seconds and dangerously closer to the earth, his shoot finally opened.

He was so close to the ground he had no choice but to land right there, in the little town of Perris Valley where there happened to be a big country fair.

So here I am stark naked steering my parachute into the middle of a full-blown carnival. I smiled at the shocked carousel passengers as I swooped naked just feet alongside the high swinging baskets on the Ferris wheel. I could do nothing to cover my nothingness as a whole wheel full of families stared at this strange sight. Crowds of people on the ground were now looking to the sky, gasping and pointing. I came in to land perfectly a few feet from Ted waiting with my bikini, but not without a circle of spectators surrounding me, stood with their cotton candy mouths, wide open.

The behind-the-scenes footage would probably have been much more exciting if included. Still, the sexy little skydiving vignette showing full frame of Larry Flynt's mansion, ran as the flagship and opener to all Playboy programming for years to come.

CHAPTER EIGHT

Guccione and Owning it All

GUCCIONE, THE OWNER of Penthouse Magazine, was in a league of his own. I had been submitting photos to his magazine for just a little while when I got an invite to meet the man himself.

Arriving one balmy summer evening at his private home in uptown Manhattan, it looked more like a hotel than anyone's personal living space. It is, "The largest private residence in Manhattan," Guccione proudly informed me later, consisting of two apartment blocks, nine stories high that created a huge horseshoe of brownstones, wrapped around an impressive garden with rambling ivy that reminded me of a grand London estate. Perhaps from a daunting black and white horror movie though. Standing at the huge oak door, I am a little intimidated to say the least.

As the heavy grand door opened, I am greeted by his long-time assistant Janet, who I'd talked to on the phone, along with his two, huge fierce looking, Rhodesian Ridgeback dogs with spiked collars whose coats glistened in the dimmed light of the candelabras.

"Come in!" she offered smiling, "Bob's in his study, working late as always. I'll let him know you're here."

I am left in the entrance that was a dimly lit Caesar's Palace, and I don't mean like the Vegas one, as there was nothing gimmicky about this. This is the real deal. Statues of Julius Caesar and Augustus on hefty marble columns, seemed like authentic Roman artifacts staring at me accusingly. Behind a massive wall of glass was a full-length lap pool, inlaid with shining brilliant mosaic.

Janet arrives back, "He'll just be a minute. He likes to work in the evenings when it's quiet. He looks through every photo himself, so he spends hours checking each image. Bob has an amazing eye. He's an incredible artist."

She offers a little about the entrance way; "Most of these statues are antiques out of Rome. Bob loves ancient art and a lot of them he acquired for movie he did, *Caligula*.

She points to the lap pool I was admiring, "Those are original tiles from the same period. Beautiful isn't it? Bob is the only one who really uses the pool, he likes to do laps in the evenings sometime. It's inlaid with silver."

I must have looked quite impressed.

"His Jacuzzi upstairs is inlaid with twenty-four carat gold mosaic!" she laughs.

Janet switches to business, "So, you sent us some beautiful photography. Bob is excited to talk to you about it."

"Wonderful, yes those are the layouts from the European photographers I was telling you about," I offered up excitedly.

"Bob used to shoot all the layouts, he doesn't shoot anymore, but he spends hours looking through thousands of chromes, every shadow, every hair, he really knows what he's doing."

At that, Guccione breaks the conversation as he arrives from his office. Sleek, sophisticated, particularly well put together and looking far younger and more attractive than I had imagined he would. He was wearing his signature silk shirt open way down, exposing his strong muscular pectorals, his bare tanned smooth chest, adorned with heavy, gold medallions. Oozing charm, he confidently shakes my hand.

"Very nice to meet you," he says smiling, "You sent us some really interesting material."

"Thank you. Very good photographers out of London." I reply.

"And I presume from the accent, that's where you're from?" he says fondly.

I smiled a "yes."

"Many great memories from my time in London! Anyway, sorry to keep you waiting. I was just finishing up the next issue. Let me show you around," he offered.

Then Bob Guccione himself gave me a personal tour of the house.

Standing in the dining room looking at a huge intricate ornate floor, Bob is delighted to show off the fine details; "These floor tiles were antique from Italy. I brought over a team of artists from Rome and I showed them exactly where to put each piece."

"Wow, how long did that take?" I exclaimed looking at this massive design.

"About nine months," he said proudly.

Then through the halls, he noted some of his paintings, "Picasso. One of my favorite pieces," he said, pointing to the painting with great admiration in his eye. Then pausing at another, "This Matisse, I fell in love with."

"And the master of all, "Salvador Dalis!" he said, stopping underneath with a sigh and looking up at this slightly disturbing painting like it was the love of his life. I must admit, it is all pretty lost on me.

A little further down the hall he stops at another, "One of my own early ones," he says smiling proudly.

I looked a little confused, and he explains, "I was an artist originally. That is my passion. Don't have enough time anymore."

"Wow, that's incredible!" I exclaimed looking up at the impressive, erotic oil, albeit a little tortured and dark.

Then the tour of his Grand Master Bedroom and the inlaid gold Jacuzzi!

He noticed my eyes wander to some framed black and white artistic nude photo by the book shelf, "Helmut Newton, a master of erotica!" Bob exclaimed admiring the photo, "You have to have an eye to capture beauty; when you are shooting, when you're creating a magazine. Now he has an eye!"

And then back downstairs, the tour continues, "And my favorite room of all! The kitchen. You'll always find me hanging out here. I find making pasta, very soothing. Do you like Spaghetti Bolognese?"

"Yes, love it." I replied

"Are you hungry, can I cook you some spaghetti?" Bob asks

"Wow! Really? That would be great."

Bob smiled, grabbing a couple of stem wine glasses from the hanging rack and pulling out a bottle of red wine. "From the Bordeaux region. A little unknown vineyard I discovered," he says, pouring two glasses and sitting me at a large wooden island while he grabs some garlic excitedly and starts chopping. He's really making me pasta!

"When I've had parties here, my friends always say they'll find me hanging out in the kitchen. I suppose they're right. People think I'm a bit of a recluse, with a rather morose side."

I smiled, not really knowing what to say.

"So, you're from the UK and you have photographers over there."

"Yes, they are actually advertising photographers that I had worked with as a model and I got them to do some nude shoots," I explained.

"A model! Well, you are beautiful," Bob said looking me directly in the eyes, "Janet didn't tell me you were so attractive. I was a bit confused when I saw you because she just told me you were an agent but when I saw you I thought you were a model!"

"Thank you. Yes, I did a bit of modeling in England and I worked with some great photographers and they were willing to shoot nudes, if it was for the States and not for the UK."

"Well, the photos are great. Beautiful girls. There are some incredible shots and I'm not often impressed. I loved the shoot with Big Ben in the background. Reminds me of my days in London at the clubs in Mayfair."

"String Fellows!" we both spilled out at the same time, and then laughed.

Pretty soon we were engrossed in conversation about his time in London while Bob chopped fresh tomatoes. He seemed pleasantly surprised to have a Brit to remind him of his wild, exciting past at the clubs in London where his empire began. We reminisced about fun times at *String Fellows* nightclub where as a Page Three Girl, I too had enjoyed holding court in the VIP area. All the while Bob was happily chopping, stirring and preparing home-made pasta for two.

"So, are you doing modeling in LA?" Bob changed the subject.

I told him I was acting a bit, doing the odd commercials and admitted I worked at the Playboy Mansion sometimes.

"Playboy!" Bob scoffed! "What a ridiculous satire! And the whole Playboy Mansion, who would live their life in such a farce?" Bob laughed. "Playboy is a fake, superficial, sell out to commercial masses. When

I created my magazine, I wanted it to be an imitation of real life; crisp, stark, erotic desire. As a photographer I wanted to capture elegance, yet raw and voyeuristic," he said, his thoughts drifting off to the images.

"I've always felt that way," Bob points lovingly to a large beautiful oil painting that hung on the back wall, "That was one of the paintings I did back in London when I was really a starving artist."

It was a beautiful voluptuous nude reclining Renaissance style.

"A man offered me five thousand pounds for that. Was a lot of money back then, but it was on the condition that I would paint over the pubic hair!"

I looked over the beautifully tasteful nude, and I wouldn't particularly have noticed the area 'til he pointed it out.

"Said it was too risqué. Said I could do 'a few brush strokes of nude paint on the lower area' to remove any obvious offensiveness!" Guccione recalled, still adamantly offended to this day. "There was no way! I didn't have a penny to my name, but I wasn't going to stoop so low as to deface my art!"

Guccione continues, "You do not COMPROMISE art. I'd have rather starved!!!"

Honestly, I'm thinking, *I can't believe you didn't take the money. I would have slapped some paint over that in a flat second and bitten his hand off for the cash, are you kidding!*

"Censorship and sexual repression is the true meaning of Pornography!" Bob said with such disdain that it was clearly the moral he would fight for his entire existence.

Wow! Bob is intense, I thought to myself

Bob continued, lightening up a bit, "Finally, though, I had a little money saved up. I was torn between using the money to open a Dry Cleaners or using it to start a magazine!" he laughed to himself, "And the rest is history!"

We had a fabulous dinner of fresh, Bob-cooked pasta, just sitting at the counter in his kitchen reminiscing about London. Later we retired to his living room with a couple of fresh glasses of wine.

"So, I really like your photography and would be very interested in taking a couple of those layouts. I still need to go over them some more to see exactly what I can use, but I would love to see more."

"Great. Absolutely!" I answered beaming.

Then Bob leaned in, a little more intimate, "You know you have an amazing look. Would you consider shooting for *Penthouse*? Becoming a *Penthouse Pet*?"

I blushed, he continued, "You have that natural European beauty, which is the type I want for *Pet of the Year*."

"Plus, there is that special spark in your eyes that is a rarity!" he said slyly smiling.

As I mentioned before I would have loved to have done *Playboy* but there were obvious reasons why I couldn't, still Penthouse Pet was very prestigious and back then the photography was still exquisite. Pet of the Year, would be a ton of money and an incredible opportunity! It was a huge boost to my ego for Bob to ask. So, I agreed, "Bob, I would really love that!"

I left that evening, not only with the hope of a stream of photography business in the future but also with a little ego boost and a commitment to shoot for his magazine.

There were certain photographers *de le jour*, of which Susanne Revalle was one of his favorites. She was based in LA, and Clive and her were friendly adversaries. She'd been bugging me to shoot with her since we first met, and I loved her and thought she was an awesome photographer.

"No way are you shooting for Susanne! I'm the only photographer that gets to shoot you naked! If you're going to do *Penthouse*, you're shooting with me! Susanne is an old closet lesbian and she just wants to lick your pussy!" was Clive's response.

Problem was, Clive was a well-known *Hustler* photographer and even though he was incredible at his craft, Bob would never have agreed to it. Finally, Clive had a scheme.

"Tell Guccione you want to shoot with one of your 'European photographers.' We'll do the test shoot and put another name on it. He'll never know it's me."

I really wanted to shoot with Susanne, her work was beautiful, always tasteful and artistic. But I knew politically, I had to do what Clive asked, so I did.

Clive shot the test of me and I submitted it under a different name. Bob absolutely loved it and I was approved to shoot the layout.

So, Clive and I went to Cabo for a week. Every day we waited for that one-hour, golden window before sunset and the photos were brilliant. I sent in the pics, and Bob loved them. I was approved for the cover and centerfold and they sent us a nice fat check.

Shortly after, I guess Clive couldn't keep his mouth shut and was bragging to Susanne. I am not sure what happened, but I presume Susanne told Bob the real deal and tried to get Bob to approve a re-shoot with her. Next thing I knew, Janet called, just letting me know that they had "changed their mind and wouldn't be running the photos." They didn't say why, didn't ask for the money back, that was ours to keep. Never asked me anything about who shot them, nothing. But when the photos were returned none had actually gone to print.

I was disappointed but even more worried that it would kill my relationship and my ability to ever sell pics to *Penthouse*. Luckily it didn't, and it was never mentioned again.

Meanwhile, things were going well in my photo biz and the naked photos were flying off the shelves. I was more excited about the art photos I represented. Horticultural and beautiful landscapes from my London photographers that belonged in a gallery were, sadly, so much harder to place than the nude girlie pics that basically sold themselves.

Still the nude girl stuff wasn't bad. They were sexy and erotic but extremely high-quality, tasteful, well-lit photos of top models, crafted with care and creativity, rather than just stimulation for a guy to jack off.

I was expanding to other countries and it seemed that all over the world in every culture, race, religion and creed the one thing they had in common was they loved pics of naked girls. They all had different styles and standards that I had to be aware of and sensitive to. England for instance was restricted to very tame reserved nudes, which fit with their sensibilities. Poor Japanese men were lucky if they could see a nipple. They seemed to be secretively into weird fetish, painful bondage and discipline but in all the nudie mags I sold to, if there were any photos of naughty bits they were quickly blurred out.

I enrolled a friend of mine to help, Mike who I'd met on an acting gig. Mike was a drummer in a pretty well-known eighties pop band, and he and his wife Mindy had become quite good friends with Clive and I. Mike was tall and slender, with strawberry blond surfer locks and had that California actor look down. As a rock star and actor, of course he had women flocking to his feet and he was incredibly charming to boot. Before his band took off he'd actually been a dancer at Chippendales, which I could not imagine, but he was a hoot. Mike and I were just best buddies and got along like a house on fire. He was a total entertainer. Could sell anything to anyone and more than anything he was a blast. He thought it would be fun to sell some nudey pics on the side and I sent him to my contact in Japan and Mike was helping me with my expansion, getting a cut of any sales he made.

Mike kept pushing my mainstream photos too, but it was my girlie pics that were always in demand. Oddly enough the same editors that did the adult mags, often did mainstream homes, crafts and collectable mags for the same companies. I'd pitch my sensational high-quality pics; my landscape photos, stately castles, amazing architecture, cultured flower layouts, for their "Home & Garden" type magazines. But they kept buying the girlie pics. Many of the editors' personal preferences were my mainstream photos. But girlie magazines were in much higher demand with far more readers so consequently they could pay much more for photos.

Often the editors were surprisingly creative and intelligent. Quiet jewels stifled away in a back office stuffed up deep into the bowels of some "dirty little publishing company." One such editor for *Swank Magazine* was the great Mario Puzo. The man who wrote *The God father!* Another editor doing girlie mags, Bob, was hired by John Lennon to transcribe his personal diaries from a mishmash of notes. After Lennon was tragically assassinated, his last diary went missing but Bob recalled it from memory in his published book; *The John Lennon's Diaries*. All the while Bob was editing the girly mags as his main-paying "day job." And the editors were certainly kept busy with their day jobs. The newsstand was a thriving and popular business, especially the adult rags.

Even though this little business was doing really well, the magazines were on a six-month payment delay. The magazines would only license the rights to publish the photos. They would not actually own the photography; those rights would stay with the photographer. So, the magazines would pay for the rights to publish the images one time. However, they would all pay on publication, which, from conception to print, was always at least six months out. I'd have to wait to get paid but so would my photographers, and many of my photographers were hand to mouth. They complained incessantly about having to wait six months and constantly asked me for advances, and I seemed to be the only one that understood and felt their pain, but the magazines didn't care, they paid only on publication.

The photographers continued to bug me. Finally, I gave in.

"Ok, if I can figure out how to pay you upfront and I wait the six months, then I own it. Lock, stock and two smoking barrels. Mine! Meaning when it comes back, and I sell it for a second time or I sell a pic for a postcard in Japan, you get nothing…

IF I PAY YOU UP FRONT, I AM BUYING IT OUTRIGHT AND I OWN IT!"

They were perfectly fine with that. I had no idea how I could swing it, but I was determined to get them paid somehow.

Clive didn't believe in my vision, partly because he was somewhat jealous of me dealing with other photographers and would continually put their work down. He told me that I'd be throwing money away and it was a "stupid idea." This of course strengthened my resolve to make this work, and it also meant I couldn't ask him for help. I once again, needed to prove my worthiness to him.

Still, I believed in buying out the photos. I thought in the long run it would be worth it. I knew I could make the most out of each photo shoot. I could repackage it, rework it and find a new magazine in another country and sell it over and over. Everything from girly layouts to postcards to advertising. I just had to scrape it together!

So, I started to own them. Just a few layouts to start. It was a huge stretch to pay the photographers and wait to get paid back myself. It meant I would have to starve for the first year or so, but I struggled and juggled through and told myself in the end I'd be much better off. While my acting girlfriends were busy spending money on makeup and handbags and normal things twenty-year-olds do, I was saving up for more nude pics. As the money started to come back, I was able to buy a little more and a little more.

Clive was not as impressed as me and noted the money was not coming back to me as fast as I thought it would. Like I could never create a dent compared to the success he had mastered as a photographer. He seemed to relish in my shortcomings and that, just as he had warned, it was "a lot harder than it looks."

This stirred a quiet determination in me that meant I had to succeed.

I believed that there would be more outlets in the future and that owning it would be key. LOL… I had no idea what the future would hold and how valuable that key would be.

I quietly started collecting.

…AND I OWNED IT

OUTRIGHT!

Several months went by and I was making it, but barely. I was finding it very hard to juggle the funds. My acting and photo business included Clive less and less, and the more independent I became, the more Clive had an issue, until there was pretty much nothing left between us.

Clive had given me every excuse in the book to leave him, but still I didn't have the confidence to make the move. That is, until the straw that broke the camel's back…

Remember those photos we took for *Penthouse* that were returned to us and sitting in Clive's filing cabinet? Well unfortunately, they didn't stay there. Months down the line, I came home one afternoon after an audition and Clive was sitting at the kitchen counter, "Not sure if I told you but I ended up using those photos we took for *Penthouse*. Thought they were great for *Hustler*," Clive pretends to nonchalantly slip it by me, passing a copy of the magazine already in print.

"What!!!" I grab the issue staring at my naked butt on the cover, "When did you do this? Why didn't you tell me!!!"

"Oh, thought I did. Anyway, you look great!"

"But you could have told me!" I am now scanning through the magazine almost in tears, "And all those artistic soft photo shots that were really nice. You didn't choose any of those. Look you chose the raunchiest pictures of all!"

"Gail, you know we can't use those soft-focus ones. What's the matter with you? It's not the first nude pics you did! And here you look amazing!"

"You even used this photo from my personal photos. This you took for me when we first met. This was for us!"

"You look stunning. I thought you'd be happy."

"But I never agreed to this. I never got paid or anything!"

"Er… you did, you got a check, like a month ago."

"I don't remember any check. I would have remembered this!"

"Oh, yeah, I think you were out of town on some *crappy movie* when it came in. Anyway, I put it in the account, it went towards the mortgage payment."

"But you've been taking my residual checks for half of the mortgage."

"Gail, honey, there's more to living here than just the mortgage. There's the gardener, the electric, do you know how much it costs to heat the pool? This is Beverly Hills and you live here just as much as I do, you need to kick in your fair share."

So, there I was, on the cover of Hustler for all my skydiving buddies to enjoy. Still the pics weren't awful, no one would really recognize me, and I told myself, *I'm planning to go back home to England eventually and no one will ever know back there.*

On a deeper level, I was hurt, and to me, it was an obvious red flag that my "boyfriend" didn't consider me his long-term love. After two years together, I was simply just another commodity.

I didn't want the usual blow up argument we'd had so many times, where Clive would make me feel it was all my fault, that I was a failure and that I could never make it alone and he'd end up convincing me I had no choice but to stay. So, this time, I waited 'til the following afternoon when he was gone and called my friend Mike who sometimes did foreign sales for me. Mike and his wife had been telling me for ages to "get out" and had been trying to get me to take the one-bedroom apartment next to theirs. In one afternoon, secretly, I made the big scary move.

So, at one of my lowest points, my confidence crushed, I was finally free and single to make it on my own in tinsel town.

CHAPTER NINE

Date with a Prince

I THREW MYSELF into acting full force, pounding the pavement with auditions. I was still trying to get those A roles but rather had a flourishing B career, frequently starring in some cheesy late-night HBO or Cinemax flick. You know, the kind with very little story line and some lame excuse for some gratuitous nudity and a steamy shower scene. The kind of embarrassing late-night movies, no one ever admitted to watching. Most appeared like real movies with enticing story lines. It was later when I was already on set that one small, innocent notation in the script, "she takes a shower," turned out to be given the same attention as an epic scene from *The Ten Commandments.*

My Hollywood agent Don DeRocca didn't know about my sexy photo sideline biz, I kept that well quiet. And, he wasn't impressed by the slew of campy movies I'd done, he wanted me in more respectable productions. However, in his book this meant that I would need to go along with the less respectful behind-the-scenes shenanigans of the Hollywood Casting Couch.

It does seem though some people were watching my B movies and paying attention to little ol' me. Some HBO film aired, and my agent got a call from His Royal Highness Grand Prince Abba Dabba, or something. Said Prince in question, having seen me on TV, now wanted to have dinner with me in New York.

Absolutely not. The very *IDEA!*

"Pays twenty-grand." My agent deadpanned. "U…S…D."

"Go on…."

"Dude is crazy rich. Oil sheikdom. Just wants dinner. He's a fan of yours. Go figure?"

"So, it's just dinner, right?"

"Yup."

I was suspect. Don had often suggested that I hook up with some powerful Hollywood producer type that could help my career, and, as it just so happened, his. Even though he himself had, ever so politely, many times tried to get into my pants, he was quite happy to pimp me out. Don was actually quite loveable; smooth, somewhat charming and not too bad to look at and although he was certainly a player in the game, he was never aggressive, just overly persuasive.

Not long afterwards another of his clients Michele who'd now become mega famous, did an exposé interview about how Don told her she'd "never make it in Hollywood if she didn't fuck her way to the top." Which to be honest there's some truth in that, which is probably why I never made it to the big league.

"You're going to have dinner with the Prince!" He said with finality. "I'm driving you to the airport and putting you on the plane myself. Now you don't have to sleep with him or anything, buuuut…" he paused with that ambiguous flutter in his voice.

"REALLY?" I said mustering all my British indignance.

"Okay! Okay! It's just dinner…if… that is all you want," said silky agent, "But… would it really hurt you to consider it? I mean this Prince could be a big investor in the future."

Don already had the payment up front and he certainly didn't want to give it back and honestly, I felt I better do him this one favor if I wanted him to still represent me.

I was flown Grade-A super first class and greeted at the terminal by a huge bald man in knee-high boots, jodhpurs and a double brass button down coat like a chauffeur who had gotten lost in time picking up F. Scott Fitzgerald. He escorted me out to a white stretch limo that took up almost half the block!

I was whisked to a beautiful suite at the Waldorf Astoria in the heart of Manhattan adorned with fresh flowers. An older Middle Eastern butler type with a posh English accent greeted me as my personal "assistant" for the weekend.

"Now Miss Gail," he said in a soft, sibilant obsequious tone, "May I take you shopping for some evening dresses? Perhaps you would like a fur coat and some jewelry?"

"Oh, no I'm ok, I have a dress for dinner. Thanks though."

He looked perfectly puzzled.

"But Miss Gail, everything is being fully paid for by the Prince. He *wants* you to have dresses and beautiful jewelry."

Now, if I could go back in time, here is the exact point in the Time and Space Continuum where jaded future twenty-twenty hindsight me would smack that incredibly dim stupid me right now! Here I was being offered, carte-blanche mind you, American Express Cosmic Black Diamond Platinum Card shopping, and the polite little ol' English me didn't want to be rude and overstep my bounds.

"All right then." He bowed and made a helpless, defeated and circular motion with his hands, a mystified expression on his face. "Very well. You have an appointment at the spa tomorrow morning at ten AM. Miss Gail."

The next morning, I was woken up with a full room service. After which I was trundled off to the spa, where I was buffed, puffed, poofed, primped, primed and ready. Ready to be now professionally dressed that is.

Then followed wardrobe fitting, and jewelry borrowing, if I didn't actually want to keep any of the galaxy of starry diamonds for some reason!

My personal attendant came down to greet me with a long sad face. The Prince unfortunately would not be able to do dinner tonight, and it was all postponed until tomorrow.

The next day I was awakened again to the exact same folderol rigmarole and Pomp and Circumstance, and taken off to another eight hours at the spa. Being British, it seemed like such a waste to redo everything.

But the Prince was busy the next night, and so it went, for several days… spa dress, ready, go. No, not now. Spa dress ready… then finally days later… our big night out.

I was escorted to the front of the hotel where a line of about six stretch black limos were waiting. They placed me in the one in the middle and within it…the Prince.

Just he and I. Finally.

Alone.

The other limos were, I supposed, carrying body guards or just decoys.

I sat a bit awkwardly at first, dressed to the nines with full evening dress and diamonds, my hair practically touching the roof of the carriage. He was surprisingly down-to-earth and I quickly felt at ease. He was dark, handsome, and swarthy, in his late twenties and actually dreamily attractive. He had just finished a stint at Oxford University, spoke perfect Queen's English, and as it turned out, we had quite a lot in common.

Wow, a nice surprise.

We went to an upscale New York restaurant where we were seated alone on a two-person table, candlelit and quite romantic. It might have even felt somewhat normal, except that all the surrounding tables were occupied by his strategically placed bodyguards.

Still it was easy to forget about them as we chattered away like a normal couple. The Prince wanted to hear all about my famous Hollywood celebrity lifestyle. I felt myself wondering if we could really have a love affair.

I was strangely intrigued at the smoothness of his hands. Had he ever lifted a finger of manual labor in his life? I couldn't get over his hands! His palms were like the finest Chinese silk.

After dinner he suggested we go to a club. As we rose to leave, the man with his back to me who sat directly forward of us, gave a nod and the entire rest of the restaurant was mobilized. A new string of limos now waited outside.

As we arrived at the nightclub, a VIP area had been sectioned off with a thick velvet rope, and once again was conspicuously occupied by bodyguards. Still we danced, ignored the chaperones and had a simply amazing time. As I snuggled under his arm in the club lounge, I fantasied that this might be the real deal. He smelled like rich musk cologne and I got fleeting butterflies in my stomach. My Prince charming come to sweep me off my feet.

Later we were back at the Waldorf Penthouse. Hardly a suite, it was the entire top floor that had been set up to mimic his Arabian palace life. Still we were surprisingly alone. He changed into a red silk robe.

After lounging in his living room and imbibing a few more magnificently exotic cocktails, I agreed to check out his lavish four-poster in the boudoir. The four wooden posts went all the way to the ceiling and a lavish fringed canopy hung from the top. The huge over-sized bed had intricately embroidered red and gold silk sheets. He gently took my hand and we jumped onto the bed like naughty children just to see what they felt like. The lighting was dim. Strategically placed red candles illuminated the room so we could barely make each other out. Just enough to be perfectly romantic.

Staring into his eyes, he took my face between his perfect silky soft hands and tenderly kissed me.

"You're so beautiful. Even more beautiful than in the movies," he whispered, "...and you're so smart and sophisticated."

I melted.

He gently slid my hair off my neck and started kissing my nape gently, working his way down to my bare shoulders.

Wow, the real deal, I thought to myself, shivers running through my whole body with excitement.

He ran his fingers over my curves through my dress. I could barely stand it. We started to kiss passionately, taking breaks only to breathe heavily on each other and stare into each other's eyes, not saying a word out loud yet communicating everything. He ran his hands up inside my dress to feel every inch of my body and I reciprocated by running my hands inside his robe and across his perfectly smooth chest. He pulled me closer to him as I sank into his arms and we slowly lay down together on the pile of lush silk pillows.

Then something horrible, something inexplicable happened. And when I say inexplicable, I mean, to this day upon my life, I really can't fully explain it.

As he was exploring the supple curves and folds of my body with his ever so soft princely hands, I slipped my hand gently just inside his robe and passing across his smooth tight abs. His robe slowly slid open exposing him fully. My hands were still headed south, and in the dim red shaded light from the candles it was hard to see anything clearly, but I got a glimpse of... something. Something horrible and shocking.

In the mid-section of his otherwise perfect body, there was a lump that looked like John Merrick. The Elephant Man. Ok maybe that's not a good and fair description, as that would indicate a trunk of some sort, which there was not. I mean, again I couldn't see clearly, but it looked like a large lump in an area of flattish hard mangled skin.

With a very brief brush of my hand, I experienced feeling something like a pile of hard crusted cow manure but made of hardened skin.

Obviously, he did not expect to be so suddenly exposed. I was shocked and let out a small involuntary gasp, as he jumped up abruptly covering up his lower area with the criminal folds of his robes that had exposed him. I questioned myself if that was what I had really seen or if it was just shadows from the low-level lights. Still, he backed away from me in shock and terror, his body language not wanting me to look or feel any farther. He quickly tied his robe and turned away from me, as honestly, I was quite horrified and didn't want to see any more.

He distanced himself and turned back towards me, but still backing away as he plopped down in an ornate Louis XIV chair in the corner of the room. He took some deep breaths, and smiled slightly again, collecting himself.

"Dance sexy for me," he ordered in a tone that was far more stern than earlier.

Honestly, I felt obligated. One, to pretend I'm still feeling sexy and I saw nothing; and two, because for twenty grand plus airfare, hotel, spa and the like, dancing and feeling silly doing it, was the least I could do. In Hollywood I had spent weeks feeling silly, doing much stupider things for way less money than this. So, I danced around stripping to my underwear pretending to be enjoying myself.

"Pleasure yourself!" he commanded, "I want to watch you orgasm!"

All I really wanted was this to be over as soon as possible. The moment had passed, and I wanted to run, but I felt obligated to follow this through. Hello? ACTRESS! I can do this! I decided faking a quick orgasm is the fastest way to Peace with Honor and an exit stage left. So that's what he got. A three-minute dance, a quick tug and rub on the outside of the ol' panties, one incredibly fake scenery chewing orgasm.

And SCENE.

He seemed to be quite happy with the end result. I kissed him quickly and excused myself.

The next morning, I woke up, the Fairy Tale now officially over. The entire palace set up, complete with staff and Prince had vanished. The coach had turned back into a pumpkin and I hadn't even taken the diamonds to remind me. Only one guy appeared to be left behind. He explained to me that the Prince had to leave on urgent businesses and that the Prince expressed his gratitude for a wonderful evening. With that the assistant put my suitcase in a Yellow Cab and handed me a coach fare airline ticket to return to my hovel.

The ride home was a miserable walk of shame. I felt degraded, and more than anything stupid. *Of course, I wasn't good enough to date a prince and on top of that I had sold my body*…sort of! Even my Hollywood agent was probably going to reject me as "not good enough."

I crawled back to my apartment where I could pretend it never happened.

"Never mind luv," my friend and neighbor Mike consoled me. "You don't need any Prince, you're going to make so much money with your photo business and you can have any guy you want."

Mike always made me feel better.

"Come over tonight, the bands having a jam session and we've got a bunch of my old friends from Chippendales coming. Gonna be a blast!"

CHAPTER TEN

Shotgun Wedding

AFTER THE PRINCE, there was a billionaire. Tod, from Des Moines. A businessman who threw exclusive parties at The Playboy Mansion for his company. I was hired as bunny, and croupier and Tod and I hit it off right away.

Tod showered me with gifts and offered to buy me an apartment in Los Angeles. "Please, let me help you out. I want you to have a nice place in your name."

The thought of having some guy buy me an apartment was, in my mind, the ultimate failure. So, I lied and told him I was in the process of buying my own condo, and that I was doing really well and could support myself, thank you very much. Now here future self should come back in time and give myself a good talking to, but she didn't.

After several invites he finally got me to agree to go for a little vacation in Iowa and came to LA in his private plane to pick me up. His mansion sat on a man-made island in the middle of his private lake. The interior was incredible and to give you a little idea of the scope, a twenty-foot wide waterfall ran through the middle of the master bedroom, cascading to the lower floors before entering the lake. The house was fully staffed including a private French chef with accent and all. Then on to his beach house, where we went sailing on his yacht and water skiing off one of his speed boats, before enjoying a sweet romantic sunset on his deck. I gazed lovingly and snuggled into his arms as he held me close and kissed me gently.

Tod was young and handsome but when he professed his love for me, I wondered if I deserved it. He was clearly many times more successful than me and in some strange way, this scared me.

He looked long and deep into my eyes and said lovingly, "I know you are the one for me and I would do anything to have you as my wife." I was very young, and it was a little scary, but as he held me close I let the fantasy take hold.

He continued gently and reassuring, "If you were my wife, you wouldn't have to work anymore. I would take care of you and spoil you."

What? Stop. Rewind. I wouldn't have to work! Oh my God! I was horrified. Suddenly the mansion on the island became a dark lonely prison with a mote and I was the dumb worthless Stepford wife. In Iowa of all places!

"But I want to work. I want to be an actress," I protested.

"Oh honey, I'd give you everything you want. You could give up the photo biz and you wouldn't have to do any of that silly acting stuff."

I wanted to run before he locked me in the basement.

I left the next day.

It was now the late eighties and I had goals to achieve and work to do and didn't need any guys distracting me.

Mike was my sounding board, and I hung out with him and his wife Mindy often. He was helping me with sales and doing an amazing job and my business was expanding in all areas. Mike, I suppose was dashingly handsome, but I never saw him that way, he was a talker, he made me laugh and we were best buds. His wife probably wouldn't have minded if I wanted something more. You see she didn't like sex, had never had an orgasm and although she loved Mike, she found his natural horniness annoying and she was always trying to pass him off to Kathy in our apartment block for sex.

"Kathy was over last night, and they were banging away keeping me awake," Mindy told me one morning.

"You really don't care if he has sex with someone else?"

"God no, Mike's been driving me crazy, I've been begging her to come over."

I didn't get it and questioned her about why she didn't have orgasms, "Have you tried…"

"Gail I've tried everything. Even went to a masturbation class through the Learning Annex."

Mindy went on to describe a class room scene with some big German woman spread eagle at the front of the class demonstrating to a bunch of women how to play with themselves. *Kinda kinky,* I thought to myself, *I'll have to use that in a photo shoot one day.*

But Mike was just a great business partner for me and I had him busy on the phone talking to potential new magazines while I was out running around.

Without having to pay my fair share of Clive's Beverly Hills' home, I found I was actually better off. I threw myself into my photography business. I was buying out the photographer's layouts up front but also any "old material" they had laying around, like entire file cabinets full of photos. Word spread, and more photographers wanted work, more wanted me to buy their file cabinets, too. Every penny that came in, went right back to buying and collecting more pics. I couldn't resist a real bargain. It wasn't cheap, I mean it was still thousands of dollars, and it took every penny I could scrape together. All the money from my "mainstream" acting and modeling and, ironically, nights at the Playboy Mansion was going right back to collecting my sexy library.

Some photographers had real gems that were just collecting dust in the corner of their studio. One photographer had shot the likes of Marilyn Chambers in classic black and white pics from the dawn of the porn biz. Others had made a career at Penthouse or Playboy UK, and after the images were published one time, their fabulous photography of some of the most incredible women in the world was just shoved in a box somewhere waiting for me to retrieve it, revive it, and give it a whole new fabulous life.

I started to arrange a few photo shoots myself, paying the models and the expenses directly and paying the photographer a day rate. The photographers loved this, and it gave me much more control over what I got. I could talk to the magazine about what they wanted beforehand and even get the models pre-approved. It was a huge risk. I had to advance all the money, juggle like hell, do all the leg work myself, and wait to get paid months down the line. Still, it was worth not eating if it meant I could advance one more photo shoot. Soon, I was advancing several photo shoots with photographers in both London and LA.

I liked the idea of being able to license future rights, odd shots and worldwide rights knowing that I didn't have to worry about paying someone else. When a photo set came back from a "first rights publication," I knew everything else was gravy. And I had the inclination that it would be worth much more in the long run.

Pretty soon I had bought out most of what was in UK Playboy. I bought the library of a famous Penthouse photographer's work in the US, and I owned layouts from Penthouse and other magazines from the sixties through the eighties.

Over time my library went from being just massive to THE LARGEST EROTIC LIBRARY IN THE WORLD… AND I OWNED IT ALL, OUTRIGHT!!!

America had proven to be, truly the land of opportunity. That is, if they wanted me…

I had been doing a shoot in a quaint Mexican beachside village and was heading back to LA by myself. Travel in the eighties was a whole lot different and I was sitting up front on an Air Mexico flight when the pilot came back to make small talk with me. He was really cute, and the sexy uniform didn't hurt. He invited me to come into the cockpit and watch him fly.

Just me, him, and a co-pilot. I told him I'd gotten to take the controls and fly the old army tank skydiving planes a couple of times. He showed a little of how everything worked and let me have a go at flying his commercial jet aircraft!

Then he got the stewardess to bring in dinner and wine for us.

"Are you OK to fly the plane after a glass of wine?" I asked.

"Yeah, it's fine!" he smiled. "And I have my co-pilot here. Right?" he said looking over to his buddy.

One glass led to another and were getting pretty tipsy.

"Grab the joystick!" he instructed me as he showed me how to fly as his joystick rubbed against my leg. Oh my God, we're both sizzled to the top and I'm flying a commercial jet full of totally unaware passengers and the pilot is sucking a hickey onto my neck. Thankfully the co-pilot had taken over, because by the time we landed we were full-on making out.

He was waiting on the other side of customs for me but that's where I got delayed. Way delayed. Perhaps they saw me exiting with the pilot, or perhaps it was the five-drinks-down slurred look, but they took me in for questioning. I had been in and out of the country so many times to Mexico they didn't know what to do with me. My work permit as a skydiving actress was in the process of renewal but technically in the interim I was a visitor. A visitor with a million stamps in my passport. I was taken into a room with two butch American Customs women. Good butch, bad butch.

They interrogated me for hours. Was I running drugs? Not getting the answers they hoped for, yelling, they ripped my bags apart and started tearing through the contents.

"Hah ha!!!" The customs officer announced as she found my notebook containing all my acting auditions.

"This is my schedule, but this was when my work permit was in effect, look at the dates on my passport."

There were so many date stamps in and out, she just threw the book on the floor in disgust and stomped on it. Bad Butch was now throwing the contents across the room at me, "What kind of drugs are you running, fucking bitch?!!!" I was able to dodge several items, then a pair of my heels was a direct hit to the face. I had to duck as they threw their office contents at me, as they grew angrier. Then a stapler came hurling across the room hitting me square on the eye.

Finally, I was released, shaken with an order to appear in court the next day at seven AM to decide if I was in violation of my tourist visa. Somehow, I made it but with visible signs of a huge black eye shaped like a stapler and stilettos. The judge was embarrassed at my treatment and asked if I wanted to prosecute. No, I just wanted to be turned loose. But that was it. I knew it was best to return to England, where I "lost" my passport and applied for a fresh one. I did a quick turn around and was back in the US shortly after, but I knew this time I would need to get my green card quick. I had spent every dime I had left on my immigration attorney, but "these things take time" and "Any day now," was the same response. The only other option was to find the love of my life and get married.

I could have married my billionaire from Des Moines. And there were equally eligible bachelors in LA. Ones who vowed to make me a Hollywood star, no less, and probably could have. But, paying a friend to marry me for a green card seemed a lot less complicated so I started putting out feelers. I asked one of the resident skydiving pros who I knew liked me, but he turned me down. He confessed he'd want more and it would just kill him. This was proving more difficult than I thought, so I was on the lookout for the true love of my life, as long as he came with a US passport.

Since finally breaking up with my Clive, I'd thrown myself guiltlessly into the love of my sport, skydiving, and signed up for a skydiving team. This is where I met Scott. Scott was an incredibly brave Top Gun Pilot and promised to teach me how to fly as he took me on an aerobatic joy ride. He was one of the four on our new, formation skydiving team. He was already a national skydiving champion with thousands of skydives and I watched him in awe. Scott was madly in love with me from day one. I wasn't truly sure if I was wildly in love or just on a skydiving adrenaline high. We'd been having a crazy love affair for about two weeks, when he shocked me, pulled out a ring and proposed.

On bended knee he pleaded with me, "Look, we're dating, I'm madly in love with you, just try it and if it doesn't work out, you'll at least have a green card. Just promise you'll try."

I felt like I was in love with him, but this was scary, this was the real deal! I wouldn't normally do anything this insane. But what the hell. It had been a long crazy road, and, in a way, it was sort of insanely romantic.

A few weeks later I married him.

Arriving back Monday morning from our wedding, I was greeted by an official envelope. By sheer dumb luck and coincidence my green card papers had come through from my application with my attorney. After years of trying, I had finally been approved and it was already in the mail while I was walking down the aisle. Scott said he'd understand if I wanted to have the marriage annulled, but I said no, I'd made a promise, I was his wife and I was going to follow through with our marriage. Besides there was something kind of crazy romantic about having married someone after only a few weeks of knowing them and perhaps it could be my fairy tale true love. I was shooting for the stars.

CHAPTER ELEVEN

Dirty Little 900 Secret

SCOTT DIDN'T MIND my acting, didn't mind my nude pic business. He went to work every day, nine-to-five as an engineer. I was beating the acting pavement doing lots of cheesy movies and my nudey pic biz was doing better and better.

I did my very best to be what I envisioned being a GOOD WIFE was all about, or the best I could interpret from the vantage point of twenty-three-years-old. He was my buddy, my confidant. It was nice to finally feel like I had a real-life partner to face the world together. It gave me more drive and ambition to do well in the world.

We settled into married life and life was good.

I was a little sad to leave my neighbors Mike and Mindy but shortly after they moved to the UK for a couple of years. Having a partner based in Europe was actually pretty useful and we stayed in touch and Mike and I continued to do deals together.

Scott was my biggest fan. He loved the movies I did and told me daily, "I'm so lucky, you're the most amazing woman in the world."

I think the magazine editors were great fans too. Not only was a girl actually talking to them, but a "movie star" at that! It certainly didn't hurt that they saw me regularly on HBO and could say they actually went to lunch with the star of *The Sins of Desire, or Sorority House Massacre II*.

I imagined being a movie star would be very glamorous. In real life, it wasn't so much. It was lots of no-frills low budget movies that didn't have the money to heat the freezing cold pool, couldn't afford a stunt double and left me buried half alive for hours with some sugary fake blood attracting vampire-sucking flies. Still, I never complained when I came home exhausted, bruised and abused. I knew I was lucky to be acting at all.

I was hired to sign autographs at conventions like *Glamour Con* which made me feel like a real movie star and I loved it. I even got an all-expense paid trip to a screening of one my movies in Rio, where my bod, cleavage busting out all over, appeared on the expo T-shirt. Collecting my own personal golden Oscar statuette. Even if it was the *Trashmania Expo*!

Quentin Tarantino was asked at the height of his fame, what his all-time favorite movie was? To which he replied, *Cell Block Sisters*, starring of course... MOI!

Still, acting was a lot of hard work for not much respect. My little sideline nude photo business was looking a whole lot easier for a whole lot more money. And I was garnering a new level of respect as a businesswoman.

On one of my New York selling trips I was introduced to a man named Alan. He met me in a busy little coffee shop, a friendly bearded man with significantly less hair on top, wearing a suit that looked slightly overused with a yellowing shirt collar clearly due to the bubble of smoke he carried around his aura from his incessant chain smoking. Sitting down he got right into business.

"I've heard you're working with pretty much all the girly mags around town," he said, hoping I'd fill in the details, "and I've been told that for such a youngster, you're very influential in this business." I had obviously been talked up by the editor who set up the meeting and told me Alan would be a great contact for me. Excitedly, I shared who was who in the adult mag industry and he listened intently in awe, occasionally making the odd gesture in between sips of his coffee. We'd only been chatting for a couple of minutes and I still wasn't completely sure what Alan did, when he exclaimed, "You have to meet my partner!"

He didn't really tell me why, "We are doing a lot of business and my partner is going to love you! Can you make it this afternoon?" he asked.

A few hours later, I arrived at the fancy Madison Avenue address for a meeting with "The Ad Agency Group." It appeared to be quite a prominent company. A pristine looking penthouse office, sleek modern furnishings in the very high rent area of Manhattan. The high circular walls of the reception were filled with prestigious, commercial ads that were quite recognizable and a large red and gold sign that read: *Monarch Advertising*.

Alan was there to greet me and led me into the grand conference room where there was a huge polished cherry wood oval table, decked out with the finest leather business chairs. His partner entered, followed by a few young obvious assistants ready with note pads.

"Hi, I'm Stuart. Very nice to meet you," he said, firmly shaking my hand with an air of pleasant confidence and a deep radio voice that projected charm and authority. Stuart and Alan were the exact opposites of characters. Stuart was dashingly handsome, tall, Nordic descent with a thick head of mousey brown hair flicked to one side, wearing a classy beige tweed suit with a crisp neatly pressed white shirt and tie that brought out his piercing green eyes, looking like he'd walked right out of one of the GQ ads in his grand entrance.

Alan beamed as he offered me up, like I was his great discovery.

"I hear you know everyone in the men's magazine business," Stuart said, as an opener, gesturing for me to sit down in his ultra-comfy, overly sized black leather boardroom chair.

"Yes," I said coyly. "I know pretty much everyone, what did you want to do?"

He leaned in to share, "Well our expertise is commercial advertising, which is great, and we're very good at it, but we also have this new 900 phone-line talk business or *audiotext* it's called."

"A phone-sex business?" I asked, quite surprised to hear this, as there wasn't a sign of it anywhere.

"Er…yes. We prefer to call it audiotext." Stuart replied, indicating his conservative nature. "It's a phenomenal business," he said almost justifying why a clearly successful man of his stature would be doing this.

"We are buying advertising space in these men's erotica magazines, but it's hard to get any more pages. They are all sold out. So, we were wondering if you might have any contacts?"

Alan jumps in, "We'd pay whatever, we simply can't get enough, the space is all committed."

"Really?" I couldn't imagine that it was that hard to buy pages in the back of the adult mags. "I don't normally deal with any of the advertising people. That's a different department, but I could ask."

"Do you know the guys at High Society?" Stuart asks.

"Sure, I do. We do lunch every month or so."

Each of the men dipped their heads and glanced at each other knowingly, twisting in and leaning over the conference table.

"Do you want pages in there?" I asked.

They lit up, ecstatic that I might be able to do that. Stuart motioned to his assistant who sprung up and grabbed a phone from the middle of the huge table and brought it around and gently placed in front of me, twisting it slightly so the buttons faced me.

"Do you want me to call them?" I said rather surprised at their enthusiasm. They almost broke their necks nodding. I called my editor friend at High Society and explained the dilemma.

"Baby doll, I don't know if I'm the guy to help you," he said, as I heard him puffing on his everlasting cigar. I work in the layout department. You need someone over in advertising."

I proposed a deal; "You know that set you owe me two grand for? Could I get a page of advertising instead?"

"Hmm…" he replied, puffing away, thinking. "Tell ya what I'll do sweetie-pie. I'll just bypass the ad hacks for ya, and I'll take out a page of editorial and give you an ad. Less work for me, helps my budget, and you get yer ad. Deal?"

"Deal!" I said, looking at Stuart who was excitedly nodding the go ahead.

In my mind I'm thinking, *This is a pretty good deal, I'm probably going to get paid upfront now by this ad agency for my photos and don't have to wait six months for the magazine to pay me. This is a win-win!*

"I could give you a couple more pages on those other layouts, maybe other issues if you wanna do the same on those?" the editor adds.

I looked up at the guys peering down on me for confirmation and they were miming a very excited, "Abso-fuckin-lutely!!!"

"Yeah that would be great," I confirm to the editor.

"Done and done, sweetums! TA!" he said making a joke about my English accent as he hung up.

I looked at my new clients who were literally jumping up and down. A page of advertising for two grand when the book rate was ten thousand! And they would have paid twenty if they could have gotten it at all, which they couldn't.

Grinning from ear to ear, they couldn't believe this little girl had just gotten them a backdoor ad deal.

Now, almost drooling in anticipation, Stuart asked, "Who else do you know? Do you know the guys from *Club* magazine?"

"Yeah sure, but they are Upstate and it is a long…."

"Can we go?"

"What? You mean now?"

"Yes, we'll get the limo."

So off we go in the limo, upstate.

A few hours and I have them in a meeting with the owner of *Club* magazine. I'm surprised to discover that my clients are correct; the publisher says they have absolutely no space. They have forty-eight pages of advertising pages all filled and a waiting list. So, tough luck guys. Call us two years from now.

Because I don't easily take no for an answer and generally ram the round peg into the square hole. I racked my brains trying to find a way around this, and asked, "What if you were to make a whole new mini-book of just their ads? Like a little insert, 'phone directory,' and then bind it into the center of the book?" I suggested thinking about some of the freebie books I had loved in the middle of my Teen Mags back in the UK when I was young.

The owner tilted his head at me, like a puppy looking at a treat, took a long pause to mull it over and see it in his mind. Slowly the vision took form and he then said, "Hmm, maybe that could work." Then he reconsidered and made a face as he shook his head. "But that's a heavy printing cost and we'd have to charge to bind it inside the book which would be pretty hefty." He thought for another long moment, "It would have to be like two-hundred and fifty thousand a month."

I choked at the price. It seemed obvious the publisher didn't want to do it, and just picked a price out of thin air to make these people go away.

To my complete shock Stuart jumped at it.

"Done!" Stuart stuck out his hand to shake on it, "Can we sign a twelve-month deal?"

I was stunned. Stuart's poker face was gone, and he was grinning from ear to ear.

Back at the ad agency, Stuart couldn't stop singing my praises. "And what a fantastic idea to do a booklet insert! That's AMAZING! How did you even come up with that? You are a GENIUS!"

Stuart took me aside.

"Just giving you a little thank you for today, for helping us. Who do I make the check out to?" He handed me a check made out for twenty thousand dollars! "Thanks for today, that was amazing."

I was completely stunned. I couldn't believe my luck.

"Would you like to do some more work for us? Like getting us more advertising and maybe doing photos for our ads?"

He had me at "Who do I make the check out to?"

CHAPTER TWELVE

Some Men are Just Weird

BACK IN LA, my husband is thrilled I'd picked up such a great new client. I've started working with Stuart, getting to hear his deep radio voice almost daily. I have added another string to my bow and not only am I producing masses of photo layouts, I'm also digging through my photo files for good phone shots and talking to all the publishers about trying to get my new clients a bunch of ad space. Many of the editors were able to give me photo trades for ad pages as well as get me really good prices to buy more space for my clients.

By now, I have a pretty good rapport with many of the editors talking to them quite often about shoots and now ad trades and sometimes just to keep in touch. The editors of the men's magazines would receive letters from their readers, but I don't think they took much notice of them, if they read them at all. Yvonne was probably one of the few who opened them, and she would read me some of the most juicy tidbits.

"This guy clearly has a foot fetish. He wants to see 'tender little pink toes' in a bowl of sticky porridge and he wants another girl to suck the porridge off her toes. 'It reminds me of my cum." Yvonne laughs.

"Weird, but we could shoot that," I said.

I encouraged the other editors to share their mail with me too. I figured if I could shoot what their readers really liked, my photos would be more popular, and I could sell more.

"Are you sure luv? Some of those letters are really strange. But there's a pile of mail in that drawer there; if you want to look through it, you're welcome," Stan offered.

I was finding it quite eye opening to get into the reader's heads. Reading their letters gave me the most intimate details of what guys wanted to see. Everything the leg man had in his fantasy; down to the perfect denier of the Cuban heeled stocking and exactly what he wanted to see her do with her peep toe heels. At the other end of the spectrum were readers who could care less about a girl's feet but would go insane over a pair of ultra-large breasts. I learned it wasn't about getting more explicit. It was that little spark, that little detail that was the gold.

I drew the opinion that sexuality takes on a vast myriad of forms and that in the end, *Some men are just weird.*

I had come to this conclusion years earlier, with my education in the male psyche starting in my early modelling years, where I had already been given a glimpse of some of the various diverse and perverted fantasies men have.

I had worked at that amateur studio which had really opened my mind. I was curious when Sandra said her regular, high paying older customer who was "a bit strange" was coming. She assured me it wasn't sexual, wasn't even nude. I was intrigued and made an excuse to get something from the dressing room, from where I could get a good view of the studio. At first, I didn't see the old guy, but my friend was giving instructions to a blond lady. It wasn't a blond lady! It was this little old man dressed up in a wig getting makeup and modeling lessons! He was learning how to pout and look sexy for the camera! Then afterwards, he pulled out a roll of BandAids!? He asked Sandra to sit on a chair as he carefully placed a Band-Aid over her lips. Then he quickly ripped it off screeching with delight.

"Oh that's my favorite bit!" He was so excited he could hardly control himself, and he jumped up and down with a pitter-patter of his feet, clapping his hands together.

There was a lot I didn't understand about men, I thought to myself.

One particular amateur I modelled for, was trying to get my photos published in a sort of a sexy lingerie magazine. He brought the outfit he'd picked out for me to wear. He carefully handed me the package surrounded in store tissue wrapping but the paper faded with time, like something you'd find in an antique store. Inside, were a pair of extremely large, ample bottomed briefs, like something my old gran would have worn. They were complemented with garter belts that looked like they really came out of the fifties, complete with original rubber tops. A plain, very modest Mary Jane brassier and original no stretch denier stockings with a knitted seam. To top it off was a fifties sweater and poodle skirt. As I put on this strange outfit, I remarked that it could be something his mother wore. He blushed a little and giggled. Oh my God! I was wearing his mother's underwear!

"It has significance to me," he said.

As I modeled the underwear, he was strangely excited. I wondered what made him want to see a model in something that reminded him of his own mother in her panties?

I thought *Some of the things that turn men on are really weird.*

But nothing would top my last gig at the ol' photo studio: I was booked by a schoolteacher from Liverpool, a three-hour trek away. He scheduled me for a usual "fashion" shoot and he was taking pics of me against some rolled out paper showing a serene sunset backdrop and making casual conversation. Joking around he says, "You better behave, luv, or I'll tie you up in the dungeon set!"

The studio was arranged with about ten cheesy backdrops; beach, skyline and yes there was a full on "dungeon" set up in the back.

"You're the one that better behave, or I'll tie *you* up in the dungeon set and take pictures of you!" I shot back laughingly.

A little later we took a break and he went back through the changing room. When he returned, he was totally naked! A little hairy, chubby man with a pale white little wiener standing in front of me, stark naked, wearing only a pair of white ankle socks.

"What are you doing?!!!" I stuttered in total disbelief.

"Well you said you'd tie me up in the dungeon set and take pictures!"

I was at a total loss for words. I was really embarrassed and in the back of my mind I was thinking, *Well I did say I would, didn't I?* I think a part of me actually felt this was my fault. Like I had told him I would take pictures, so now I had to do it.

"Well not naked – put some clothes on!" I finally managed to say.

So off he trots back to the makeup room leaving me totally bewildered. My heart was racing, and I just felt so clueless. When he returned, clothed…. well sort of, he was wearing a school uniform complete with shirt and tie, short skirt, and white girlie panties peeking out underneath. Shuffling across the room with a big toe in each of my high heels!

Ok, now what do I do? I reasoned to myself, *After all, he did put clothes on.*

Before I have time to say anything further, he's set his camera up facing the dungeon set.

"Handcuff me!" he ordered, holding out the cuffs.

I was reluctant to do it, but I didn't really seem to have a reason I could give him as to why not, so I just seemed to go along with what I was being asked. And these were real handcuffs apparently.

He instructed me on how to operate the camera – "Just press the black button on the top; that's the shutter."

I simply had no idea what to do. I just pressed the shutter.

He, meanwhile, lights up, switches into his glamour role, completely in his element. He starts squirming in a "Do I look sexy?" pose. Pouting his lips and lifting his skirt to expose the little wiener hanging out of the side of his panties.

"Yes baby," he moans.

"Ok here's what you do," he explained, preferring to remain handcuffed while he directed me on how to change the roll of film. I took out the exposed film. I was about to load a new roll, still wondering what to say, yet words just don't seem to come out of my mouth. And with film in hand, I excused myself to the bathroom for a moment where I could perhaps regroup, rethink, recover. I walked through the changing room past the agent, past the bathroom and then in a complete London fogged in daze, just kept going…and going...and going… until I found myself at home. And I had left this guy handcuffed to a rack on a dungeon set!

The agent waited and waited and finally went in the studio to find this man in a school uniform, heels and panties, spread eagle against his rack! Consequently, I didn't dare show my face to the agent again. And you would have thought this would have put the guy off for life, but apparently, he came back a couple of weeks later, asking for me again and when he couldn't book me he asked for other girls who would tie him up in the dungeon set.

I thought I didn't really understand men very much but strangely it seemed most men were clearly just as clueless about the female species…

Even amongst the professional photographers, there was the occasional thing that threw me for a loop. I was hired to do in Barbados with several girls in a scene all shot completely underwater.

The photographer picked me up at Heathrow airport and I spent the night at his country cottage near London with him and his wife before an early morning flight out to the islands. I chatted with the photographer on the hour or so drive about the shoot and other normal stuff. Then, just as we pulled into the driveway he handed me a neatly wrapped little box.

"This is so you don't keep my wife up with the noise of a vibrator," he said, as if it was a completely normal thing to say.

I didn't want to appear naïve, so I just thanked him for the gift. As soon as I was left in my room alone, I opened the box, thinking I would now understand what he meant. Only now, I was more confused. In a fancy Chinese style, silk lined, box lay two steel balls. I thought they might be a musical thing or something, but the label read, "Love Eggs."

What was I supposed to do with these and why had he given me them? I think I finally realized they were sexual in some way, but for the life of me I couldn't figure out how.

He leered knowingly at me over breakfast and I wondered if he was fantasizing about me having some wet screaming orgasm and I felt insecure that I wasn't sexually experienced enough to even know what to do with them.

Later the other models joined me on the trip.

"Did you get some of those ball thingies?" was the first question, one of the other girls had when we were alone.

"Yes! What were they for? I didn't have a clue what to do with them, did you?"

We were all baffled and I was quite relieved. We all agreed on the universal feminine mantra:

"Some men are just weird."

—⚬⚬⚬—

My early days as a model had proved invaluable for me now behind the camera to get into the psyche of what men really wanted. I was starting to realize that men didn't all want your usual top models. In fact, men could be far more complicated. It was all about hitting on that "thing." And the more "things" I saw, the less and less I noticed how outrageous it all was.

My bizarre experiences in the past had given me an edge in the sex magazine industry and I was taking note of exactly what the guys would like. Information I could use to find exactly what would make my photos sell.

For the leg enthusiasts, I had ridiculous seven-inch heels custom made in Europe that no one could possibly walk in but seemed to be every leg man's wet dream. I bought out a whole warehouse in the Midwest that made stockings in the fifties and had been left untouched until some crazy collector (me) was willing to buy everything. There was a whole lot more care being put into the photo shoots than you would ever imagine. It paid off. My photos were loved by the readers and so the magazines were eating them up. My layouts were selling quicker and I was getting top dollar.

What else would the reader really like? I contemplated one day while watching one of my models. *The guys love to get autographs from the girls. I bet they'd die to get the panties that she's wearing.* So, after the shoot I carefully placed the bra and panties in a plastic baggie and included it with the photos. I later called the editor, "I was thinking if you like you could run a contest for your readers. Win Wendy's Wet Panties! Encourage them to write in or something."

The following month it ran and the sales for that issue were extraordinary. Readers' letters piled in, all giving their opinion in the hopes of being the lucky winner. It was a huge success. And from there on I'd often take the models panties, or sweaty stockings or some other garment that contained her perfumed odor and carefully seal it in a zip lock baggy and enclose it with the photos. I presume some of the editors kept certain items for themselves, but I didn't care what they did with them. It was all just that little added incentive to get them to buy the pics and it worked!

CHAPTER THIRTEEN

Meeting the
Phone Sex "Investors"

I WAS ADDING on a few phone advertising shots to every photo layout, paying the models some extra bucks to hold a phone and smile seductively to the camera. Stuart was my new best friend and I was his golden goose, cutting deals for every ad page I could lay my hands on. Things were going great with the ad agency. Stuart would wire money to my bank to pay for advertising space and I would spend it. And, of course I got to keep a percentage as an ad placement fee.

I couldn't keep up with the amount they wanted to wire me! I was up to a half a million a month and Stuart was begging me to spend more.

"That's all the ad space I can buy right now Stuart, believe me I'm trying but please don't send any more money."

The more ads I could place, the more money they could bring in and there seemed to be absolutely no spending limit. They wanted every page they could because for every ad they placed, they were getting ten times back.

I was not that impressed by the ads coming out of their New York office. I mean they were slick, colorful and eye catching but from my experience in what men wanted, I knew the ads were missing the mark in the turn-on department. At this point I felt I could be pretty open with Stuart.

"Stuart honestly, some of the photos don't make sense."

"What do you mean?"

"Well, for instance that full page ad your guys just sent over with my girl Kim, cute fresh-looking girl on the beach. That photo is really going to appeal to a guy who likes young girl-next-door types, but the copy your guys put on says, 'busty girls will do something or other.' If you're going to do an ad with that girl, it should say something like, 'beach coed looking for fun,' or something that matches the picture better. Kim's not even busty!"

"Well, honestly Gail my guys are really good at advertising but maybe not in this field, it's not exactly our expertise. You seem to know an awful lot about this, could you help us?"

Inadvertently, I had just created myself a whole other project. That is, overseeing all the phone sex ads. At first, we were faxing back and forth ads that I would tweak and direct with the art staff at the ad agency until pretty soon a large portion of the ads were just entirely turned over to me and I was creating much of the advertising out of my office.

I applied a simple technique; to match the photo with some copy the reader might actually like. If the reader likes this girl, then what would turn him on? What would make him pick up the phone? With just a little finesse, it worked big time, the calls increased dramatically, and I was a goddess in the eyes of my ad agency!

Then one day, I was checking in with Stuart on how my ad production was going when I mentioned something else, "Stuart, your ad guys gave me a list of numbers to use and I noticed if you look up the letters a few of these numbers spell out something. You know like they do on a car commercial like 1-800 ALS CARS."

"We can actually get ones that spell something on purpose, they are called 'Vanity' numbers," Stuart replied.

"You mean you can get things like 1-800-IMBUSTY?" I said excitely thinking immediately about all the possibilities.

"Yes, absolutely. Wow, that's a great one!"

"Can we get anything?" I asked, now getting very excited.

"Well some might be gone, but pretty much anything, if you know what numbers to ask for."

"Wow, Stuart, this is amazing! We can get numbers to match the ads, like a busty telephone number for a busty pic."

I was then set about coming up with literally hundreds and hundreds of names and their corresponding numbers. Shortly after they owned a whole portfolio of these "Vanities," everything from

1-800-LEGLOVE to 1-800-BOOBS4U to 1-800-COEDS69.

The ads were certainly looking better and this whole phone sex business seemed to be making a ton of revenue for my clients. But how? I didn't really understand who would call a phone sex number. Out of curiosity, I tried calling some of the phone lines. They were totally lame. I mean really stupid; "Naughty Confession Line" was some girl breathing heavy and then she finally said "I have a secret. I once had a naughty thought." Then lots more breathing. Then another stunning girl confession; "I stole five dollars from my mother's purse." Followed by lots more heavy breathing. I mean, it was crazy! Who would call these numbers and pay actual hard-earned MONEY for this!?

Obviously, a lot of men were calling them. For every one-dollar I spent for my agency on advertising they were bringing back ten. So, a half a million was bringing back five million! I just didn't get it. There must be so many really lonely men out there. Because men were calling… millions of them!

Still there was room for a lot of improvement.

"Stuart, have you listened to any of these? They are really bad. How can anyone stay on the line and listen to these?"

"Well, we are trying to improve our hold times," he admitted, knowing they are junk.

"And don't people call and ask for their money back?" I asked.

"Yes, chargebacks are a huge issue for everyone, but you are going to get that, it's the nature of the business."

"Yes, but the recordings could be way better and keep the guys on the phone much longer. Even our models could make better recordings!"

"Great idea!!!" Stuart exclaimed.

Oh, no I had created myself yet another job and Stuart set me on producing audio recordings to go with the photos. You know, these heavy breathing, "I confess to something stupid" tapes? From then on, every girl that came through the door to take nude magazine photos was now being paid a little extra to hold a phone and pose for the camera and now record a couple of heavy breathing tapes. They laughed through most of it and got paid to boot!

Stuart was thrilled.

On my next trip to New York Stuart insisted on covering my expenses. His assistant was instructed to book me first class all the way with a lavish suite over-looking central park. Stuart took me out to all the best restaurants and insisted I made time in my busy schedule to go to a Broadway show with him and his girlfriend, best seats in the house of course.

Stuart's girlfriend Laura was nice enough to me, in a sort of superficial upper class, high society sort of way, more interested in showing off her newest channel outfit to other high society acquaintances she bumped into and generally picking at Stuart, rather than actually engaged in the show.

"Stuart tells me you're running an ad company out of Los Angeles," she says, "I have a lot of friends in Beverly Hills, we should visit sometime, Stuart."

I hoped she wouldn't.

"What does your husband do?" she asked as a sort of a way of judging how high I had climbed up the ladder.

"He's an engineer."

"Oh," she mumbled in a demeaning manner and didn't seem to want to have any further conversation about it.

While I was in New York, Stuart also wanted to introduce me to Micky, a guy he spoke very highly of, who Stuart said was the brains behind their audiotext business.

It was only a couple of blocks from Stuart's prime Manhattan address, but Stuart insisted on taking the town car. Alan joined us, and we arrived at an equally impressive building, in fact a much larger spread than the ad agency. Stuart acknowledged the front desk person as he showed me through, giving me the impression, that this was at least partially his office.

"I'll give you a grand tour of the place," Stuart said as we entered.

Micky came out to greet us, "Welcome Gail, nice to meet you. I see you've been doing quite a lot out of Los Angeles," he said with a warm sincere handshake. Micky was a well-groomed business man with obvious Italian descent. Dark brown, almost black greased hair and honest looking sweet brown eyes. A confidently quiet man in about his forties. I took an immediate like to him.

Stuart took the lead as they showed me around the office. A sprawling, tropical fish tank divided several plush executive rooms from a main office floor of cubicle workers.

"Is this where they handle phone calls?" I inquired.

"No," Stuart replied, "That's all handled out of Wisconsin and Micky's building a new warehouse switching station there. It's state of the art, nothing like it anywhere." Stuart looks at Micky, who confirms proudly with an excited nod, "But this office is where Micky runs the operations for our audiotext business."

I didn't know exactly what that meant, but there seemed to be a lot of staff, all keeping busy and I could have easily gotten lost going to the restroom. I was shown around and introduced to all the department heads as if I was a very special client or something.

"We have a reservation at twelve-thirty," Micky mentions to Stuart checking his watch, "Our table."

"Gail is going to join us for lunch," Stuart confirms to Micky.

"Great! The Investors are dying to meet you," Micky adds, making me feel terribly important.

So, after the office tour we head out to meet "the investors." We arrive at an upscale but old-world style, Italian restaurant with dark oak wood and stain glass windows and a large sign out front, "Viggiano's."

As we are walking in, another group of suits are just leaving the restaurant. My guys obviously know them well, and they all stop in the doorway to shake hands and there is a moment of professional acknowledgment, hand shaking and patting on the back. Their group appears to be led by a very tall, stocky guy, who holds out his hand to me, "Johnny," he says, grasping my hand and shaking firmly. Meanwhile eyeing me up and down in an extraordinary sexist manner. "You must be their girl from LA! Yeah, very nice," he remarks out loud, nodding his approval in a drawn out, deep and controlling voice, his eyes scanning my body and with a tone like he knew all about me.

"It is very nice to meet you, Johnny," I answer wondering who he is.

He cracks a sly smile.

"Glad I didn't have to break those pretty little legs. That would have been a real shame," Johnny says.

I give a little polite laugh, thinking that is a very strange way to compliment a woman.

Johnny's group exited.

As we walk inside, I whisper to Stuart, "What did he mean by that? Was he joking?"

"Well not really. But don't worry about it. We took care of it," Stuart assures me.

"Ciao bella!!!" the maitre'd exclaimed loudly, throwing his arms around Micky and then acknowledging the whole group like we were old friends, "Welcome, come in." The Maitre'd led us around the bar through the main part of the restaurant and to a more secluded dimly lit private area where a group of about six or seven guys were already seated at a large round table with a crisp white table cloth.

The group immediately jumps up to hug Micky and the rest of us like long lost friends, "Ciao, Micky!!!"

"Yo, Tone!"

There was a mass group hugging, some back slapping and I was kissed on both sides of the cheeks by almost all of them.

Stuart announces me to the group, "This is Gail, our superstar from California!"

"Wow!" they say in unison and nod in approval.

Micky introduces the guys to me, "This is Big Tony!" Big Tony opens his arms inviting me to hug this bear of a guy. Probably six two tall, with huge square shoulders that made him look really massive and an oversized waist. "Bella!" Tony exclaims pulling me to his chest and hugging me tight. He seems to be somewhat the leader of this group and the others hold back to wait their turn to greet me.

"Joey," Micky introduces next, a slightly smaller but outgoing energetic man who's face full of lines portrays a lot of emotion. Joey immediately jumps up and is lined up waiting for the next hug, instantly throwing his arms around me as soon as I am released from Big Tony, "Yo! We've heard so much about you!" Joey exclaims with enthusiasm, nodding and kissing me firm on each cheek.

"Then there's Vinnie and Lou...." Who stay seated but lean fondly from the back of the table to greet me.

I sit down to lunch feeling totally pampered and the star of the attention as delicious Italian delights are piled up on my plate.

"She reminds me of Sasha doesn't she Joey?" he says looking for a response from Joey. Tony explains to me, "You look just like my niece."

"How old is Sasha now, like sixteen, seventeen?"

"Something like that," Joey replies

"I'm twenty-four, I just look younger," I explain to Tony, apologizing slightly.

"Can't believe a sweet little thing like you is the one getting us all these amazing ad deals...." Big Tony laughs, doting over me.

"Still, I have no idea who would call these phone numbers!" Tony sniggers at the idea looking over at Micky.

"Yeah well they're calling. Millions of them! Literally!" Micky adds, proud as all heck.

The "investors" I met that day were a group of guys that struck me as real old school New Yorker types. They all seemed pleased to meet this young upstart who was making them shit loads of cash. They absolutely loved me and accepted me like "family" as they phrased it.

"Anything you need... You're part of the family now," Big Tony says like my new protective uncle.

Joey jumps in, "Yes, anything you need out there in Cali, anyone messes with you, you just let us know. We'll take care of you."

"You don't got any problems out there do ya? Cos if you do, you have us now, ya know," Lou pipes up for the first time. He's older, more reserved with a very heavy accent.

I got a ton of hugs and hand squeezes in a very genuine family kind of way. *These New Yorkers are so sweet,* I thought to myself.

"Hey Micky, you just missed that agent guy Johnny, that dick from the magazines. He was in here," Big Tony mentions as a quiet aside.

"Yeah we saw him on the way in," Micky replies, "Scared Gail a bit though."

"Hey, don't worry about him Luv, he's harmless enough. Anyway, Big Tone will take care of you!" Tony winks at me.

I discovered at lunch that Johnny who we had met passing on the way in, was a media agent who had some kind of exclusive on advertising space in these top shelf men's mags. The pages that people were dying to get, offering triple the book rate, and waiting for months. He had the pages so tied up that you couldn't get near one of these without Johnny's approval and his Vig or the hefty commission. That was until this little English girl had somehow backdoored him and stolen ad pages in his best mags. You see that first day at the ad agency when I managed to get advertising pages from the editor and circumvented the ad people, the very dangerous man I had circumvented was Johnny. Luckily, my guys had reasoned with Johnny, showing him how it was all a Win/Win situation, and that he wasn't losing money, because now they'd also added the booklet inserts which were icing on the cake, and they had come to some greasing the palms agreement with him, giving him a cut he was happy with.

Still, I naively presumed the "breaking the legs" comment was just said in jest.

I had a new group of Investors to watch over me. Father figures who made me feel like anything I wanted, anything I needed, they'd be there.

Back in LA, I'd upped the ante to every magazine and every page of advertising I could lay my hands on, way beyond the scope of Johnny. But my clients wanted more. I needed to find more places to buy ads. I just couldn't spend enough.

I had an idea for extra advertising but wanted to check with the editors first to see if they would agree before I promised it to Stuart. With a little persuasion, almost all the editors agreed.

"Hi Stuart. Listen, we're maxed out on the number of pages that we are buying but I've got something else... You know how the centerfold usually has some phony signature across the spread? Like "Samantha, Love and Kisses?"

"Yeah, I guess." He was probably being nice and had never actually looked at these magazines other than when his assistant put a page in front of him to check his ads.

"Well I just asked the editors, if we could put 'Samantha call me 1-800 ...'"

"Yeah...?"

"They said yes! Meaning you can have your phone number right under the centerfold. It's no longer an ad in the back of the mag, its right there on the girl!"

"Seriously! That's fantastic!!! You should try to get as many magazines as possible! How much do they want?"

"Well I told them they could have the layout for free if they put the phone number on it, so like two or three thousand, the price of the layout."

"Gail, do you know how huge this is?!!! That's prime advertising! Do you know how much that is worth?!!!"

And so, I had phone numbers in almost every magazine out there; placed under the centerfold, and then in the copy, 'til there were phone numbers popping up all over the place. I even shot a few photos of our models on the phone, so when the editors ran the layout they could include a couple of pics of the girl with a phone in her hand and of course our 1-800 telephone number was printed below the pic! And, it was easy enough for me to attach the real model's voice recording to be heard on the other end of the phone line!

My tiny little home office had turned into full service phone sex production! Photos to ads to phone recordings. One would think I had an ad team coming up with ad copy but there was no time for that. The ads were literally thrown together between me and an art girl I hired. I'd look at a photo and just think of a catch phrase I thought would go with it. Like a model with big boobs might get "Suck on my swollen succulent breast 1-800..." or a more down to earth looking girl might be tagged, "Real housewives taking calls while their husband is at work 1-800..." Either way it was probably the same operator at a desk in Wisconsin, for all of them.

Sexy, slutty copy as pretty easy but many of the 900 phone carriers would only accept tame copy. This took a little more ingeniousness on my part. Try making an ad sound sexy when you couldn't say anything sexy. You couldn't even use the word *legs*! Even the word *hot* was too much. *See My Hot Legs* would've been pulled in a second.

And the girls in these 900 ads had to be completely clothed. These phone carriers were worse than a Catholic school. No nudity at all, no cleavage and legs only showing to just above the knee. I was paying my models to put more clothes on!

The sheer volume of photography that was needed was now insane and I had a real shortage of pics of girls with enough clothes on! I had to outsource. This was where my contacts in Hollywood came in. Who better than Hollywood photographers who shot headshots of actresses all day long! Up and coming actresses seemed quite happy to actually get paid to have their head shots done in return for throwing in a phone and letting us use them in ads.

CHAPTER FOURTEEN

Shooting Sexy Grans

MY HUSBAND, SCOTT code-named me *The Secret Weapon*. He said men would look at me, take one long gander at my boobs, and think they were dealing with some dumb blonde. And while they were busy looking at my chest, I was busy striking the deal. By the time they'd come to their senses I'd be out the door with a contract in hand and they'd be left wondering why they just gave me the best deal ever. I thought that was a little exaggerated, but the label caught on.

I was interviewed a couple of times for various newspapers and asked if it was harder for a woman to get ahead in business and did I experience any issues with sex inequality? I laughed, "Are you kidding, I love being a woman. Sex inequality? Yes! Absolutely- it's such an advantage!"

It was an advantage all the way 'round. The couple of women in the industry, loved me and supported me. We had that woman to woman bonding thing. And men, well men are just men! Gotta love 'em! And I really do! Sorry guys, but those with the pussy hold all the cards. This might have been a man's world, but it was directed in many ways by the women.

Then there was the Dragon Lady. She held the iron fist on all the ad space for a very large New York publisher. She'd seen me in and out of the office selling pics but now I needed some of her domain. She suggested lunch.

She was a self-confessed Chinese butch bull dike, no bones about it, lesbian. She dressed like a man, acted like a man and looked like Chairman Mao on steroids. She arrived at the restaurant in an Armani suit and tie, opened the door and pulled out my chair at the table. We had a great time at lunch as we chatted and got to know one another.

She told me about some Korean spa steam place where all the women seemed to be mandated to go nude and there was some great deep tissue, massaging going on. "I could do with a hard, naked massage," I must have said out loud. My genuine interest was really what did it for her. At the end of our long lunch I suggested the advertising deal I wanted. She thought she could do it, so we stopped by her office and I asked for a twelve-month commitment and left with contract in hand.

She was, after all was said and done, very sweet. I wondered why they called her the Dragon Lady. A little later I had reason to talk to the head honcho, Mr. Simpson.

"Well Miss Thackray, seems like you got the Dragon Lady's panties in a tizzy this afternoon."

"What do you mean?" I asked naively.

"After you left she was standing there in a whirlwind saying," and he scrunched up his face and did this overblown Chinese accent, "I don't know why I agreed to that! HUFF! But I did! I even give her twelve-month commitment! AHH! WHAT WAS I THINKING! AHH!"

He laughed, and I couldn't help laughing with him.

Stuart was calling daily trying to get me to buy more ad pages, but I was getting all the space I could lay my hands on, I couldn't spend more! So, with every inch of every spare magazine page in the US covered, Stuart asked me about Europe, "You're from Europe. Who do you know in the magazines over there?"

"Well, I sell photos to a lot of the European mags but as far as I know they don't even have phone sex lines over there!"

And there it was, my next project. And off I went to England, then to Germany, then France, then Holland. I was correct, most countries didn't even have phone sex lines.

I called Stuart.

"Well just figure out who the phone carriers are over there and try to make us a deal."

And so that's exactly what I did. I got the ad agency deals for phone lines all over Europe. Once that was set the world was their oyster. They had no competition. No one had bought the advertising pages yet because the business simply didn't exist. So, I was able to lock down every men's magazine for Stuart, buying out their entire advertising space for years.

In every country. It seems men all over the world were just as crazy. And really lonely. The phone lines worked. I mean they really worked.

Meanwhile the number of photos, recordings and ad copy was insatiable and now we had to have a bunch translated into German! I hired myself more office helpers and had a stable of freelance photographers.

Doing audio recordings that sounded sexy with no body parts and not even the word *hot* made it very difficult to ad lib. I needed to write "scripts" and the sheer mass meant I needed help. Where else? Back to my contacts in Hollywood. This time I hired Hollywood screenwriters to script write phone sex ads. I had mainstream, now very well known, Hollywood writers, writing phone sex copy!

Suddenly I needed to make a hundred audio recordings for the new UK ads. They had to be even softer than the soft American ones and still sound sexy! Plus, I needed them all with English accents! And they couldn't all be me! I had exhausted every friend I had with a British accent, getting them to record sexy tapes for me. I even used my mother who happened to be over on vacation!!! (My mother, good sport she is, doing sexy phone sex recordings with moaning that sounded more like Boris Karloff, is an image that is unfortunately burned into my memory forever!)

Now I was auditioning real Hollywood actresses for voice over phone sex ads!!! The scripts were genius. Very creative… with titles such as *Horse Riding Lessons* which went something like… "Wow big boy, steady while I mount you, you big stallion, you. Now I am going to ride you hard, up down up down…!" Or my personal favorite *The Cockney Grocer* which went something like … "I was in t' supermarket feeling my juicy melons when this young man from the 'meat' department, said 'nice pair' and slipped me some tongue…"

On one such recording session an older lady named Dalston showed up for the voice over work. She had the Queen's English stiff-upper-lip English accent and she didn't seem to mind these odd scripts we gave her. Dalston admitted to being seventy-five years old but I suspected that meant she was at least eighty! As I watched her delivering these non-sexy lines in this sexy English seductive accent, something occurred to me. If my experience with the mags had taught me anything, it was that there is someone for everyone. I looked at her quizzically for a moment, then the words just left my mouth.

"Dalston, would you be interested in doing some modeling for us? Nude modeling that is?"

My assistant shot me a look that said, *Have you completely lost your mind?*

"Oh, that sounds fun! I'd be delighted to," she replied in an awfully, awfully posh British tongue.

My entire office looked over at me, stunned and confused.

I decided to set her up with my photographer Mark the next day. I didn't exactly tell him what to expect. He was already shooting another girl, so I just told him, "You have another model coming over."

Imagine his surprise!

Oh, our office was full of fun surprises! I half expected her not to show, but sure enough she did. After Mark got over the shock, confirmed that I really did want her shot and it was not a practical joke, she got herself ready. She had brought her own selection of sexy lingerie!!! Her eyesight wasn't very good, so I had to fix where she missed her lips and drew lipstick on her cheek. And she was half deaf and couldn't hear direction and without her glasses she was blind as a bat so couldn't see direction, but somehow, they managed.

"You are SO going to hell for this one!" Mark remarked.

But Dalston was loving it! Clearly there had been some posing in the bedroom at some point in her life. She had a great time, we paid her, and she offered if we needed her again she would love to come back.

It took a lot of persuasion to get an editor to run the photos but when they did, the publisher was absolutely amazed. An avalanche of letters arrived as the guys went crazy and wrote in droves. We simply had no idea the massive response Dalston would create! She brought in at least ten times the mail of any other model…ever! She was beyond a fantastic success. I hired her over and over and the photos just flew off the shelves.

Thanks to her and the response, the magazine *Forty Plus* was born.

We had for a while been shooting soft little single girl videos of the models that came through. Especially the newbies and the mega boob dancers and we'd created a video line of a few hundred titles. They were very tame, just girls by themselves stripping off and talking to the camera. I decided to ask Dalston if we could do a video of her. It was softer than soft core. Just stripping off and talking to the camera about her fantasies. The videographer said he expected a hundred years of cobwebs when she pulled down her panties and he was a bit traumatized by the whole experience, but I knew there'd be a certain group of guys that would absolutely love her. Young guys aged eighteen to twenty-six to be more specific! — No, I'm not kidding.

Again, I had no idea of how successful she would be. That video outsold our entire video library put together. And we would crack up, every guy would call our eight-hundred order line and we knew they wanted her video, but they were too embarrassed to ask, like teenagers asking for condoms at the Seven-Eleven. So, they'd order this girl and that girl until they plucked up the courage to say, "Oh and just throw that one of Dalston in…um… for my friend!"

Dalston went on to model for me for about three years. Then one day she came and said her big Hollywood agent forbid her to do it anymore. She was a regular recurring character on Seinfeld at the time and the agent was freaking out.

"I really am terribly sorry," she said. "I do love doing it and thank you for the opportunity…and all the FUN!"

After that, there were other older ladies that crossed our path. With Dalston we had opened a whole new genre.

But then I stooped to a whole new low. We had another _very_ older lady modeling. I was at the shoot and in the lunch break she was moving her teeth trying to get some piece of salad out.

"Do your teeth come out?" I asked, out of curiosity.

"Yes, I have false teeth."

Hmm… I thought …. for a moment, the squirmy, evil side of my brain taking over.

"Would you take your teeth out for an extra fifty dollars?"

She whipped those suckers out faster than you can say "granny gum-job." I have a simple headshot of her smiling with her teeth on the pillow next to her. That shot would sell over and over and over. I thought, *Now, I'm really going to Hell.*

The recorded phone lines were now humming along. So, what about the high-ticket Live Operator lines?

"Stuart, how do the live operators know what to talk about with the guys?"

"What do you mean, they talk about sex I suppose."

"Yes, but do they get a screen that shows them the ad, or who they are supposed to be. Like a screen that says, 'you are now Debbie with big boobs' or 'you are now Mistress Mandy who will spank you?'"

"Honestly, I don't think there is anything like that, I think they just answer the phone," Stuart thinks for a moment, "I suppose if the girl knew what to talk about she could keep him on the phone longer."

And of course, I had now created myself the job of meeting with live operators and what followed…creating screens and prompts and training scripts!

The trip was more than eye opening;

Janice, a middle aged short stocky lady dressed in a bad Christmas sweater months too late, black sweat pants and slippers was one of those phone answering ladies who filled me in on the details.

"Most of them never even talk about sex," she said with a southern drawl.

"What?" I exclaimed, confused.

"Yessiree, most of the time they talk about things they have to do. You know, like how they have to walk the dog, pick up something from the store and go shopping for their mother…."

I looked very confused.

"Like Dave, he's a regular, he always gripes about his boss at work. He has a crush on this girl at work but never dares to actually talk to her. I've told him what to say, and maybe he'll dare to do it one day…"

"What, you mean guys call just to chat and they don't even talk about sex."

"Well eventually they might. Or if they've had a drink. But they usually have to pluck up the courage to get down and dirty."

I discovered that most of these guys just called for someone to talk to. Either that or they were too scared or too polite and felt like they had to chat the girl up on the phone for ages, before they were allowed to talk dirty. All the time paying $2.99 a minute!

Didn't they realize that the girls were getting paid to talk sexy? All the phone operators said the same thing, guys would call in several times a week just to have someone to talk to!

This is why, when the girls hit it right, the hold times were insane! I couldn't understand why a guy would stay on the phone for forty-five minutes. It was forty-three minutes foreplay talk! And maybe, just maybe, two minutes of action. And some perhaps thought it was worth it to pay hundreds of dollars a month just to talk to some hot girl about shopping for their mother! And now I understood, with guys calling at an insane rate and staying on the phone for whatever crazy reason, my clients had a money-churning machine.

Plus, they didn't really have that hot California beach babe in the ad photo on the other end of the line. They had some housewife at a switching station in Wisconsin somewhere who was probably way better on the phone.

Still they were able to implement better systems, so the guys could connect with their regular girls more easily and the operator could know who she was supposed to be.

And what the girls really wanted… a switching system that allowed the calls to go straight to her home phone when she was on call. This way Janice didn't have to be at the call center, she could be cleaning house, making dinner and watching her favorite Soap, all while entertaining some guy at $2.99 a minute! And a network of housewives across America was launched, all earning a ton of extra money talking to some lonely strangers about shopping for their mothers.

Now those phone numbers placed under the actual girl on the centerfold where it said, "I'm Bella call me!" or something, were going great. So were the give-away panty promotions I had sent to some of the mags. This led me to another idea.

"Hi Stuart. I was thinking. You know the magazines sometimes run a contest and the winner gets the panties from my model? Well, since we have access to the models and I am sure I can pay some of the girls to do it, how about 'Win A Date with Centerfold Candy'?"

"Really?! You could get a girl to do that?"

"Yes, I mean a chaperoned dinner date."

"Sounds great, so how do the guys compete?"

"Well, they have to call in. And pay of course the $2.99 a minute for the phone call."

"You mean, they have to listen to a very long list of instructions, staying on the phone…."

"Yes! And I was hoping they can actually leave messages."

Several girls agreed, and thousands of guys spent ages leaving message after message, hoping to be the chosen one.

Months later audio recordings were shipped to my office to choose the winners. Tapes were piled high, *Oh my God, how am I going to choose a winner? I am not going to listen to all of these weird freaky phone messages!*

Stuart had been talking me up to his girlfriend, who decided she should get in on the action.

"Gail," Stuart called, "We were thinking about doing some of those late night infomercials and I know you probably have some contacts in Hollywood but Laura also has some experience in TV, so she's offered to fly out and help you."

"Great," I said, hoping it wouldn't happen.

Unfortunately, she came out.

She was checked into some high-end expensive hotel on the West Side, where we met to discuss the ads. I had pulled some serious Hollywood strings and had booked a sound stage, crew and props for a fraction of the price.

Laura had her own ideas of exactly how the infomercials should be shot, which were not really in alignment with mine. Anyway, somehow I had managed to work around her expert input and after two weeks of exhausting hell we had some pretty good quality footage in the can.

Laura wanted to go over the final bills, "Gail, if you can write up an invoice for the sound stage and the production costs and the models as one flat fee for seventy thousand."

"But we got a really good deal on the production, it was less than twenty K all in."

"Yes, I know but I told Stuart we would come in under one hundred K, so he's going to be happy."

"Yes, but it didn't cost us anywhere near that."

She snorted, annoyed with me, "Don't worry about it, I'll just write up the bills."

I talked with my husband later, "She's going to screw her own boyfriend, I can't believe it!"

"You should tell him," Scott advised.

"I'm going to stay out of it," I decided.

I was in New York and Micky invited me out to dinner with Big Tony and the rest of the group — Vinnie, Joey, Lou and Pepe and his friend, a couple of youngsters I hadn't met before.

We are seated at a cocktail bar which was quite noisy and Big Tone insists that I sit next to him where he can hear me. He was dying to know all about what was going on as far as their phone biz in LA.

"So, tell me, how does this work? The guys call a phone number and they get to talk to a real girl or is it a recording or something?"

"Well, they have different programs; they have live operators and they have recorded lines and then they have these date lines or party lines."

Pepe pipes up cheekily, "Do you know these girls? Are there any around here?" which infuriates Tony who shoots a look throwing his hands up, "What the fuck is wrong with you?!!! No, she don't have no girls! You wanna a broad, go to a fucking strip club!" Pepe is put in his place and backs down.

Turning to me he continues, "And guys really call these numbers?"

"Yeah, apparently tons of them."

"And what do the girls talk about?" Tony asks totally confused, "I mean do the guys really get off from these calls."

"Well actually, you'd be surprised. A lot of them just talk about boring stuff, like shopping for their mother," I tell him.

"What?!!!" Big Tone scrunches his face in disbelief.

"Yeah some of them just want someone to talk to."

"Yo, Micky is this right? Some of these phone sex calls are about shopping?!" Tony shouts across the bar.

"We don't care what they talk about, as long as their credit card goes through," Micky replies in a very matter of fact way.

"Okay Gail. Let me get this straight..." Tony continues trying to wrap his head around it, "Some geezer calls a phone sex number and pays like a dollar a minute to talk about shopping!!!" Tony's shaking his head in disbelief.

"Yeah. But more like three dollars a minute," I correct him.

"What da fuck! Joey, have you heard this, some guy calls a phone sex line and talks about shopping with his mother, and we're getting like three dollars a minute!!!"

"Yeah bunch of sick fucks if you ask me," Joey snorts.

"This don't seem right. You're not pulling my leg are you?" Tony asks yet again.

"No Tony, I'm serious and some of them call like three times a week."

"What!!! Get the fuck outta here!"

We sit through a two hour dinner and Tony keeps bringing it up, "And it don't matter what he talks about we still get three dollars a minute?"

Big Tony is trying his best to understand the business and Micky is patiently explaining all the different programs which are completely going over Tony's head.

Vinnie in the back is getting sick of hearing about it, "Why the fuck do you care Tone?!!!" Vinnie pipes up for the first time.

"Just trying to understand OUR business!" Tony shoots the group a look and they all instantly go silent.

"It's a great business," Micky intervenes to calm everyone down. "And Gail's been cutting us amazing ad deals. Pages in magazines we couldn't even get in and now she's even got them to put phone numbers on the centerfolds."

"Yep, she's our super star, this little one," Tony says fondly squeezing my hand. "And they're taking good care of you right?"

"Yes, absolutely."

"You want anything, you let me know, right?" he reiterates squeezing my hand again.

Later that evening, we drive to a strip club somewhere in Philadelphia. I'm pretty tired but felt I should make the effort to go. Tony seemed excited to talk to me and he was obviously a big backer of some sort for Micky and Stuart, so I tried to keep myself awake.

We're seated around a club lounge table, the guys in worn but comfy leather chairs drinking whiskeys and smoking cigars like it was their regular hanging out. We had been there hours and they'd all had a ton of alcohol, but were pretty good at not showing it. I'd switched to soda a while earlier. Some regulars came over and hung out and occasionally some of the dancers they seemed to know.

One of the girls came to talk to Big Tony and he smacked her fondly on the butt. He was nice to the girls, but I felt like I was treated very differently. I was like one of the guys. Not just one of the guys, but like Tony's golden child.

Then there was a bit of commotion at the bar as a "customer" seemed to be raising his voice and getting a bit out of hand. He was sitting on a bar stool clearly mouthing off and there was a tense moment with the bartender. It was enough to catch the attention of Tony, who looked over to Joey. Joey nodded as if to say, "I'll take care of it." And he got up to sort things out. He was gone for just a few minutes, and they must have gone out back somewhere. A few minutes later he returned. Nothing was said and there was just a nod and a look between them like "it's sorted out."

"It's time to get outta here," Joey notes.

I agree, I'm tired out! Thankfully that was the cue to exit.

CHAPTER FIFTEEN

Milk Money

THE "ITALIAN FOUNDING Fathers" were taking very good care of me, protecting me from having my legs broken and probably other issues I was happily not aware of.

In addition to the usual fees they paid me to find them advertising, there were other projects thrown my way. Stuart seemed to like to work on a very loose handshake arrangement and was always more than generous.

"What do you think is fair for the ad layouts you did? Like a Grand each?" Stuart would ask.

"Sure!" I'd answer.

"And for that trip to Europe? What was that worth? Like, Thirty k? Is that good?" he'd say, check in hand.

"Yep! All good with me!"

It was all so good our lifestyle at home had gone up considerably. Shortly after we started, I bought my husband an airplane for his birthday. Just a little four-seater Cessna type. Sounds impressive but it was very old and cheap as far as planes go. Still it wasn't much longer before I upgraded that to a still old, but six-seater jet.

I loved being able to provide for my family and to make my husband happy. Between the magazine sales and my phone clients, I was doing so well it was kind of silly for my husband to keep working his nine to five engineering job. I desperately needed help around the office, and really, if I was making ten times what he was making, what was the point in him going to work anymore?

He agreed, quit his job and came to help me, "Besides I have a Business Degree," he pointed out. "I'll manage the operations and I actually know what I'm doing," he laughed.

Perhaps he was right, I didn't really know what I was doing. I was just winging it.

He figured he could do photography just as well as anyone else and, being an engineer, was able to figure out the technical aspects pretty quick. He didn't have an artist bone in his body so as long as I was standing behind him doing the posing and everything except actually hitting the shutter we were okay. He was now officially in the sex biz with me.

With all this pent-up sexual energy, in a business of constant tease and arousal, you'd think my sex life at home would have been off the hook. Really it was pretty nonexistent, unless I instigated it, and it was nothing to write home about even when it did happen. Vanilla, missionary, lights out.... you get the picture. The fantasies I'd play out in directing the photo shoots and writing phone sex copy, was way more exciting. Sex with my husband was five-minutes of missionary, then he'd roll over and ask, "did you cum?" The answer was, of course not, and he made me feel like it was some inherent flaw in me. It was easier to have some wild sexual fantasy in my mind, masturbating next to him, while I tried not to wake him up, and these fantasies never included him. I could get turned on at my desk in the middle of the day and reach in my panties and have a wild orgasm, or in my studio makeup room, or wherever, but he was never a part of it. But this was more of a sexual release. The real deep love feelings I longed to have for him, honestly, on my part were just lacking. Still, my mind was focused and in work mode most of the time anyway.

My husband however, really wanted us to have a baby soon and kept pushing for it. I was only twenty-five, focused on my career and had loads of time ahead but I finally conceded and so the boring missionary must have happened at least a few times.

I am now pregnant with my first child Rachel. Perhaps the hormones gave me a push of determination, drive or just sheer ballsiness, as my business had gone through the roof. My hormones rocketing off the charts as I seemed to have insatiable business drive or perhaps it was because I was just hornier than hell all the time. On the other hand, pregnancy didn't bode well for me as morning sickness set in. Did I say "Morning" sickness? I was throwing up all day long. On the phone wheeling and dealing with a puke bucket next to me. The most successful, busiest time in my career so far, and I've got my head in a trash can half the time! I tried to get my husband to be more of a front person and deal with my clients. Unfortunately, they weren't having any of it.

I decided to take Scott on a trip to New York with me, figuring if he could meet people and have a personal relationship with them, he could take over a lot of my business and really help me out.

Scott was very happy to have the responsibility, and he is getting into all my invoices, "Why are you only charging the ad agency two k for these ad pages, I thought the book rate is like eight?"

"Yes it is, but I pass on to them whatever deal I get. I got them a really good deal."

"Yes, but they'd pay the full eight!"

"Scott, they are more than fair with us, they pay us really good for placing the ads and making them. I want to keep them happy."

Scott shrugs his shoulders, "Well I am going to do an hourly flow chart on the phone recordings you did to present them an invoice," Scott said authoritatively.

"Well, they are more loose than that. Stuart is usually like, 'Shall we say twenty k' or something like that and then I just send him an invoice for that amount."

"Yes, but that's not proper business. The way it's done correctly is to calculate the hours and add a management fee," Scott said adamantly throwing his new authority around.

"But, they're not like that, they usually just do a flat fee and Stuart is always very generous."

"Look, I'm the one with the business degree, all this slap hazard stuff needs to stop."

Scott had just taken an additional degree in business at some satellite college, so I figured it couldn't harm.

So off we go to the Big Apple. First stop was of course Stuart and the ad group.

"Wow look at this place! Shit they got some bucks!" Scott remarked upon arriving at their reception.

As we were taken back to the board room, Stuart came in, "Wow, congratulations guys." Stuart said looking at my pregnant bulge and meeting Scott for the very first time, after well over a year of me doing business with them.

"I'm hoping Scott can help out with a lot of things with the baby coming."

"Great!" Stuart said excitedly.

"So those English phone recordings are going great," Stuart said getting straight to business, "What do you think is fair for those, like thirty K?"

Scott cleared his throat and interjected, "We'll actually here's a spread, it shows the hours and the expenses and then there is a management percent…," he said handing Stuart an official looking cost breakdown.

"What is all this for?" Stuart gestures throwing his hands open to me in a confused and slightly agitated manner.

Scott continues, "Well this is the correct way this is done in business, and the spread shows…"

Stuart is now getting quite irritated, "Well Gail and I don't do it that way. I just asked if thirty k is good?"

"Yes Stuart, that's great. Scott just wanted to…"

Scott is now getting red in the face, "Look Stuart, it's not like I'm trying to Jew you down or anything! In fact, this comes out to quite a bit less."

Stuart jumps up staring at Scott, "I take great offence to that derogatory statement. It's an insult to my heritage."

Scott continues making it worse, "Well I didn't mean anything by it, it's just a saying. I didn't even know you were a Jew!"

Stuart gets up refusing to look in Scott's direction and looks at me, "Gail is the thirty thousand Okay?"

"Yes Stuart, sorry."

He hands me a check and goes to leave, "Gail, we're good and I don't care what he does for you in the office, I just don't want to have to talk to him, okay?"

Scott did a little better with some of the other editors he met on the trip, not much though. They all wanted to deal directly with me.

On our return home, Scott got to answer the phone and it was always, "Hi, how are you? Great…. put Gail on please."

He tried his hardest but there were obviously things I needed to do myself in the business. At home we could use some help too. My husband always got along with my very sweet mom and suggested with baby on the way we invite her out to live with us. My mom took an early retirement from her job in the UK, sold her house and came out. Pretty incredible that she didn't get cold feet. She'd been out a few times to try it out. The last time she'd visited we were on the Bay Bridge in San Francisco in eighty-nine, when the earthquake struck, and the Bay Bridge went down. Amazingly, we survived unharmed, on the bottom deck, just a few hundred feet from the section of concrete that collapsed. We had both been interviewed on the San Francisco news outside a building that later imploded.

The next day we flew home in that first plane I'd bought. Did I mention it was old and crappy? Well, on the way home the engine gave out. There were a few final spats as the propeller slowed spurted out black engine oil, soaking the window and within seconds the view was completely covered in a layer of black oil. My husband was luckily a great pilot and pulled off an emergency crash landing in a field full of corn, miles from anywhere. We hiked out and finally hitched a ride.

It was quite a story mom had to tell friends back home; earthquake, being on the news, and surviving a plane crash. Still my mom must have been up for the excitement because she still moved out to live with us. She was here to help with her grandchild on the way, but she was a good sport and I put her to work around the office sorting naked pics and the likes.

My first daughter Rachel popped out. I felt like some Lakota Sioux maiden leaving Crazy Horse just long enough to wander into the woods and squat. I tried to take one day off work but even then, Stuart called me a bunch in the hospital.

"Thank you Stuart for the incredible baby gifts! Wow! And for the beautiful flowers, that was so sweet," I said, looking around at my hospital room that looked more like the Ritz brimming full of the most exquisite flowers and the mass of the finest baby gifts one could imagine.

"Absolutely. Congratulations! And….er… I hate to ask you while you're still in the hospital but wondering when we can talk about that ad campaign for Germany."

"Yes, it's Okay, I can talk, I can't fax you from here, but I'll be back in the office tomorrow, I can fax a copy then."

Stuart heaved a sigh of relief. It was back to the full rat race the next day. The Buffalo Calf Woman, baby in one hand, phone in the other. I had puked all the way through the pregnancy, so I had no baby fat, but the excess of milk made my boobs spectacular.

I was living a bit of a dual life here. One-minute sexy business lady, next minute Hollywood actress and then, most of the time, just mom. It may sound like I was so busy with my other lives that I didn't have time to be a mom. But my baby Rachel came first. Turns out I loved being a mom and I was very much hands on. Breastfeeding my daughter and my overproduction of milk came to be a bit difficult sometimes. I'd been to a mammary specialist to try to figure out how to reduce my milk production and was walking around the home office following some suggested home remedy of frozen cabbage leaves pressed on my swollen breasts.

I was on the phone one day donning the cabbage leaves, complaining to Yvonne. "I keep trying to get my husband to suck on my boobs, but he says that's disgusting! I need someone to milk me! I just need a little relief here."

"Oh, my God!" Yvonne screams, "I can't tell you how much my readers would pay to do that! Sit on your lap and have you be their mommy! You could charge like a thousand dollars, maybe two, for, like, twenty minutes!"

I must admit the thought of having my breasts sucked was very appealing. It wasn't in the least bit sexual to me, but I knew it was some boob guy's extreme fantasy. I do confess I had used it to my sales advantage and I'd given Morgan a little squirt across his desk, which was enough to have him quivering on his knees, drooling at the mouth and begging like a wild animal. And my real intention, giving him the incentive to buy whatever pile of photos I'd brought that day.

Here I am trying to get sympathy out of Yvonne. "I have a freezer full of milk and my baby can't get through that much. My boobs are ginormous and bouncing off my knees. I tried to donate my milk to the hospital, but they said they'd have to collect it at the hospital and I don't have time for that."

Then Yvonne has a brilliant idea.

"How much milk do you have in the freezer? We could advertise to my readers and we could sell it! What about it? We could get like five-hundred a bag."

"Really?" I said skeptically.

"Are you kidding!" she exclaimed, "Your freezer, right now, is worth thousands!"

There wasn't even a question as to whether that was weird or rude or unethical at all. I was so far past that at this point. If someone wanted to pay for it, why not?

We went into full production. I researched it, she advertised it. Then my husband noticed the FedEx, cold ship boxing piling up.

"What are these for?" he inquired innocently.

I explained my new money-making venture, thinking he would be quite happy. ......He was anything but. He hit the roof!   "You do know what they are going to do with your milk, don't you?"

I supposed I did. Drink it? No, maybe not. Put it on themselves, somewhere…? Honestly, I didn't really care. I was supporting our family. Why did he care? It was anonymous anyway. It was not like they even knew it was coming from the scream queen who starred in *Sorority House Massacre II* or it might have been worth more. Anonymous or not, he was adamantly against it.

"No! NO! Absolutely not!" he stomped his words with his feet.

"But there's like fifty thousand dollars in our freezer just sitting there," I argued.

"That is… disgusting!"

And unfortunately put the dead stop to our little Lucy and Ethel scheme.

I really couldn't understand why he was being so prudish. I remember one of the girls we photographed sharing about a little business side deal she had. She was a famous porn star or something. She told me she was selling her pubic hair clippings.

What?! I thought she was kidding but she wasn't.

She said she had serious fans in Japan. Said one guy was making a love pillow out of them!

I thought at the time, *Some men are just weird.*

What was a little breast milk compared to pubic hair clippings? She even told me she was selling her used tampons to customers in Japan too. At that, I thought she was pulling my leg. But maybe not.

The weirdness had only just begun.

CHAPTER SIXTEEN

Women with Agendas

ONE WOULD THINK that the girls in these shoots are poor innocent girls coaxed or conned into doing it. Actually, there was a steady stream, knocking on our door to work. But then our photos were all pretty "soft-core."

Some of the girls were looking to be in the magazines to promote their career, such as the mega boob exotic dancers. These girls had fantastically produced professional strip shows and were bringing in the big bucks. They'd work as a "featured dancer," Las Vegas style, with elaborate shows and costumes. But the rate they got from the clubs depended on their exposure. That's where we came in. If we could make them a Busty Beauties Centerfold, their rates could double!

I had girls on the other end of the spectrum, too. I found little Bridgett in a strip club doing some kind of "young girl" act. One might have thought her to be a teenage boy. She was actually twenty-two, but looked much younger. Completely flat chested and very petite. I brought her into town to shoot and let her stay with us. She knew I was an actress and that I occasionally hung out with a couple of celebrities. She begged me to take her along, so one night I took her to a bar on Sunset Blvd. Sure enough my friends were there. Hanging out with John Daily and some other producers was Mickey Rourke, and this was when he was all hot and pretty before he took up boxing.

Just like the other guys were mesmerized by boobs, this one was mesmerized by the lack thereof. Oh, she played it up big time, looking all coy with her head tilted, sucking seductively on carrot sticks.

Oh, he's not really falling for this, is he? I thought.

He sure was! He was smitten. She was supposed to be staying with me but over the next few weeks I only saw the occasional glimpses of her. I had loaned her my beaten-up old ranch truck and one day, Mickey showed up at my house driving her around in said beat up pickup. They'd come to the ranch get some things and then play out some fantasy: "guy picks up a little fresh young babe hitchhiking and then fucks the shit out of her in the bed of the pick-up." Mickey's bare ass slamming this newbie's spread wide legs over the back of the cab, was probably the last image I saw of the two of them.

And the New York editors were just as starry eyed to meet the girls, so from time to time I'd take one of the models with me. Wows! That was a real treat for these lonely, love starved editors, getting to meet a real-life model in the flesh. Most of the editors were very respectful. Even, perhaps a little nervous. The girls made the most of it and used these visits to help their careers. Getting a nice layout in a magazine meant as much money to the girls as it did to me. I didn't discourage them when they started flirting with the editors, sitting on their lap and giving them a bit of a titty dance action in their cubicle.

But the one that most impressed me with her business forte was Penny Plentiful. Huge breasts that were clearly fake. It didn't matter; men would fixate on those bosoms and trip all over themselves. She was older, admitted to being forty but that was probably as big a stretch as the miracle boob grow cream she sold to guys at seventy-five dollars a jar "to rub on your wife's boobs and make them as big as mine." We've just arrived in town when she asks, "Do you mind if we go meet 'Lick-n-Stick Dan.'"

Who is Lick-n-Stick Dan? I wondered, but agreed, "Sure."

So off we go to a little coffee shop on the West Side. We are met by a very grateful, geeky chap who's probably been waiting hours. Penny, by the way, has dragged this suitcase across town, which he immediately takes off her hands. Dan is totally mesmerized by her breasts, trying hard not to salivate as he talked to her completely spellbound and in awe. His gaze fixed at mid breast, fluttering between her lips and God forbid glancing down at her heaving cleavage.

He doesn't give me but the slightest glance. As Penny leaves to powder herself, I finally get to know Dan a little. Dan is an accountant. A simple man with no social life but works in his little bean counting job all year round saving up for the one day a year he has the honor of taking Penny out to lunch.

You see Dan was the "Penny Plentiful New York Fan Club President." His role was to pay for her lunch when in town. When presented with the suitcase, he lovingly took it with such gratitude. Inside were thousands of flyers. Dan's job was to buy envelopes, fold each flyer, address each envelope and "Lick-N-Stick" the stamps (which of course he had to purchase). Hence the *nom de guerre'* "Lick-N-Stick Dan".

This was his entire savings for the year, but well worth it to him.

Apparently, she had a Lick-n-Stick fan club president in every city.

Wow this girl had it down! Why couldn't I have a team of men all over, lined up to work for me and pay for the privilege?

Later I talked to Yvonne about this. "Yeah of course, you can get guys to do your chores and yes they'll pay you! I can get you some slaves in LA if you like?"

I looked confused.

She continues, "Do you have a maid to clean your house?"

"Yes, sure."

"Well, I can get you a ton of guys who will do that for free."

"What, really, like real housework?"

"Yeah, they're great. They do laundry, wash your windows, they work really hard."

I didn't get it, what's the catch? "And you don't pay them?"

"Fuck, no, they pay you! They'll pay you like two hundred dollars a day."

"What?"

"I mean, they probably come in a rubber diaper and thigh highs or some shit, but if that doesn't bother you… and you just have to scream at them and slap them once in a while…"

It seemed like a good financial deal, I just couldn't imagine what the family would think about some guy in a rubber diaper on his hands and knees scrubbing the kitchen floor…Perhaps I'd stick to paying my regular housecleaning lady.

Meanwhile back at the New York hotel room, Penny wanted to go out shopping. She pulled out her Rolodex and started to call different men. In a very affected Marilyn Monroe voice, I heard her say; "Hi Bill… It's Penny, I was wondering if I could run your credit card for a hundred, for a new sexy outfit. I know you'll wanna see me in it."

She did this with four or five different guys, till she had enough in her account and then off we'd go.

I mean, I have big boobs and I am very aware that a certain group of guys will just trip over themselves looking at your chest. But we're talking ginormous boobs here.

Penny had definitely gotten down how to work that boob fetish thing, but she wasn't the only girl. There was something about boobs and their control over men. One Erotic Dancer said she wanted a boob job but desperately needed her teeth fixed. She couldn't afford both, so she went for the boob job. After that no one even noticed her teeth!

It's true, those that liked boobs, couldn't take their eyes off them and you could hear them going, "Yes, sure whatever you want…uh-huh…uh-huh!" in a state of trance. Editors were not immune to such spells either.

I took advantage of this in a big way. I'd arrange trips for these editors to come out and spend a week or two with me in LA. I found for a mere airfare and putting them up, I was able to have an editor completely captured for a week. Their bosses, the publishers, were very happy that I was paying all the expenses and the lure was that the editor got to direct the shoots which would give him exactly what he wanted for his magazine.

In reality, I was going to shoot way more material than the editor needed. The model wanted that centerfold badly and she'd be all over the editors showing them a good time. So, instead of doing one layout on the girl, we'd shoot six, and after Tanya Tatas had worked him over and he was totally in love, there was no way any other magazine was getting a hold of photos he'd directed, and he'd have to buy the whole lot. The editor would leave with a big smile on his face and enough material to fill his magazine for months. Then the next editor would come into town….

I've talked about Morgan in LA, he was one such editor who was a sucker for a pair of boobs. Boobs were his thing. Ok that's not really fair, it was actually just any girl who would talk to him was his thing. The depths of degradation he would stoop to for the chance to maybe have a girlfriend was so very terribly sad. He was not bad looking, pretty good income, intelligent, but when boobs came around he was a sad, sack in a sorry state. He had the worst of the worst luck. He had once had a girl who genuinely wanted to date him but there was a bit of an issue because she had a split personality and only half of her was in love with him, the other half couldn't stand him. But hey, half is better than nothing. But the day she was about to move in with him, he waited at the airport, but she never showed up. Finally, he called her house. Her "husband" answered to his shock and horror and went on to explain that she never got on the plane because, you see, the night before she checked herself in to a mental institution. Not kidding! Absolutely true.

He was one of my very best clients and it was imperative that I kept him happy. Plus, I felt sorry for him and it became a personal quest to help him with his love life. And of course, if he had a personal obsession with any of the girls, I knew I could sell him every layout I had of her.

I often tried to set him up on a date. He really was quite a catch, but he'd degrade himself so much with, "I don't know why you would be interested in me. I'm down and out and have no prospects. I'm really depressed most of the time. Haven't had a girl in years...." Blah blah sob story that I suppose, he thought would make the girls think he was "honest" and that was supposed to make them feel sorry for him and then want to date him. He was so self-deprecating that every blind date I set him up with was, by the end of the dinner, ready to slit their throats, not sleep with him.

Occasionally I stooped to paying the girls five hundred dollars to "make sure he had an amazing dinner." And they were instructed that they could never tell him they were paid. It worked pretty well, except the girls would come back for another five hundred the next day and the next and it was all getting a tad bit expensive.

One girl however, Fluffy Mounds, actually liked him. Wow, finally my match making had worked, and he was head over heels. I had shot a bunch of layouts of her and of course he wanted to buy every one of them. It was a whirlwind romance while she was in town, and as she left she promised to be back soon. He was still on cloud nine when only a week later her agent called me with the sad news, "Yes, sorry, Fluffy blew her brains out." Sadly, I am not making this up.

It took him quite some time to get over the devastation of that one, and I was stuck with a bunch of great layouts of some poor dead girl.

Finally, Morgan was back on his feet and mentioned a girl at his local bar whom he was swooning over. Morgan talked about how he would love to date her, but in his words, "She would never be interested in me." Ok, personal challenge, plus I really felt for him and wanted to help as his gal pal. So, I concocted a little scenario where I accompanied him to his local hangout. I dressed particularly sexy in a tight top accentuating my breasts, plus a black-mini and ultra-sexy-heels. At the bar I cooed over him and hung on his every word and appeared to flirt with him incessantly. Debbie, his local bar girl was clearly intrigued as she served us. Then as planned, I gave him a big smacking kiss and left him at the bar alone. It worked like a dream and within minutes Debbie was leaning over the bar, talking to him. As soon as closing time came, she was back at his apartment making out on his couch. They were at third base, about to digress to his bedroom, when he decided it was best he confess that the girl at the bar was not really a date, rather it was a friend of his who had done this to try to make Debbie jealous. What!!! He did what!!! Yes, he did! And that was the end of the road with Debbie.

So unfortunately, it was back to greasing the palms.

Then out of nowhere he met a model, who he was reportedly dating. This time nothing to do with my matchmaking skills. Wow, I was happy for him! I invited them over for dinner with my husband and me.

He showed up at our house proudly touting his "new girl," a mega-boob exotic dancer. He was over the moon, thrilled she was really dating him and, actually they were already planning to get married!

Ten minutes into dinner, I knew he was going to get badly hurt.

She starts to tell us about the upcoming wedding; "We're going to have a very expensive Disneyland wedding with the crystal coach. I am going to be Belle from *Beauty and the Beast.*"

Scott leaned over and whispered to me, "So does that make him The Beast?"

Still, on the surface, all seemed bliss. She moved in, he paid for her to have a bigger boob job that she wanted, he paid for her new wardrobe, he bought her jewelry and she left on the road, in his truck, for a little stripping gig, insisting he had to stay home. A week or so turned into a month, but still, she'd be home soon. His wife-to-be, needed a little extra money so he was wiring money every week or so. Till one day, and I swear that this is a completely true story; he's at home and happens to be watching *Jerry Springer*. This particular episode is called, *How Stupid Can Your Boyfriend Be*. As he is watching, he sees his girlfriend come on stage, and he can't believe his eyes, but there she is! And there is some guy with her. She then proudly tells the whole world she has this stupid idiot of a boyfriend back home. She's on the road stripping with her real boyfriend, the one back home is footing the bill and she's even driving his truck!

Fortunately, most of the girls were not like this. Many of them were really nice. I just pointed out the stereotyping of a poor innocent girl drawn into this business by these leering men, is quite far from the truth.

Girls seemed to pull the strings on their own careers and in one case, even a dramatic exit: I happened to be at Larry Flynt's office when Traci Lords and her mom popped in to say hi and had another little surprise announcement. Traci's mom said, "It's Traci's Birthday today." To which Larry replied, "Oh...err. Okay. Happy Birthday Traci."

Traci's mom repeated with emphasis, "It's Traci's EIGHTEENTH Birthday today."

You see Traci Lords was the hottest, sexiest thing to hit porn, being in almost every adult movie around at that time. With hundreds of pornos out, she had also graced the pages of most men's magazines. And on any particular day, she was in at least a phone sex ad in every single publication on the newsstands.

And now the world was about to find out Traci Lords had been underage the entire time!

We walked straight from the office to the local video store and bought every Traci Lords video in existence.

By the next day every movie was pulled from the shelf. Every magazine, anywhere, was taken off the newsstand and shredded. That month there was not a single men's magazine on the stands.

Traci was far from the sweet innocent child, and don't tell me this hadn't been orchestrated by Traci's mother long before. Still, it was brilliant marketing.

But then my business wasn't the porn business. My girls were a whole different breed. I told the girls never to do "porn videos." To me that was crossing the line.

Traci's mother had done something amazing. She had taken her daughter out of the business in an instant. I must admit, I had inadvertently done something similar to what Traci's mother did, a few years later. I happened to be at Larry Flynt's office doing some deal with the then-president, Tim. I noticed that there was a magazine sitting on his desk, with the back cover face up, or should I say, ass up. You see, the entire back cover was a close-up photo of my butt. Remember they had photos of me in the archive from ages before. A very attractive-looking shot, I must say, with a bunch of Cabo sand dripping off a glistening butt, with some slogan about, "get a subscription to Hustler."

"Oh, that's my butt!" I announced, picking up the magazine and admiring it. Tim looked at me sideways. I continued, "Yeah, wow, I shot that years ago with Clive, when I was probably like seventeen."

Tim didn't really say anything just, "huh," and I went about my day. I hadn't really cared if they had run that shot, no one would recognize me, it was just my butt. Yet, I had dropped a bomb, without even meaning to. One of the editors told me, the moment I left the building, it was like sirens went off. Tim was on the phone frantically screaming at everyone. Within hours all these pre-copies were destroyed and every photo they could find of me. Years later when I had access to the photo room, I went to remove any other images of me and I took just the couple that were left.

CHAPTER SEVENTEEN

A Walk on the Sleazy Side

QUITE OFTEN I'D meet girls just out and about, like Brandi, whom I met at a club.

I was in the bathroom doing my makeup when I notice a really pretty girl and struck up a conversation; "You're so beautiful, have you ever considered modeling…"

"Oh my God, thank you. You are too! I'm Brandi."

We hung out on the dance floor together, and we chatted at the bar. I explained what I did then passed her a business card, "If you're interested, call me."

And she did!

I'd find girls when I was in town shopping, at the beach, really anywhere. I could just walk up to a girl and start chatting. Guys could never have done this.

Still with such a massive demand for layouts even I'd stoop to use the sleazy agents sometimes. This meant crossing paths with the video guys, when I'd go to the famous *Empire Model Agency*. This less than upstanding group were the suppliers of girls for the pornographic movie industry.

The owner of this establishment was an old crotchety cowboy Texan and not an agent around could compete with them. Or should I say would dare. His office was a hangout for the sleaziest of the sleaze waiting for some fresh meat newbie talent to walk in. I must say the stereotypical porn producer weighed down with a mass of gold chains and smoking a big fat cigar was alive and well, every afternoon at Empire Modeling.

All the directors of course wanted girls to go all the way. That was their biz, so girls that wouldn't, were happy to work for me instead. I got into trouble many times with the Big Texan Burrito for recommending to girls that they shouldn't do the "videos." I could understand why a girl would sell herself in Hollywood when a multi-million-dollar career was at stake, but for a sleazy porn movie? Why?

Even during these casting sessions I'd slip into the Ladies bathroom and give these poor newbies some advice. I wanted to scream, "GET OUT." Still I had to ride a fine line and I was barred more than once from the agency for "helping the girls" with my advice to not do the movies.

An afternoon open call at Empire Modeling was always an experience. Sitting in this smoke-filled office with a bunch of old time porn producers as a line of newbie girls came in each day trying to land a job.

Any new video director would always presume I was "talent" and try to hire me.

I wanted to take a bath after an afternoon there. The ingrained smoke in my hair would wash out but the real filth I wished could be washed away.

Often these porn chicks would come with some loser boyfriend who was managing them. One such girl was Lola Mercedes. A porn star known as the girl with the biggest boobs in the world, and they were ginormous! I remember she was just starting out her career. Her husband/manager/ suitcase carrier/pimp was there controlling the whole shoot. He gave me her driver's license to copy and I was shocked. How could she be only twenty-five years old, she looked at least forty-five!

Her breasts truly were a sight to behold. I chatted with her suitcase manager while she was getting ready.

"Yeah, I make her implants and then we take them to a doctor to have them put in. We have them redone every six months, bigger. The doctors only get them up to a certain size and they don't make them bigger, so I had to start making them myself."

I was blown away.

This was a business that had gone completely out of control. These girls with the humongous boobs were going to extremes to out-do each other. They were exotic dancers and the bigger the boobs, the bigger the bucks. Finding a doctor that would make them big enough had become more and more difficult. I knew girls were going to other countries to have them done. You see they had to be silicone, as saline were just too heavy at that size. I'd heard horror stories of the skin becoming so stretched and thin, under the fluorescent lights, the girls were having problems because you could see the implant bags. In one case, a girl was stripping, and they were so heavy the skin split and the implants dropped out on stage! I bet that scarred some poor guys for life!

But Lola had the biggest things you had ever seen. I mean forget thirty-four triple-D, these must have been seventy inches around! I was intrigued by this whole process of her boyfriend making silicone implants. "Oh yes, I do everything. I inject her lips, cheeks, everything. I'm working on her forehead."

"What's wrong with her forehead?" I asked.

"Well, you see it used to slope backwards, so I injected it, so it leans more forward now. I do her cheeks as well."

I was in total disbelief. This guy was injecting silicone directly into her face, on an almost daily basis.

"I could do your forehead while you're here if you like," he offered, looking at my head.

"No, I'm good, thank you. Rather live with a …sloped forehead."

Was this guy nuts? Clearly there was some kind of silicone fetish going on here.

In a quiet moment alone, I tried to talk to Lola, to give her the advice that she desperately needed. I tried to empower her that she didn't need all of this. I really wanted to explain that this bizarre world she was living in was not real and longed to scream at her, "GET OUT!" But like many girls who had teamed up with these looser suitcase boyfriends it was hard to help them. So intrenched and repressed in the whole situation with these co-dependent unhealthy relationships with some blood sucking leach, it was as hard for them as breaking a heroin addict. And this one was married to hers.

Anyway…we shot some great layouts of her and she was very sweet. As for her boyfriend/husband/suitcase-carrier/silicone doctor/pimp, well I thought, *Some men are not only weird, but some are stupid and devastatingly damaging.*

I remember a year or so later reading that Lola Mercedes had been found dead from "unknown causes."

I thought, *Unknown causes, my ass!*

CHAPTER EIGHTEEN

Hollywood Casting Couch

MEANWHILE I WAS DOING a different kind of acting myself. Something I considered legitimate Hollywood.

I found the highest level of Hollywood, the big TV shows and blockbuster movies almost all came with the barrier of the casting couch. My photography biz was a straight up professional business, any sexism was me flirting a little to get the really good deals I wanted. Never did a magazine publisher try to get into my pants. In stark contrast, mainstream Hollywood seemed to be nothing but, "Oh, I'll cast you in this role if you sleep with me."

It was quite the norm to get hit on during an audition and after all, if the producer was looking for a girl with sex appeal to carry the lead in his movie, hopefully they were going to find you attractive! Sometimes they'd cross the line though and get a little out of hand, desperately trying to grope you under the pretense that it was part of a scene.

If I was invited to some producer's hotel to read, you could guarantee I was going to get hit on. It was usually a sure sign when they opened the door in a bathrobe, "Hey, I was just getting out of the shower, let me get you a glass of wine and we can discuss this amazing role I think you'd be perfect for." But honestly it could have been in their office, on the studio lot, or anywhere else too.

The smaller the production, the more nudity in the role, the more professional the casting. They were just happy to have you. But if a guy could offer a star-making role that would change a girl's life, he had extreme power. Often, I was offered the deal, "I can make you a big star if you want to be my girlfriend." And if future me could go back to being twenty-two, knowing what I know now, I probably would have gone for it.

They were just being guys trying to get some, but none of them were actually threatening or anything and no one was ever forceful.

And to be fair, on the flip side, a lot of actresses were holding out the same carrot on a stick. Actresses had been winding guys up and "working" them from the days of Marilyn Monroe and it had become "industry standard."

Usually a producer would give you a typical come-on line, but occasionally, it would come out of left field with a strange twist. I auditioned for on a big-budget movie helmed by a well-known producer at the time. The "sides," as audition material is known, was dialog of an argument between a girl and her boyfriend. After reading the script the producer asked me to, "Do it again, but this time ad lib. Take it a step further. Really tell me what for!"

So as directed, I am shouting abuse at the producer who is pretending to be the boyfriend in the role.

"You don't deserve me. I'm done with you!" I act off the script, pretending to forcefully push him away.

The director shouts at me, "More! Yeah baby! Give it to me! MORE!"

"You're a lying bastard!!!" I take off my high heel as stated in the script and lash out towards him, purposely missing him.

"No, really hit me with your stiletto," he directs me

"Give me more abuse. NOW SPANK ME!" he shouts, leaning over the couch to be spanked.

At this point, I realize he's getting awfully carried away and excited about this.

With a raving hard-on protruding through his pants, this well know executive starts dry humping my leg screaming, "Hit me! BEAT ME! Tell me I'm SO BAD!"

He pulls down his pants exposing his butt crack, "Now really spank me!"

Clearly, I thought as I peeled him off my leg, *this has gone way off the page.*

In many auditions I was told my top would just "have" to come off, even though there was no nudity in the role. On one such occasion, I had gone for a role dressed basically as a hooker, in a tight red leather mini and a croppy top with it all hanging out. Although a trashy broad role, it was actually a great role, with good dramatic lines. Yet the director keeps trying to persuade me to take off my top,

"I just need to be able to see your body type, it's very important to make a casting decision," the director says, pretending to be very professional.

"Even though there is no nudity required and I'm dressed almost naked as it is?" I questioned.

I finally stop arguing and let him see me nude, no biggie, just a little frustrating. He got a quick thrill and I probably got the role, I don't remember.

Still I was having quite a day of it. I hadn't been able to park out front, so I had parked on Sunset and Vine a few blocks away. Unbeknownst to me this was a prominent hooker pick up place. Already pretty stressed, I arrived at my car to find I had locked my keys in the car. ARRRGH!

Okay, so I've called AAA and I am waiting by my car for help. I'm still donning my red leather mini, patent heels and crop top, when a car driving by, screeches to a crawl and the driver rolls down her window, a black woman dressed to the nines and layered with makeup, screams, "Yoh bitch! This is my territory, get the fuck out of my area…." Her bright blue eye shadow glaring at me and dripping red lips screaming obscenities, as she hit the gas. I have absolutely no idea what she's talking about.

Several cars passing by, honk at me, then one guy burns tire to stop at the curb in front of me. He rolls down his window.

"How much?" he says.

"Huh?" I am still clueless

Another car pulls up behind the first and honks, he leans out his window, frantically waving for my attention, "I'll pay you more babe!"

I finally catch on and I'm horrified, "Oh no! Oh my God, I'm NOT a hooker!!! You see, I locked my keys in my car and I'm dressed like this because…"

Another car pulls up behind the second and honks, he leans out, "Hi gorgeous."

And this is all in the space of about five minutes, mind you!

I continue to tell my story, "No but really, I'm so sorry but…." the guys obviously think I'm being picky and just turning them down or something. Confused, finally they drive off.

I turn to see another "lady" strutting out of a nearby diner, making a beeline towards me, clearly pissed and I have an inkling of what she wants.

Just then a gentleman in a suit approaches from across the street.

"My boss sent me over. We've been watching from our office across the way there. Are you ok?"

"Oh, my God, thank you. Thank you so much. You see I locked my keys in the car…."

He extended his boss's invitation to wait in their offices across the road.

I was so relieved and continued my story as we walked to refuge. I was invited into what looked like some film production office. His boss greeted me, and I was ever so grateful as I related my story yet again. The big cheese led me into his beautiful office with large movie posters plastered on the walls and glass wrap-around windows with a great view of my car, as I continued to explain. He seemed genuinely concerned.

"Yes, we don't see girls like you on that corner," he remarked. He offered me a glass of water and I felt very relieved and safe. After a few minutes, when I was finally settled and calm, he shut his door and chit chatted with me a little.

Then he leans in, "So…… how much really?"

"What!! NO!! I……No!!! I'm really, really not a hooker."

At that, not a moment too soon, I saw the AAA guy arriving at my car, so I thanked him and scurried out of the office.

One day, my agent Don DeRocca sent me in for a role on a TV show called *Charles in Charge*. The casting director read me and was unusually quite nice and professional. Then he looked at me quizzically and asks,

"Why are you with Don?"

"What do you mean?"

"You know he has a bad reputation." Then he continues, somewhat reluctantly but he knows he would feel guilty if he didn't tell me, "Look, you seem really sweet, you have a great look, you can play young and you read really well. I'm going to give you some advice: There are some girls in this town that are very aggressive about getting ahead. When an actress comes from Don we have … let's say a certain expectation. You're a good actress, you could get a really good agent."

I didn't tell Don why I left him.

I arrived at CAA (Creative Artist Agency), one of the top five acting agencies in town. I had heard it was incredibly hard to get in, but I happened to walk in when Blue Cross wanted to renew my very lucrative contract for another year of national commercials and I needed an agent to negotiate it. So already generating good agency fees, I was in.

And it was true, on a CAA backed audition there was a noticeable decline in the unwanted advances. It was a large agency and I got lost a little, so it was less personable than Don. They very rarely sent me out, but when they did, I almost always bagged it. They clearly had clout and it meant it was a lot less time wasting.

Still it was harder to fit in any real acting when the lure of the sex biz was pouring in the money…

CHAPTER NINETEEN

The Phone Sex Shakedown

I DIDN'T HAVE a whole lot of interaction with Alan, my initial contact at the ad agency. I was more closely working with Stuart and his advertising execs. But on one trip to New York, I was in my hotel room, just about to turn in for the evening when Alan called unexpectedly and asked if we could meet in the lobby bar. He didn't say much on the phone, he seemed particularly rushed to get off the phone.

"I'll just see you in a few."

We met in my hotel lobby bar. He didn't seem his usual laid back relaxed self. He chose a dark corner booth and seemed particularly paranoid, constantly looking around. He was disheveled, sweating profusely and I wondered if he was on coke or something but that really wasn't like him. Alan was always a consummate chain smoker but tonight he was barely taking breaths between puffs. He made small talk about his family and told me he wanted to meet about a new project he was doing and wanted to make sure we could do some good business. I would, but…it seemed as though there was something else he wanted to tell me under this surface talk.

"Look, I'm going to be running some business at Penthouse and I want to make sure you can help me."

I was surprised to hear this. I wondered if he was doing this on the side or if he was moving away from the ad agency. I knew Alan had other projects of his own, but this sounded like a more involved position. I didn't ask but he volunteered.

"I'm not sticking around that place to one day have my brains blown out!!!" He blurted out in an emotional explosion, like it was the first time he'd been able to share it with anyone and he wasn't over being pissed. "It's fucking crazy and it's not what I signed up for!"

I was more than puzzled. He continued spewing his guts:

"I'm just sitting at my desk and four guys come in and put a gun to my head." He's now visibly shaking as he is clearly reliving the experience. "This is insane shit and it's not like it's the only time. Plus, there were other people and they're not around anymore. I have a daughter I need to support, and I don't want to turn up like them."

I felt a little like he's not had anyone to share any of this with and I'm really not the right one to be talking to, but he had no one else he could trust.

"Mobsters, fucking mobsters!" He grimaced in a panicked controlled whisper, the veins on his neck popping out as he leaned into me. "He should never have taken money from those kinds of people. Not the right kind of people to take money from."

I'm not saying anything just listening.

"Just watch your back." He warned, pointing at me,

"WHEN YOU RUN WITH THE WOLVES, YOU'RE GONNA GET BITTEN!"

He grabbed his jacket to leave, "Anyway, I've said too much. I gotta go. So, we're on? I'm gonna call you about that Penthouse deal."

For a moment I asked myself if I should be nervous. I'd never experienced anything of this kind of thing with the ad agency. Stuart was amazing, and his operation was particularly upscale and professional. The other investor guys I had met or been out with socially were great and I thought, so sweet. I chalked it up to someone that Alan had gotten himself in trouble with and that it shouldn't be any concern of mine.

Not long after I saw Alan at Penthouse and he was managing their videos. He had cut all ties with the ad agency as far as I knew, and we didn't say much more about it, just "be careful" was his advice, and "glad to be outta there" kind of comments.

Maybe six months after that I heard he passed away. They told me he had cancer. I wondered back to that strange conversation we had. I did give it a second thought, *but after all, Alan was a perpetual chain smoker*, I reasoned.

Still, it wouldn't be too long before I found myself in hot water with the ad agency.

—⟨⟨⟨⟩⟩⟩—

I had a beautiful compact streamlined production humming along at my office. One of my largest suppliers of the tame shots for the phone biz was Karen Amariman, a well-known headshot photographer for Hollywood actresses and a good friend of mine.

Every week I'd get literally hundreds of headshots of girls on the phone that we could browse through for potential nine-hundred squeaky clean ads. Rather than have a mountain of releases in my office, whenever we were about to use a photo, I would let Karen know by faxing her a copy of the ad and she would provide me her model release on file and of course an invoice for an extra photography fee.

Production ramped up exponentially, but as to be expected, things occasionally would fall through the gap. The "gap" suddenly came in the form of the ad agency in New York, who had decided to do some of these ads in house. No problem, they would just fax me a copy of the ad before it went to press, and I would pass them on to Kathy as usual and send the ad agency the model release. Unfortunately, they did not mind the gap, as they say in the London tube, and in this one, teeny, tiny case…they forgot. They forgot to fax me a copy of the ad asking for the release. They forgot to include the releases when they sent it to the magazine and the magazine forgot to do the usual paperwork check. A photo was published of two cute girls on the phone promoting a 900 number dating line in Penthouse magazine.

Unfortunately for us, the first ones to notice the ad were the photographer and the girls' sleazebag agent.

They filed a lawsuit.

Clearly, even though I was sued and rowing the same boat as everyone else, they really wanted to get to my clients, the deep pocket Ad Agency and Stuart.

Depositions were set, and I was the one under fire. Every question was designed to follow the source of the money and the profits from the ads. Luckily, I really didn't know the intricate dealings of the money chain. I just got paid for placing the ads or making the ads and other jobs but not any actual phone profits. I was not a partner in it. This was infuriating the hell out of the opposing counsel.

"Did Company X or Y ever make a profit out of this ad?"

Of course, I thought so, but I had never seen any of the accounts, so I really had no idea.

He was clearly not so interested in me, but each time he kept coming to a dead end, he'd sweat more profusely, and more color would come to his face. I was the most irritating defendant he'd ever come across. He drilled me from nine in the morning and it was approaching his last few minutes before the five o'clock cut off, and I was exhausted, when he completely lost his mind. He lurched over the desk, literally grabbing at my neck screaming, "LYING BITCH!!!"

He was immediately ordered off me. The judge was infuriated with this attorney and I am sure felt very sorry for me.

The next day was with the witnesses Karen the photographer, accompanied by the agent.

I cornered Karen in the ladies' bathroom.

"How could you do this to me? I'm going to lose everything! For a year you've been getting a ton of business from us. You've been getting paid off all these photos and now you're ruining this for both of us!"

Karen knew she'd done me wrong. She broke down shaking and crying and confessed.

Finally, on the stand she told her deeply regretful story, "The agent Reynold told me to say I didn't have a release, but I didn't know they were going to cause problems like this..." Karen is now starting to sob. "We were going to do a movie together. Reynold promised me that I could produce it and the girls were starring in the movie, but I didn't know this is where they were getting the money from. They showed me this great script and I just thought..."

It all came out, how the agent and attorney had convinced her she should pretend she didn't have the releases. She confessed to the judge that they had even had meetings at her office on how they were going to split the millions from the lawsuit. They'd even slated the money for this movie they were going to produce together!!! They'd even gone as far as writing the frigging movie script!!! What the what?!!!

It all came out like gouts of vomit in front of the judge.

It couldn't have been better. It was all proved that these were not some poor innocent actresses being exploited by some huge ad agency. Rather it was a scam that included a sleazy Hollywood agent, a stupid but conniving photographer and a couple of gold-digging, wannabe actresses.

Then the call came from Stuart.

"Look, Gail, we had to settle."

"What, NO! Not Now!!!"

I protested that we'd just proven our case. To settle was beyond ridiculous. That we should NOT be taken advantage of like this and that we had proved beyond any shadow of ANY DOUBT this thing was an entire con, from Jump Street to the Pub, and this case was going to get thrown out. It had been proven in front of the judge.

"It's done. It didn't matter. The legal fees to fight it would have ended up being the same. Penthouse was threatening to cut off our entire ad account. Look, it's done, we paid them two-hundred and fifty thousand. It's over."

There was no convincing him. He started to talk about how I was to blame, and I continued to point out if someone in their office had not dropped the ball this....

He cut me off, "You need to feel the pain as much as we did. So, you need to pay half, you need to pay one hundred and twenty-five thousand."

"But Stuart, I don't have that kind of money!" I yelled, beside myself with the injustice. "This wasn't even my fault. We got PLAYED!"

There was just breathing on the other end. I took a long deep breath of my own and spoke into the silence.

"Stuart... I'll work for you and waive my commission to pay it back. I can get you extra advertising for my layouts and we can work it off over time...."

"You're not hearing me," he said with a deadly menace in his voice, that wasn't like anything I had ever heard from him. "You need to *FEEL THE PAIN*. You need to pay one hundred and twenty-five thousand. TODAY. IN CASH."

"But I don't have that kind of money. I only make ten percent of what you spend and for every dollar I spend for you, you bring in ten times as much," and so I tried to point out they were making one hundred times my money and I simply didn't have it.

"Look," he went on with a cold unfeeling tone, that was completely foreign to the Stuart I knew so well, "This is not a negotiation. You need to feel the pain. The pain must be shared." He paused for effect to put more weight in his words, "If you don't pay the cash, we cannot be friends anymore. Do you understand? We will not be...FRIENDS."

I thought it meant he wouldn't want to do business with me and this would be absolutely devastating. Stuart was my friend. More than a friend. There was a hook of fear in my belly so strong it felt like I was being ripped apart. My lifeline, my income, everything could just disappear and more than anything our friendship?

But still it was a strange term for a grown man to use.

"Well...Stuart I absolutely want to be friends," I said weakly, having no clue what I was saying, "but I just don't have that in cash. You know that, and, I mean, who does?"

"Then we can't be *friends* anymore," he said coldly.

And the phone went dead.

"What, wait, NO!!!!!!!!!"

It was too late.

I was sure he was just angry, and he'd call me back when he'd cooled off and we'd work it out. I was certain he didn't really mean it. I mean it was Stuart! We'd talked on the phone, almost daily for years now. I was making them so much money, this didn't make sense.

At this point, I had given them direct contacts with the magazines and they could place ads without me, but why? This was a pittance in their world, so why was he doing this? Was it someone else making him say this? And why?

But, as I continued to put out calls he wouldn't return, and the days kept slipping by, reality set in. I was scared I'd lost this incredible business.

And what about Big Tony and all the times he said he'd take care of me? Obviously, he knew what was going on right? But the truth was Stuart was my contact and the buck stopped there. The message was clear:

If I was going to run with the wolves, I better step up and take the consequences like the rest of the pack!

I tried to keep a stiff upper lip. I was about six months pregnant with baby number two, my daughter Kyla on her way, so I knew I had to figure it out how to provide for my expanding family. I had other avenues like selling photos and even publishing my own magazines.

Still, I was saddened that on a personal level that Stuart didn't want to be *friends* anymore. I was completely oblivious to the actual meaning of his statement, otherwise I should well have been terrified.

CHAPTER TWENTY

Creating Barely Legal

WHEN THE AD agency stopped wiring money we were in the process of buying the ranch. We had bought airplanes, horses, cars…I feared we were going to lose everything. There was no time to sit around crying, I had a good photo business to run and I had to get back on my feet quickly and hit the pavement running.

I also had ad pages I'd already traded layouts for which were now useless to me, so I found a few other advertisers that wanted them and eventually created a small phone sex business of my own with a handful of vanity numbers.

By now I'm still only in my mid-twenties yet I own a good portion of all the soft erotica in every men's magazine. I seemed to have a knack at knowing what worked. I noticed that many readers had their go-to type: big boobs, small boobs, big girls, skinny girls, black girls, long leggy girls… you name it.

The male editors also had their "type."

I, on the other hand, as a woman, did not possess the male ego of what was beautiful. I, as a girl and an actress, could get myself into the heads (or pants) of all men, like playing a part really.

Many sexual fantasies seemed to be tied to a young man's first pleasurable experiences. Whether it be mature heaving breasts of their mother's friend or a little innocent girl at school with pert little newbie nipples who'd pulled down her panties behind the shed. Or as a little boy, from the perspective of the floor, seeing the neighbor in their high heels. His first rumbling feelings, that program his later desire to enjoy older women.

And, what was the most popular?

The not so pretty chicks!

You think I'm kidding?

A publisher friend launched a magazine based on amateur photo clubs in England. It wasn't doing very well, and I told him the girls were way too pretty. A professional photographer would go to the studio to shoot the pics. I told him not to make them look too good. He didn't believe me at first but after much convincing he took my expert advice and let me pick the ones with a few "realities." The magazine numbers went through the roof. Why? Because these girls looked real. A normal Joe would be totally intimidated talking to a Penthouse model. A girl with slightly inconsistent teeth, eyes looking a little off, and a less than perfect figure. Now THAT is a REAL girl that would talk to a regular bloke. Not saying all men are into unattractive chicks, but certainly a percentage of men like a few imperfections! And the magazine that could really cater to whatever the man really wanted, well… there lies the pot of gold.

You're probably thinking my photographers had it made. And yes, sometimes the girls were insanely beautiful. But I also worked the photographers really hard, and for every amazing girl they got to shoot, there were others. Let's just say they had to do it all; the pretty and the not so pretty. But remember, what's pretty is completely subjective.

We were always on the prowl for your typical gorgeous Tens. But it was not always the prettiest girls that sold. The Eights and Nines were actually the hardest to sell. Now give me a four-hundred pound, pretty, plump girl, or something else a little off the beaten path and it would sell like hot cakes.

You may be thinking that heavy girls would not be considered, but there are guys that love plump girls.

Gina and her husband were a prime example. Husband Dan, like most typical plump-girl-lovers was tall, ultra-skinny, a hundred pounds soaking wet. Mega-plumper Gina came to do a layout for us and Dan was just along to enjoy the ride.

I decided to put Gina in a kitchen baking scenario, cooking and eating donuts. Oh my God, you think I'm a horrible person. No actually, this is what plump-girl-lovers like. They call themselves "feeders!" It's all part of their fetish. I was learning here myself. My long-time friend and photographer Mark was shooting this, and we were both learning together.

Mark asks her to bend down, ever so sexily as if she is taking off her sexy strappy heels. But Gina tries and tries. She can't reach her shoes.

"Yeah, err...I usually wear slip-ons," she says. Mark and I are slightly embarrassed for asking.

"Ok just play, dance around and do some sexy poses for us," Mark suggests. And with that Gina squirms and writhes and Mark snaps away. Dan is in Mark's ear, "Oh, baby...Yeah. Oh my God my wife's so hot! Fuck baby yes, that's such a turn on...."

Mark shoots me a look like, *Is he looking at what we're looking at?*

Trying to look professional, I direct, "Ok darling..." I say encouragingly, "Now play with your pussy."

Her hand goes south but it can barely reach to where the rolls of flesh are covering what must been a navel under there. She literally can't touch her own vagina.

I have an idea and run and get a wooden spoon for her. Holding the tip of the handle and stretching her arm as far around the side of her rolling belly as she can, to her husband's delight, she is just able to touch her clit with the spoon, to pretend to masturbate.

Pics in the can, it sold like crazy!!!

You think we are horrible, but Gina and Dan had such a great time they sent over their friend Doris. Doris was about five hundred pounds. Thing was she hadn't gotten out of her little Fiat in quite a while. She came for an interview, but it was too great of a problem to extract her from her car, so we talked through her rolled down window.

Mark looked at me...... "Oh, no" he said, shaking his head.... "don't EVEN CONSIDER IT...!"

The thing that most of my photographers dreaded and I made them do anyway, was public flashing. This is where we would have a girl walking in a crowded street or sitting in a very public restaurant or busy amusement park and then flash passersby. This required a couple of extra team members. A cop lookout and a getaway driver. All the photographers were shit scared and almost all had experienced the cop lookout not paying attention and some very close calls.

Our model would be, say, sitting in a restaurant with a dress on like she was eating lunch and then when camera ready, she'd open her legs, showing she had no panties on and was completely exposing her pussy.

Most of the public around her had no idea but we'd usually catch a few guys on camera, breaking their necks as they whipped around in disbelief.

The dresses I had made with the butts cut out, were pretty entertaining. As our girl is walking down main street Hollywood Blvd. to most of the busy street, she's wearing a tight slinky dress, while those from behind got a whole other view.

John, one of my English photographers, was one of the most brave and trustworthy to get real pussy shots in the middle of say a McDonald's. He was in Spain trying to do the same thing but there were police everywhere. Finally, he said to a cop, "Can I take a photo of my girlfriend with you?" So, while the officer was posing to the camera and looking directly at the lens, the girl, arm linked with the cop, lifted her skirt to reveal absolutely everything. This was a great issue, about ten different police in full uniform, each totally unaware that they were posing next to a hot model, tits and pussy out to the world.

Then there was Janet the sex surrogate who came to shoot. I sat next to her and she started to shake and went into wild convulsions. "I'm very orgasmic," she said. No one was even touching her! She ran a masturbation club in San Fran which I thought would be a great connection and she had a Tuesday night "Jack-off Circle," where her clients, both male and female, would masturbate watching each other in a group. I sent a couple of photographers to shoot some of her female clients who wanted to do layouts. The day of shooting went really well and at the end, Janet tried to get the photographers to stay for the evening festivities. They were scared to death. They couldn't pack up their equipment fast enough and the Jack-off Circle was already forming, as they were trying to get out of there.

Still sometimes my staff would get their own back on me. Young new chickies, often would find their way to my office to take test Polaroids. I very rarely took these myself, rather I'd have my office girls do it. One day, only the guys were around so when I came back from lunch they told me there was a new potential model waiting for me. She seemed a little shy, so they said they'd waited for me to take the pics.

Ok, I thought, *No problem*, and I took her in the back to take Polaroids. She seemed a little nervous, so I started with a couple of shots clothed.

Finally, she took her top off, but she seemed reluctant to take off her tight mini.

"Ok, we'll need a full nude shot if you want the magazines to consider you," I said, trying to be as reassuring as possible. She shuffled nervously and started talking about some poem she wrote about butterflies and transformation. I was totally confused. Until finally the penny dropped, and I went out on a limb; "Do you have a penis under that skirt?" I asked, somewhat nervous to hear the answer.

"Yes, I do," she finally admitted, relieved that I hadn't made such a big deal about it. "But... err...the thing is it's really embarrassing because, well you're a really attractive woman and I can't help myself...and err... I have a hard on."

I tried to keep my composure and a straight face as she slipped off her mini to show me her very impressive erect penis. I took a couple of shots professionally, then quickly ushered her out. As the door shut, I turned around to see the guys in my office hysterical on the floor laughing their asses off!

I noticed there was a real hole in the marketplace and decided to come up with a couple of my own magazines. One was *Maxim*, but under a different name at the time.

The other idea *Barely Legal*. I pitched both to the president at Larry Flynt Publications. I actually had the whole first issues laid out. He was only mildly interested and put them nonchalantly on the backburner to simmer while he "thought about it". I shopped them around to all the other publishers too; same thing, all were too unimaginative or just too lazy to really make a move.

After much persuasion and months later, the Flynt's Exec cautiously took it off the back burner and agreed to finally take it to a boil and to publish.

"We could try one to start," Tim, the President said.

I chose *Barely Legal* to start!

It was a very loose handshake deal, but I was happy just to get it out, finally. I put the whole publication together out of my little office and presented it as a finished magazine. It was published by Larry Flynt Publications and out on the national newsstands.

Within weeks the "Little Magazine That Could" made publishing history. *Barely Legal* outsold every other magazine with the sole exception of a close second to Playboy. The publishers were going crazy, they couldn't believe the massive success. It was even mentioned on *Seinfeld!*

I tried to hire people to write the girly copy for *Barely Legal,* but it seemed these older male writers just didn't get it. I wanted real girl confessions, not what some dateless editor *thought* a girl would fantasize about.

I threw up. It was easier just to write it myself than try to explain it...so I did.

Part imagination, part what models had told me over the years or just an intuition about what men wanted to hear. This was supposed to be real girl fantasies. Hustler magazine's editor, the raunchy expert of the industry, got to oversee everything before it went to print. I was a little concerned he might find my copy too unbelievable, especially since I'd stretched the truth telling him they were real girl fantasies, when I had often really, just made it up. He wrote for Hustler, so you know his mind was in the depths of the gutter. As his personal sideline fantasy, he asked me if I would like to produce a *dog training video* with him. He was animated about his idea that didn't include dogs at all. Rather it featured scantily clad girls on all fours begging for a treat in their dog bowl.

This gave me a flashback of my formative school days and the Physics' teacher who had punished girls in his dog cage.

The sexpert editor is reading some of the girl confessions:

"Shit! This stuff is great! You can tell this stuff is real. You just can't make this stuff up!"

This sexpert mind, awash in pure filth, was most impressed with my young girl confessions.

I guess it was convincing enough!

As *Barely Legal* took off, I was suddenly the expert of the industry and I was inundated with offers from other publishers to create magazines for them — and I did. Even a bunch of spinoffs came out; *Just Legal, Just Eighteen, Barely 18…* and who was putting these together?... I was! *Barely Legal* was my main priority but all the lesser photography went to other magazines that I packaged for other publishers.

I had a whole mail order line to go with it and every girl we shot for *Barely Legal* was put in our soft-core video line. It didn't need to be hard core and we were not competing with porn, this was some little innocent newbie playing with herself for the "first time." And other spin-off merchandise that I thought guys would like, such as selling the models' panties. In reality, I'd buy two hundred pairs of the same little white cotton panties and the girl would wear one pair. The other one hundred and ninety-nine pairs were ones my office staff smeared a little dab of mayonnaise with a hint of tuna juice, on the crotch before shipping them to some guys house in a plain unmarked brown envelope. Yes, readers who ordered these weekly–sue me for false advertising–you jacked off over some mayonnaise!

Then there were other genres of magazines I started. So now I had a photo business, my own phone lines, a mail order biz and a complete magazine company.

Now I don't want to give the impression that the sexy biz was my only life, or that I was some uncaring, uninvolved parent. My daughter Kyla was born and now I had two little ones I was devoted to. As my girls were growing up, I was attending PTA meetings, with my hubby and volunteering on school trips. I was living a double life. Hiding the naked things going on around here from my daughters but also any "normal" people in our lives. Other mothers would always politely ask me what I did for a living, or more important what did my husband do? There was no way I could possibly have a friendship with these school moms and share details of my very successful sex biz! I would skirt the issue and talk about my work as a Hollywood actress.

After about a year of *Barely Legal* magazine and its dynamite success, Flynt wanted to bring more of the magazine into their office rather than out at my place. They tried to coax me with a full-time office next to Larry's.

The corner penthouse no less. I was having none of it. They wanted to throw bigger budgets at the magazine, shoot in tropical locations. No! It was not supposed to be high budget! They were missing the point. It was supposed to look like it was shot and published in some dirty-kid-down-the-street's basement. We used lots of Polaroids, and shag carpets with blankets on the wall. The fantasy was some little chickee high school dropout hitchhiking for a ride, getting picked up by some guy and happy to screw on his bare mattress in his basement for the ride. Cheap, cheesy and "real."

Still everyone in their corporate Ivory Towers all wanted to be part of the success and just had to all come and put their dicks in the pudding. I was assigned more and more people I didn't need. More of the magazine was done in the Flynt office and I became more the overseer of the content. Finally, I gave in, allowed them to do their thing and became more of a consultant, basically collecting a check every month while their in-house staff took the credit I could care less about.

It was probably into its second year and *Barely Legal* was on its way to becoming the mega-multi-million-dollar brand it would ultimately become, when I got a letter from Larry Flynt's office. It read something to the tune of:

"Since it seems you have become more of a consultant on the magazine and you don't have much involvement anymore we feel that you are no longer needed. Therefore, we will pay you for three more months and then please cease and desist."

I promptly wrote them a little note back something to the tune of:

"Thank you very much for this opportunity. However, I own ALL of the trademarks and copyrights on EVERYTHING. I own the magazine! So, YOU can now please cease and desist….I will continue to publish it without you."

I took my attorney with me to the meeting. In the hall, my counsel tried to downgrade my expectations, "Gail don't expect any kind of agreement today, these things take time, it's going to be a substantial legal battle and you probably won't see anything for years."

"We are walking out today with a very big fat check," I assured him.

We are shown into the President's office, where Tim sat behind his big desk which was surprisingly clear except for the one letter sitting directly in front of him. My letter. He got right down to the matter at hand.

"Errr…. I received your letter and I understand that you have the rights to publish this anywhere, but we really feel that Flynt has and can continue to be your best asset and…"

"Tim, I am willing to sell it to you."

Tim breathed a sigh of relief, now it was just down to how much.

"You know this magazine isn't the only amazing idea I have. Let's cut a deal today that makes everyone happy and I can do other magazines for you," I offered to try to resolve this amicably.

I was correct, and we walked out of his office check in hand. By the time I got home, Tim was calling me, "So Gail… what are these other ideas for magazines you have?"

That was the start of their next bestselling magazine; *Hometown Girls*. This time with an actual contract! The deal I wanted, and a nice buyout clause.

Every publisher in town wanted "The Secret Weapon" to consult for them or create a new magazine! So here I was, well into several successful magazines and a booming photo business that fed them all.

CHAPTER TWENTY-ONE

My Exciting Sex Life

I RAN AROUND town, back and forth to New York, jet setting, meeting publishers and still one foot in Hollywood, so I flirted to get my way a lot, but in the end, I was married, and nothing ever seriously drew me astray. Even though honestly coming home to lights out at ten o'clock. and not an ounce of sizzle, was a bit depressing at times. And even if I had wanted him to go out "partying" with me, there is no way, that was totally not his personality. Still, I kept my passions in my work, and it was not like I met anyone that was interesting enough to me anyway. That was until I met Tom….

Tom owned a huge phone sex business and since my New Yorker guys were no longer needing my services, I had taken over running all his ad campaigns. He was from South America where he was a mega business mogul, living in some kind of compound and followed around by bodyguards all day, so we always dealt over the phone and in over a year, we'd never met. I happened to be in New York and he was too, so he suggested dinner.

He came to the lobby of my hotel and as I descended the grand winding staircase, I saw him standing there. Oh My God… was that Tom?!!! Time stood still, and it was like the scene from the movie *Blow*. Our eyes met and locked and shivers ran down my spine in a flurry of unexpected excitement. There was something so magical, like that moment they talk about where your souls recognize each other. Okay, something like that. Either that or it was just 'cos I found him so strikingly handsome. I think we stood there staring at each other for like ten minutes both in shock, speechless and sparks flying. Talk about instant chemistry!

All through dinner we looked starry eyed at each other all night. He kissed me good night, which I felt guilty about, but fireworks went off for both of us. The kind of deep incredible butterfly tingles, I had forgotten once existed. If only we were both not married.

We promised not to see each again other but a week later he couldn't help but fly out to LA and find some business excuse to have dinner with me. This continued on, back and forth, Los Angeles to New York, for weeks, just flirting and kissing on the premise of new business that kept coming up. We were both floating on air but knowing that it could never actually go anywhere. When, one day he asks me to meet him for dinner at the Bel Air hotel, in LA. "I have something really important to tell you," he said secretively.

Over dinner he explains that he caught his wife screwing the tennis instructor and it was official, he had already filed for a divorce. "Please leave your husband and let us be together, we could have an amazing life." Up until this point I had been flirting with disaster and getting very near to crossing the line, but suddenly this made things very real. Although I knew I wasn't in love with my husband, I also knew that I couldn't do this to him.

In that moment I realized that I had a responsibility. To my husband, to my kids, to my mom, my family….no guy was worth that.

I cried, but I just knew that I had to say goodbye to Tom. I told him I'd give his ad account to someone else, because I knew I couldn't continue to deal with him and be strong enough to not go back on my word.

I went back to the miserable husband who knew nothing about this. Watching Scott, snorting and venting around the office, wondering, *Did I really make the right decision?*

They say that fifty percent of women are divorced, twenty five percent of women are getting divorced and ten percent of women are thinking about it. That only leaves about fifteen percent that are happy. I wondered how many other women were in the same place that my head was at, right about now!

"Hey. What happened to that Tom guy? He hasn't been doing any ads with us recently, you need to call him," Scott demanded a few weeks later. But I never did.

Oh, how I wished I could have the same spark with my husband. I wished I could somehow create that kind of feeling with the person I was already committed to.

But oh well, plenty of sparks in my business to keep me occupied.

I was very interactive with the photo shoots; choosing the models, arranging the shoots and art directing them. At this point, we had a ranch. Our house was on one side of the property and across the stream, on the other side, we had an office and a full-blown film studio. Sometimes, I arranged shoots on location but there was always plenty of shooting going on at the ranch.

With plenty going on, I always could use an extra hand and my Cousin Ric from England decided to come over with his friend Clint for a couple of months sightseeing. And boy did they see some sights! The first morning up, still jet lagged, I handed them both a reflector, "If you could please help out this morning, we have a girl-girl shoot, so if you can each hold a pussy reflector, and make sure you bounce the light, just right there into their pussy lips, that would be great...."

Two twenty-one-year-old lads from England were standing there shelled shocked, which I must admit quite tickled me. Later that evening I dragged them nightclubbing around Hollywood, where I instructed them that they had to pick up girls with me.

"Boy your cuz is crazy awesome!" Clint declared to Ric. Yeah, welcome to Gail's world, and I was excited to have a couple of young handsome Brits I could tout as bait for a few months.

Never would my husband step foot in a club, he was way too conservative for that. He'd stay home but he didn't seem to mind what I was up to. Yeah, I was a bit of a tease but at the end of the day, I didn't do anything.

Even though I was always busy, I was on set for many of the shoots. The photographers loved this because I knew exactly what I wanted and all they had to do was press the shutter.

When I was there, I would take over much of the posing. I knew what I needed for the editor in mind. The photographers were becoming heavily reliant on me, to the point where it was taking up far too much of my time. So, to ease myself out of this position, I made a "Posing Book," where I printed out pictures of different poses we had done in the past. It was a guide for the photographer to get a core twenty or so, standard poses. The photographers were dependent on me and when I wasn't around they were dependent on the posing book!

The photographers would get really upset if someone took the "Posing Book" and would be panicked, like "Who has the book. I NEED it?" I think eventually I made three.

The girls loved me to be behind the camera because it was far easier to just mimic me, rather than to try to figure out the photographer's directions, and way more fun. I'd say, "Darling do this pose" and "do this with your boobs," caressing my boobs through my clothes. "Undo your bra a little bit…that's gorgeous darling…" I would be teasing them for sure. Can't say it didn't have an effect on the photographers, and yes, I got really into it, too, sometimes.

My photographer Mark complained to me, "These girls all want you. How come they don't come on to me? You get all the action." But I never took the girls up on it.

A lot of the girls liked other girls anyway. When I spent the whole day with them, posing them, and oiling them and being sexual, they were totally turned on.

A few told my husband that they wanted to be with me and offered to have a threesome with us.

"Oh, please let me do your wife, she's so hot."

"Do you wanna try it?" I asked my husband.

"It's not a good idea. Emotions get involved, it gets complicated," he argued.

I could imagine that would probably be true with someone you really cared about but honestly with him I couldn't imagine being fazed at all.

But one particular girl named Jamie was too hot for him to resist. She was absolutely, drop-dead gorgeous. She had long brunette hair, an amazing body; tight but soft, with incredible natural breasts and we were shooting her for Penthouse.

I worked with her all day and by the end there was a certain connection between us.

We went back to the house and a natural progression occurred. My husband and I ended up in our bedroom, with one of the most beautiful women on earth. We all started kissing, teasing and gently fondling. She was soft, sweet and feminine, a touch I was not used to. An unfamiliarity that was uniquely exciting. Jamie's long silky hair brushed my thighs as she descended, her long delicate painted nails gently running down my leg.

As my husband is kissing my breasts, she started to go down on me and I said, "Oh my God, I'm not going to last very long!"

I told myself to think about something I had to do in the office, so I could maintain in this zone of Heaven for at least a while longer. Anything! I tried my best to hold off, but I couldn't control it.

My husband and I went down on her together, slowly descending her body we both kissed her firm abdomen before going lower. The most perfect, pristine body. Her skin still glistened with baby oil from the photo shoot earlier.

Scott, who had been reluctant now had a ragging hard on and was completely and totally involved. We grabbed his cock together, side by side…

We all played 'til we were completely exhausted. She went off to the guest bedroom and my husband and I were quite content.

—◦◦◦—

A week or so later I'm in my office filing model releases. My husband enters leaning on my desk, "Jamie was so sick. I sent her some flowers from both of us."

"Who's Jamie?" I asked, getting another stack of the releases off the top of the cabinet.

"The girl we made love to!" he snorted in disgust.

"We didn't make love to her. We had sex with her."

Oh my God what was wrong with him?

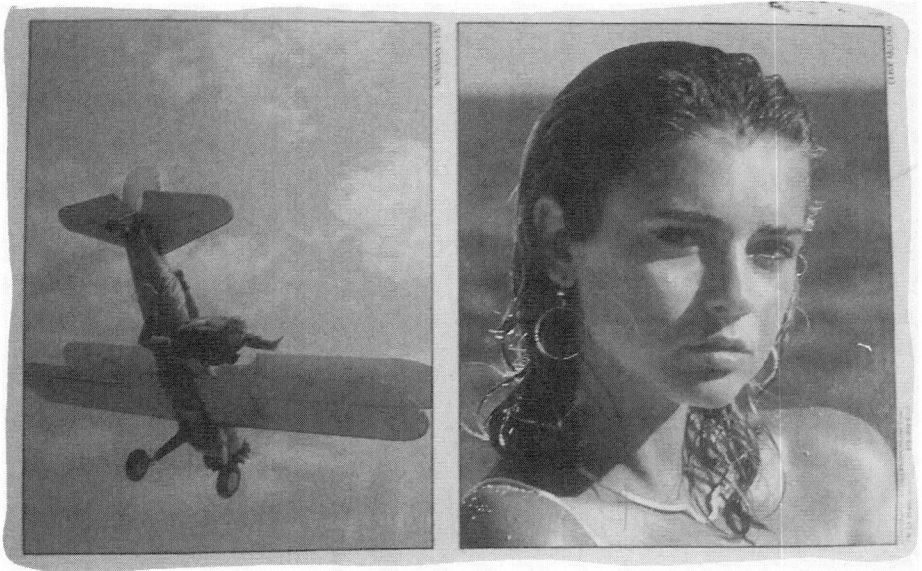

Modelling & travelling – a hard life

Skydiving pass to Hollywood

Baywatch beach fun

Playboy line up

Acting classes in good use!

Photo for the Tribune by Stephanie Diani

Gail Harris works with her operations manager Ken in editing digitized film from a photo shoot.

PORN:
Psst mister, want to buy a picture?

CONTINUED FROM PAGE 1

industry.

Today, the privately held company owns 1.5 million mostly soft-core images, yet it remains one of the best-kept secrets in the constantly expanding world of adult entertainment. The www.falconfoto.com Web site offers consumers and other Web masters dozens of niche photo galleries from which to choose, plus streaming videos, CD-ROMs and stories.

Changing face of industry

By acknowledging the niche market for sexual fetishes, and playing it for fun and profit instead of shock and shame, Falcon Foto also effectively changed the face of the adult magazine industry over the last decade. Harris' vision inspired dozens of Web masters to follow suit, using Falcon Foto content to help launch their online businesses.

Harris said she wouldn't be averse to taking what she has learned about the Internet up the street to a major studio. If there's one thing about which Hollywood doesn't have the faintest clue, it's how to make money on the Web.

"What's worked for the adult industry is that we're a close-knit community," Harris said. "Even though we're competitors, we share traffic with each other and steer business to other sites. Hollywood is much more proprietary in that the studios want to keep everything to themselves and they don't want to have anything to do with another studio's products."

Or, as one panelist put it at a recent iHollywood seminar in Santa Monica, where the question was asked, "Does the adult industry know something about the Internet that Hollywood doesn't?"

"They [studios] are afraid of giving away the crown jewels," said Taylor Marsh, editor of Danni's Hard Drive and a columnist for LA Weekly. "They think that once they give away a song or movie clip, it's gone. The opposite is true in our business.

"Gail has one of the biggest libraries on the entire planet, and I have a part of it, other people have a part of it. It's all about licensing, repurposing and repackaging."

"Gail's smart," said Mark Hardie, who analyzed the adult industry for Forrester Research Inc., before entering the online music industry. (He suggested that Falcon Foto may be worth at least $50 million on the open market.) "She brought some products to the major magazines when they weren't even thinking about them, and those products took off."

"A few years ago, we opened up the whole niche market with a magazine we put together in-house, called Barely Legal," said Harris, the divorced mother of two daughters. "A lot of publishers were concerned about the title, but Larry Flynt was willing to take a shot at it. Overnight, it became his second-best-selling magazine, behind only Hustler.

"After that, everyone wanted their own niche magazines. And, because we worked with so many different publishers, we were able to get a world view on the demand for various fetishes."

First-rights ownership

Casual observers might assume that skin magazines retain the rights to the photographs they use, and, as such, have stacks of pictures stashed away for creative dry spells. In fact, with the exception of Playboy and a few other publications, most skin magazines only own first rights to the handful of images they pick from each portfolio.

Freelance photographers, then, can peddle the dozens that are left unsold to other magazines and Web sites. Or, they can make deals with archivists, like Falcon Foto.

Stable of veteran photogs

Harris also has her own stable of veteran shooters, who continually replenish the company's inventory. She also buys pictures from photographers who have done pictorials for such publications as Hustler and Penthouse, and from photographers who work in Europe, where things are far more hardcore.

Today, adult stars openly pitch their Web sites on popular drive-time radio shows, and one sure way for a young musician to show he has hit the big time is to cavort in a music video with a half-dozen strippers (all of whom probably take home as much money as he does). Meanwhile, supermodels have kept black-leather micro-minis, see-through blouses and visible-thongs in vogue long enough for porn-chic to qualify as a "classic" look.

"This isn't the '40s and guys aren't coming home from the war, looking for a cutie to pin up in their gas stations," Hardie added. "Teenagers and preteens, today, are looking at stuff that would spin the heads of their grandparents, and they don't go out and buy Playboy. Britney Spears rips her clothes off on prime time, so why should they pay $4 to see someone else in fishnets?

"The stuff they want to see now are the seemingly unproduced products . . . the amateur and voyeur stuff . . . the real girl next door. With the Internet, there's no reason anymore to go to the local porn shop to buy a magazine . . . and the porn shops, in turn, are forced to diversify by selling sex toys and cheesy lingerie."

Meanwhile, established content providers, like Harris, prosper because they have the one thing everyone — magazines or Web sites — wants: photos and videos of naked women (and more than a few men).

Still, nothing strikes fear into the heart of the adult industry more than the possibility that the new Republican administration might use federal Act 18 USC 2257 to harass producers and publishers. Simply put, the law requires a company to keep two pieces of ID and age-verification documents on hand for every model used in a photo shoot or movie.

Not surprisingly, Falcon Foto maintains extensive computerized records and documentation for its clients. Harris said it's available at a moment's notice. This is another plus for Falcon in an uncertain business climate.

"We've always been very cautious," said Leg Show editor Dian Hanson, who has worked with Falcon Foto in the past and said she appreciated Harris' attention to detail.

Hanson's magazine is noted for highly stylized pictorials in which the artistic display of stockings, pantyhose and high-heel shoes is more important to readers than any gynecological posing.

"There was a law passed in 1996 — the Child Pornography Protection Act — and, up until then, we went milder, to eliminate any hint of hard core. Back when Traci Lords got herself a fake ID, and got into the business, people were more trusting."

Gail Harris, who lives outside Los Angeles in the foothills of the San Gabriel Mountains, hopes to strike it rich with her collection of X-rated photos. She plans to put her entire collection of 1.3 million photos on the Web.

can offer valuable marketing lessons to the likes of travel agencies and auctioneers.

"I don't think the big, legitimate marketers have much to learn in that regard," said Dr. Davidson, author of the 1996 book *Selling Sin* — *The Marketing of Socially Unacceptable Products.*

But Dr. Davidson and others concede that porn helped develop methods for luring and trapping "looks-loo" traffic. Early on, it honed techniques in snaring "referrals" — customers sent to porn pages by clicking on banner advertisements elsewhere on the Net, including on street-sized sites that are paid a finder's fee.

Porn Webmasters perfected tricks for temporarily disabling "back" buttons, which causes a page in constantly reload. They also figured out how to launch a seemingly endless series of windows when a casual visitor tries to exit a site.

Less devious was porn's groundbreaking use of third-party contractors — known as "wallets"

— that bill Web surfers' credit cards with a promise of confidentiality.

Net authorities say porn was similarly quick to exploit Web cameras (for live peep shows) as well as "rookies" and "spiders."

A rookie is an embedded browser code that monitors an individual's Web-surfing habits. The copyright-protecting spiders are electronic signatures that determine whether an image has been stolen.

In addition, porn is considered a force behind the growing demand for digital subscriber lines, hyper-fast links that can deliver movies to computer screens with minimal choppiness.

There is talk that, before long, Web video will bury brick-and-mortar retailers in porn tapes.

"They tend to lead the way in new technologies," Robert Sterling, an analyst for Jupiter Communications, said of the porn crowd. "They're a mature industry online."

Relative terms

Mature is a mild term for the material being uploaded at Wicked Pictures, a $6-million-a-year company that makes hard-core features. It is based in San Fernando Valley, America's porn-production capital.

"In the next year, the revenue from the Internet will pass just about everything we're doing," said Aaron Karacas, Wicked's Web guru.

"The whole Internet is still sex, sex, sex. When a guy buys a computer, the first thing he types in is 'sex.'"

The 31-year-old Mr. Karacas, who hinted at a previous life as a hacker, is expanding and refining Wicked's site.

On this day, he was hunched over a Compaq desktop in a crackerbox industrial building, the lights down low. His online laboratory is tucked behind Wicked's warehouse, where video titles such as *Pandora* and *Los Angeles* were stocked nearly to the

ceiling.

"The whole thing is creating marketing tools and traffic," said Mr. Karacas, a clean-cut type who would look at home in an online division of Disney, where he actually worked for a while. "It's all about traffic."

On his screen, he demonstrated how a hapless surfer would find it almost impossible to escape the Wicked site. Every click on "exit" spawned another lewd window.

"We finally got you to Wicked, and you want to leave?" Mr. Karacas said mock-cheerily. "Without paying!"

Wicked charges its 10,000 Web subscribers $24.95 a month. It hopes that its upgraded site — Mr. Karacas is fashioning a free casino page as a traffic bait — will soon attract 100,000 customers.

"We can make an unbelievable jump," said Wicked president Steve Orenstein, a 37-year-old redhead who was wearing a Wicked Pictures T-shirt (his BMW's license plate reads WICKED1 [?]). "We're a year away from people being able to watch our movies on the Internet."

He was perched at a modular Formica desk, in a tape-clutter room across a parking lot from Mr. Karacas' geek digs.

Mr. Orenstein's phone rang incessantly. There were deals to be struck and lawsuits to juggle, including an e-piracy complaint against someone who allegedly violated Wicked's copyright.

On a shelf over Mr. Orenstein's shoulder were several gold statues of a winged woman — Adult Video News awards, porn's Oscar.

"We feel proud of what we're doing," he said.

But he acknowledged that Wicked is not ready for Wall Street — or, rather, Wall Street is not ready for Wicked.

Initial public offerings remain rare in porn. Underwriters are squeamish.

"I don't think people will bite on an adult IPO," Mr. Orenstein said.

In the case of Ms. Harris, however, Mr. Hardie disagreed.

"She's got a more legitimate business than three-quarters of the content businesses on the [Web]," said.

A modeling gig for Merit cigarettes brought the striking blond Ms. Harris to the United States in 1985. She started ...

Please see ...

B-movie actress Gail Harris used the Web to help create a $50 million business empire.

X-rated photo czarina shows how to market a body of work

By Gary Dretzka
Tribune staff reporter

SUN VALLEY, Calif. — Falcon Foto, practically unknown outside the adult-entertainment industry, may seem an unlikely business model for moving media to the technological cutting edge.

But in the 10 years the Los Angeles-based firm has existed, Falcon Foto has built what is reputed to be the world's largest library of pornographic photographs and videos. And it has helped fuel the $10-billion-plus U.S. sex industry's move into cyberspace and beyond, a transition still daunting to a wide array of more conventional companies. No Fortune 500 CEO is likely to have the resume of Falcon's founder, president and chief executive, former B-movie Scream Queen Gail Harris.

"I was working in made-for-cable and 'B' movies before I developed this sideline business," said Harris, 36, who broke into the skin trade as England's "Marlboro Girl" and posing for a tabloid's "Page 3" feature. "One day, I asked my boyfriend, who was a photographer, if I could take the images he'd thrown

in the trash, and try to find a use for them. I went down to a newsstand, collected a bunch of men's magazines, and shipped off the pictures to the addresses I found.

"I sold everything."

While also acting in such straight-to-video epics as "Cellblock Sisters: Banished Behind Bars," "Sorority House Massacre II" and "Virtual Desire," Harris used her modeling connections to initiate an exchange of photo collections with agents on both sides of the Atlantic Ocean. Instead of paying the photographers she represented a small commission on occasional sales to magazines, she would agree to a flat fee up front for all rights to the images.

It didn't take long before Falcon Foto owned the copyrights to tens of thousands of photographs, which she then syndicated to magazine publishers around the world. When the Internet began to explode in the mid-'90s, Harris already had viable business and distribution models in place, and she prospered, along with the rest of the adult-entertainment

PLEASE SEE **PORN**, PAGE 7

Adult is big biz

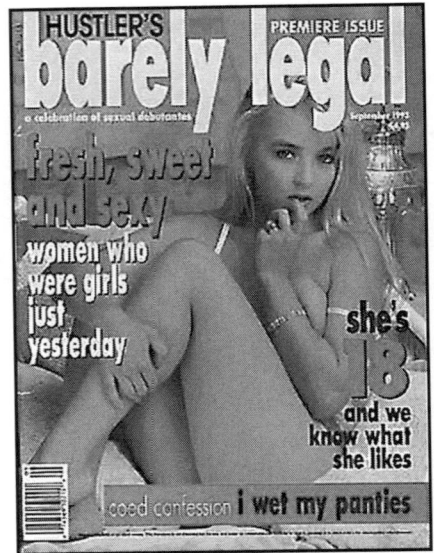

Premiere Issue
rocks the stands

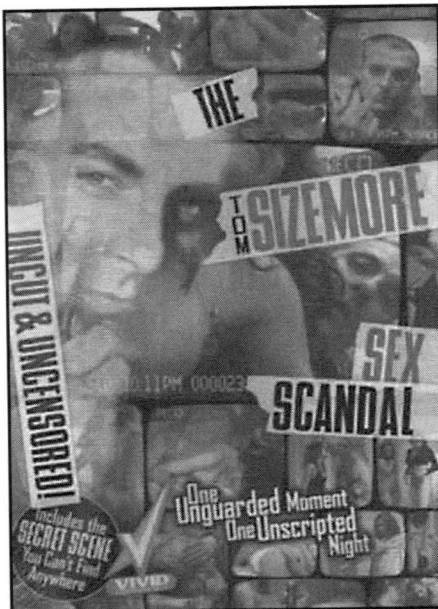

Tom Sizemore
Sex Tapes
"leaked by Heidi"

"Gail's smart," said Mark Hardie, who analyzed the adult industry for Forrester Research Inc., before entering the online music industry. (He suggested that Falcon Foto may be worth at least $50 million on the open market.)

In the case of Ms. Harris, however, Mr. Hardie disagrees. "She's got a more legitimate business than three-quarters of the content businesses on the Net," he said.

Harris' vision inspired dozens of Web masters to follow suit, using Falcon Foto content to help launch their online businesses.

Falcon Foto has built what is reputed to be the world's largest library of pornographic photographs and videos. And it has helped fuel the $10-billion-plus U.S. sex industry's move into cyberspace and beyond, a transition still daunting to a wide array of more conventional companies. No Fortune 500 CEO is likely to have the resume of Falcon's founder, president and chief executive, former B-movie Scream Queen Gail Harris.

My New Life as a motivational speaker

The Largest Erotic Library in the World,
then and now

CHAPTER TWENTY-TWO

Stupid! Stupid! Stupid! List

IT WAS AROUND the year ninety-three or ninety-four, when one hot California day, an ultra-shiny red sports car pulled into the rustic dirt drive at my ranch office. In a cloud of dust, out stepped Calvin in full suit and newly shined black shoes. I knew Calvin as the owner of a very successful phone sex biz. He was a shrewd businessman and had made a fortune in the audiotext business. I'd get regular visits from his staff to license my images for his phone ads; this time he was here himself for something very different.

"I wanna buy photos for this brand new thing they're calling the WORLD WIDE WEB."

I had heard of some new "Bulletin Board" thing on the computer. Someone else had contacted me recently about a fan site with my cheesy B movie acting pics. I was a little miffed at the fact that guys seemed to be sharing images of me and I wasn't involved in collecting any money out of it and my wheels had already been turning on how this could somehow turn a profit.

Calvin explained excitedly about what this new "Internet" thing was and how there could be thousands of people looking at these places called "domains" and how he wanted to make some of these domains with sexy photos. He was convinced this thing was going to be massive.

He wanted me to license him some new rights no one had ever heard of; THE RIGHTS TO USE IMAGES ON THE INTERNET

I offered to license him images at the same rate as the phone pics; for a hundred a photo.

"I'll take five hundred."

It took a millisecond to do the math and figure out that I was getting fifty thousand dollars!!!

So convinced was he about this new Internet thing, he chose five hundred pics and left me with a whopping big check!!!

I was not technically savvy at all. Couldn't even type a letter; I had a secretary I relied heavily on for that. But I was intrigued to know why this man would invest so much. He had made millions before and it wasn't on bad decisions. I had my secretary look up these things called "domains," and soon discovered, you could get one of these for about fifty dollars. I started to dream about what this could mean if computers could be connected all over the world. Not only for sharing and looking at sexy pictures but everything, the incredible things that could be possible. And if this was true, and ultimately, we'd all be talking over computers, like Calvin said, what other kinds of services might be on there?

I made a list of potential names for "website" domains that might be useful in the future if this really happened. I gave the list to my secretary to try to figure out how we would go about registering these things. There were a hundred names on my list. Some sexual yes, but also general things that might be useful. All were available:

Boobs.com, Girls.com but also *Cars.com, Flights.com, Movies.com, Tickets.com, Books.com, NewYork.com*…all were available!!! At that point you could've registered *CocaCola.com* (I thought probably would not be wise, but you could!). *Sex.com* had just been taken; everything else was up for grabs and low hanging fruit, ripe for the picking.

I went to run it by my husband and showed him my one hundred wish list.

"I want to invest in this. I want to buy these names. They are fifty dollars each. The entire investment is five thousand."

My husband went ballistic!

"You are stupid, stupid, stupid!!!" he snorted in the middle of my office in front of all my employees.

This wasn't the first time I'd been called this. He was an arrogant know-it-all that made everyone wonder why I married him or continued to stay with him. This was a huge argument. I wanted to invest five thousand dollars, a pittance really, of MY money. Money I brought in, and money I had earned, NOT HIM!

Of all the times I'd been right, all the times I had that sixth sense, but no, I was still the one that was "Stupid!" He knew about computers, I knew nothing! I didn't even know how to turn one on (yeah true actually).

He went on...

"This is a ridiculous idea, something like that could never work, it would take massive infrastructure. It would just crash. I know! MS-DOS rules everything and this is a piece of shit! No! Forget it! It will never work... oh... AND.... it's STUPID!"

It was a huge sore point between us for several weeks as I tried to convince him, but he wouldn't budge. I finally backed down. After all he was right, I didn't know about computers like he did and perhaps I was "stupid" when it came to that.

Several years later after we got divorced and the dot com boom was in full swing, my assistant Ken found my old list and hung it on the wall, titled "The Thirty-Five Million Dollar Stupid! Stupid! Stupid! List." As each domain sold my staff would cross it off the list and write the amount next to it ...

Cars.com $2.2 million.

Flights.com $1.8 million.

Movies.com $3 million...

This was my "Sick to my Stomach List."

So, as you know, gentle readers, the Internet hit, and hit big! Now I might have missed those domains but what I did have was a mountain of material. Remember I had bought out all the photographer's rights and I owned that Largest Erotic Library in the World! When I sold photos to companies like Penthouse they only bought one-time print publication rights, they never really owned the photos. The originals were with me. So, at this point if Penthouse wanted to run their photos on their website it was me they had to crawl back to, to buy the rights.

Overnight my library had multiplied in value... exponentially!!!

Lucky for me, during our quite amicable divorce my husband had been given the choice of what he wanted. He wanted all rights to my magazines, the business that was bringing in all the cash. The library full of old photos, that had already been licensed and printed, was "a bunch of old crap," in his opinion. In the end, he got the magazines he wanted, and I got the old crap photos.

Once again, there is gold in that thar trash!

But how exactly did I get to that happy point of divorce and freedom?

CHAPTER TWENTY-THREE

50 Ways to Leave Your Lover

"YOUR PROBLEM IS you are too optimistic!" Scott yelled at me.

"What do you mean?" I replied confused.

"You set yourself a goal and then you reach that goal, and then you set yourself another goal. Then you reach THAT goal and you set another one and it keeps going!!! At what point does it stop and are you just satisfied with where you're at?"

In those few sentences, I realized how different we were. All these years, I was the one running around, ambitious to grow the business with my desire to expand. I wanted to provide for my family, so my daughters wouldn't have to work so hard. He wanted us to fire all the staff and run a small mom n pop biz.

My friends always wondered why I stayed with him. Even though his fuse was short, he was so in love with me I rarely bore the brunt of his cruelty. He told me daily, "My wife is the most beautiful woman in the world." And this would melt my heart and keep me in the game. But, now, his frustration was turning on me.

After his up bipolar rages I'd broach the subject, "Look, there's not a lot of love here, why don't we think about getting a divorce?" Then he would swing to the other pole and burst into tears and beg, "Oh my God, I'm so madly in love with you. Please don't leave me."

The last few years had been an emotional roller coaster, but the feeling of guilt held me back from moving on. Wishing and hoping I could leave him without hurting his feelings. Finally, the perfect opportunity came along.

We had a stream of different models coming and going but occasionally we'd fly one in from out of town for a week or two. This one particular twenty-one-year-old, beautiful, blonde haired, blue-eyed girl I'd brought in from the mid-west. Her name was Jennifer. She was gorgeous, natural and with a body to die for. She was very sweet, albeit lacking in the brain department somewhat.

We got along really well, and it was clear that she idolized me. I took her under my wing and helped her around town, getting her some real modelling connections on her non-working days and introducing her to Hollywood. She was staying in our guest room, so she was hanging out the whole time with me and evenings with the family and my hubby.

One night we all went out to dinner; my husband, Jennifer, a couple of other people. Jennifer was not feeling too well with some kind of stomach pain and my husband, very concerned, thought she should go to the emergency room and offered to take her to the hospital. They left, and I stayed at dinner with the other friends for a few hours.

I came home around midnight and as I came in, my husband was just exiting the guest bedroom, looking a bit sheepish, wearing only his underwear.

"Are you guys back from the hospital?" I asked, not thinking the obvious.

"Once we got in the car, Jennifer was actually okay, so we never ended up going. She's feeling a lot better now."

"Oh good," I said.

It was very out of character for him, so it wasn't until we were upstairs getting ready for bed that it finally dawned on me to ask, "So, what were you doing coming out of Jennifer's bedroom in your underwear?" I inquired, not in a judgmental way, more just out of curiosity, "Were you guys...getting it on?"

"Err...no," he stammered.

Knowing there was something more, I continued, "Was something about to happen when I came in? Were you about to get it on and I interrupted you?"

"Well, err, yeah, kind of," he said cautiously, wondering how I would react.

Partly I was shocked; he'd never given me a moment's doubt about how faithful he was to me and how much he loved me. But other than that, I didn't seem to have a reason why I would actually care.

"Honestly, I don't really mind. If you want to have sex with her go ahead. Can't blame you, she's beautiful, I'm tired out, I'm going to bed!"

He climbed into bed next to me, "Really? You wouldn't care?" he said excitedly.

I reiterated again, that no, I really wouldn't care, I just wanted to go to sleep and it was fine.

He didn't need much more, he had the permission and quickly left to go downstairs to continue what they'd started. I rolled over and went to sleep.

I had presumed that would be a one-night thing. But I guess he took it as a continuing permission, every night, so the next few nights the same thing happened!

Now during the day, I'm working with Jennifer posing her for the shoot etc. when she very coyly says, "Listen, your husband told me that you know about me and him and that you're okay with it?"

"Yes, I know, and yes, I'm okay with it," I said in a friendly matter of fact way. She looked quizzically.

I explained, "Look, we're more like friends now. There's not a lot between us anymore and I really don't have a problem with it at all."

She looked slightly confused but she had been given permission by the Lady of the House.

That night my husband came into bed with me and again asked, "Do you mind?"

I said, "I don't mind." And off he went downstairs for his midnight snack. We could probably have gone a year without sex with me unless I instigated it, now he is doing it night after night.

After about the fourth or fifth night, I was in bed fast asleep when I am woken up, ever so gently by a soft naked body crawling into bed with me. Sweet gentle feminine hands are caressing my breasts and I can feel long fine hair running along the curve of my back. I realize it's Jennifer, but I am quite liking it. This soft feminine energy, slowly starts to pull down my sheets, and she's sweetly licking my neck, waking me, as she holds the curves of my breast in her hand. Scott's at the other side, stroking my leg and kissing my thighs. The two of them have gotten into bed with me and they are giggling naughtily.

"We thought it only fair that you should get a little action as well," she says seductively.

My husband is with her caressing her as she takes the lead on me. I'm now a little more awake and quite aroused. She is on one side and he is on the other side. She's playing with me, teasing me, and laughing, playfully as she kisses me lower and lower, now breathing on my bare tummy just below my navel.

As her tongue goes lower and lower, finally stopping and doing circles. I am now nicely awake and moaning with deep pleasure. Scott pulls down his pants and exposes his stiff cock as he watches us.

We played for a good while, him clearly knowing her quite intimately by now, "Jen likes it here, like this...."

Finally. we were all nicely satisfied, and they left me to go back to sleep as they disappeared together back downstairs.

With any guy I would have had feelings for, I know I would have been devastated and hurt by his intimacy with her, but with him, I honestly didn't care and at that point I knew I had no deep emotional feelings for him at all.

That was our one group night of pleasure. Shortly after that it was time for Jennifer to go home.

My husband decides he might as well fly her home in our plane rather than her going commercial, "Plus I thought I could stop via some places see if I can find some local amateurs and do some shoots. And I was really thinking I could use Jen as my assistant on the road. You know I can't pick up girls, but Jen can. She can do makeup and can help me out."

I was fine with it, and at this point I was starting to hope that he might really be falling for her. *Wow, if he was interested in someone else this would be my perfect way out of this marriage,* I secretly wished. I was more than okay with it... I was encouraging it!

I honestly didn't really get what Jennifer saw in my husband. She was only twenty-one and drop dead gorgeous and he was about forty and not so much. But from her vantage he had this great photography business, no, an empire. Little did she know he wasn't the real brains nor drive behind it. Plus, Jennifer idolized me, and he was married to this hot woman, so he must be the bomb.

He started traveling with her. And this goes on for weeks, in fact, months. With a few stops home, then he's back on the road with Jennifer again. At home, nothing was amiss. As always, I took care of my girls full time with help from my mom when I needed it and I had an insanely busy business that was going just fine. Business continued as usual and he was barely missed.

I was aware of where he was going, but there was also a trail on the credit cards. Lots of stops for clothes he bought her, extravagant dinners, bars and fancy spas. Oh my God, Fancy spas!!! You had to know my husband to know how totally out of character that was. This redneck, literally, white from the neck down was going to tanning salons and getting spray tans and man manicures. OH MY GOD!!! And on his brief visits home he looked like a Cheshire cat grinning from ear to ear…. He was clearly in love.

Wow, I thought to myself. *I've been asking for a divorce and he's begged me not to, telling me he could never be in love with anyone else and I felt so bad and here look at him!* Secretly I could see my exit coming.

Then one day, while my husband and his new "assistant" are out "working," Ken, my office manager storms in, all pissed off and upset. He slammed an envelope down on the desk and yells, "What the hell is this?!!!"

"What do you mean?"

"It's a corporate American Express card with Jennifer's name on it. I've been working for you for over ten years and I don't get an American Express card! This little slut traveling with your husband gets a card?"

It was okay to fuck this chick and buy her a few things but giving her a company credit card was another thing. Now I was pissed. Sex is one thing, but a credit card account is unconscionable!

A few days later he was back, and it was time for us to talk. I presented the Amex card as he sat there with his fake suntan and out of character outfit, fit for a teenager.

I launched in, "Look. Obviously, you have feelings for this girl and clearly if you have feelings for her then you can't really care that much for me. I really think it's time we get a divorce."

Reality suddenly hit him. "Oh my God. NO!!! No, please! No, I mean, God, I'll give up Jen in a second. It was just fun, but you can't leave me I love YOU. I don't want to be with Jennifer anymore."

Finally, I could do this without feeling guilty, "Honestly, we've had this conversation over and over and you clearly can be in love with another girl. You are and it's time."

Still he was shocked and protested, "How can you do this to me? Just cos I had sex with her? That's not fair. You had sex with her, too!!!"

REALLY?!

He regretted everything in that moment. But I persuaded him that it was all okay and all was good, that we would have an amicable divorce and he would live happily ever after with Jennifer who was the true love of his life. We did just that. We had the perfect friendly divorce. The girls were doing great, mostly with mom but Scott was a doting father who often had them over.

Oh my God, the sun came out, the clouds parted, the Angels sang. After almost ten long years, I was finally FREE!!! I was SOOOOO HAPPY!

We amicably split the business. I was willing to give him everything, lock stock and barrel to get him out of my life and offered him anything he wanted. He chose carefully, the magazines that were bringing in the obvious income and anything else that was making the money. He was willing to leave me no income and the crap used old photo library. I was secretly laughing my ass off at his assessment of the most valuable asset we had.

He did move out and Jennifer moved in with him. To her chagrin, he wasn't the business mogul she thought she was sleeping with! It took her about two weeks to realize that he wasn't the mastermind behind the business and sadly she dropped him like a hot rock. Shame, but she'd done me a huge favor.

I was free at last! Free to run wild. And I did...

CHAPTER TWENTY-FOUR

Bait at the Swing Club & the FTC

WITH SCOTT OUT of the picture, many clients came, in a bigger and better way. Scott had not been the most likeable character, so his exit brought back many old customers who disliked him and a lot of new ones. News spread fast that I was now single, so there were suitors lining up that wanted more than to make money with me. This didn't hurt my business either. I was pursued, wooed and downright chased by these wolves like a fawn in the woods and I was quite happy to turn these into new business opportunities.

In some ways though, being married had been a bit of a safety net for me with some clients. I had certainly been running around, flaunting it, flirting and holding myself out as a "maybe" so I could rope in the deals, but now there were some clients I didn't want to know I was single. You know the ones, I'd dangled the carrot for but declined them, saying, "Oh, you're wonderful but unfortunately I'm married." Now I had to be a little careful about who knew I was officially single and available and for certain meetings I even put my wedding ring back on.

I was so happy to have freedom in my life. Freedom to make my own business decisions. Freedom to make crazy out on-a-limb investments, without arguing and getting the third degree. My incentive to leave the marriage was not to date other people, hadn't even thought of that. I just wanted my life back.

I had presumed that being a thirty-year-old, single mom, with two kids, would be a big put off for most serious contenders. Boy was I wrong! Men seemed to genuinely want the whole package, doting over my children who were loving the extra attention. Still I was married to my business so any geezer who was going to capture my heart in a serious way, would probably have to capture my business sense too. Meanwhile, I intended to enjoy being single.

American men I found to be the most chivalrous adorable creatures, who would shower you with compliments. Hardly a day would go by without some random guy offering to buy me a drink or outright asking me out. Barely ever paid for anything—guys would run to pick up the check, even my groceries sometimes! I'd be sitting in a restaurant and some stranger at another table would pay my bill. Even when I was out with my kids! I was always flattered, very polite and always thanked them for the compliment, but still I'd never gone for it. It was just part of being female, and that thing I adored about American men. Now, I was waking up to see the guys coming on to me and what was being offered; there were young guys, older guys…all kinds of amazing guys. It was like the candy aisle in Harrods.

I thought, while single, it was a rare opportunity to try somethings. I had written about fantasies for so many years for the magazines, I thought I might want to try some of these.

It started to hit the proverbial wall when I learned my staff had for years been fantasizing about me. Huh? Really? My long-time assistant Ken confessed he'd had a crush on me since the day he was hired. It turns out he probably would have been working for me for free if I had carried out his ultimate fantasy. That was if he could spend most of his work day under my desk while I wore seamed stockings and six-inch heels. And, oh yes, if I would also pee on him once in a while!

He shared that many of the photographers and various men that worked for me seemed to have had quite an obsession in guessing my personal sexual desires. Ken, argued that I was into that in-charge look. After all, one of my magazines was called "Business Class Women" and I seemed to know exactly how to fulfill their fantasies.

Brian was convinced of quite the opposite; that at home I for sure played the *Barely Legal* girl. He fantasied that I wore full-bottom little-girl white panties and my partner would play dirty old man who would finger my bare pussy in secret.

But personally, I really longed for a man who would admire and appreciate me, play to that part of me that needed constant validation, to be told I was beautiful every moment, but someone who would take charge and take care of me. Spending most of my time around the office taking charge of every detail in my business, in my personal life I longed for the opposite. A real man to sweep me off my feet and spoil me. Someone I could feel totally vulnerable with. But someone I could admire and RESPECT (now that seemed to be the biggest challenge). Still I didn't have time to drop my guard. My business was full speed ahead and I didn't need any emotional distractions.

My pseudo sexual experimental stage was short lived and pretty soon, I fell back in my pattern of serial monogamy, when I met Gary through business. He wasn't that much to look at, but his charm intrigued me, and he was the ultimate family man and great with my girls.

I got to know him during my many visits to his office to sell him images for the audiotext side of his business. He was smart, and I had a thing for smart men. He was pretty good in the sweeping one off one's feet department. His favorite thing to do was to take me on lavish spa weekends or to some tropical island to pamper me mercilessly and lick my pussy five times a day. Finally, I'd met someone who knew where the G-spot was and what to do with it!

He loved to role play and I'd raided my studio wardrobe in my leg fetish department as well as trying out the Barely Legal closet. He especially liked the virginal full bottom white cotton panties, old man gropes young girl fantasy, while I whispered, "Shhhhh… be quiet or you'll wake my parents up." So needlessly to say I was having a whole lot of fun in the bedroom.

It was nineteen ninety eight, still the early days of the Internet and as the pioneers flooded in, there were no rules yet. There was nothing to base rules on. It was truly the Wild West. Rule number one was formed; if you were a newbie webmaster you needed to license some nude pics and the place to get those pics was Gail. And who had bought out "all rights in perpetuity" — Gail! It didn't matter if you'd run those pics in your magazine, you now needed "Internet Rights" and that meant you had to pay Gail.

A library of now over a million images was categorized into niches; big boobs, old women, plumper girls, skinny girls, hairy girls, not hairy girls, peeping Tom, girls that look like boys.........

It was a whole new industry. Photos were placed into categories, scanned onto CDs and mass produced.

A flood of new website owners sprung up. But who were these website owners? They didn't come out of the porn video business as one might expect. No, those X-rated movie guys were left standing in the dust, still working on their Betacam masters. A new breed came in. The young college tech geek! At an average age of twenty-two and an IQ far above most, this was to be the fastest breed of multi-millionaires the world has ever known. They weren't interested in sex! Well, no more than any other twenty-two-year-old. They were interested in how many ways you could stretch a credit card.

Was it membership sites where subscribers would pay a monthly fee? Was it free sites that would drive traffic to the memberships and get paid from the guys with the membership sites? Was it supposedly "free" trial sites that would back door you into some never-ending tunnel? Either way you slice it, it was The Gold Rush and I was selling the shovels and pans!

The phone sex guys were the most prepared. They'd had the most experience in trying to stretch a guy's wallet. They knew how to bill any credit card, twelve ways 'til Sunday, and if that didn't work they'd take your checking account or even your phone number and bill through your phone company! And if that didn't work they'd open their own bank and issue you one of their own credit cards and if all else failed, they'd sell your number to someone offshore who had some program to suck out a few more cents.

Data and technology was king. I mean good content was a must and getting exactly what would hold the guys attention was paramount. But knowing the data on a man's masturbation habits was highly important. For instance, you would think, weekend and evenings would be peak site viewing time. Right? No, it was completely the opposite. Weekdays with peaks at 5pm New York time and 5pm LA time. We found this to be true and it matched everyone else's info. Clearly the guys were rushing to log on at work right at the end of the work day. You see there was two reasons; firstly, at least back then, the workplace probably had higher speed computer power than home, better for viewing their adult sites. Secondly, wife and family were likely at home. It was quite obvious that most men were logging on from the office. A few were starting to come in earlier at 8am but most seemed to be having to work an extra hour every night! So presumably they weren't actually masturbating in front of the computer. Unless they had a really weird workplace. They were curiously logging on and viewing porn at the office. And we are not talking little numbers here. We are talking a massive spike as millions of guys all of a sudden, logged on at 5pm and server banks crashed everywhere! The weekend was slow family time and by Monday morning at 8am they were desperate to log on again. I say men, and of course there were a few women that were curious, but women were way more complicated and unpredictable. Men, well they are creatures of habit and you could set your clock by their horniness.

The more information the webmaster could get about their customer's viewing habits, the more they could deliver them the perfect product.

But there was still room for the newbie upstart. A couple of college roommates could start their own site with just a photo disc from me. It was here I made hundreds of young guys rich.

I am now dating Gary and we are developing website features and technology together. We are in Las Vegas checking out the annual CES or Consumer's Electronic Show while also attending the spin-off Audiotext event at the hotel across the street. This smaller 'adult' show was nothing to be sniffed at, and quickly being turned into the adult web industry, the profits were already growing on a massive scale.

Perusing CES, the mainstream technology floor, we bumped into some mutual friends. They were an up and coming processing company about to go huge on the web. The owner Malcom asked if we wanted a quick drink in the bar.

"It's going amazing. We created this Finding Friends connection site and it's massive. We have hundreds of thousands of users so far and we just launched," Malcom explains. "But we've got this huge issue, these people are trying to 'hook up' all the time. They can exchange photos, but half the photos they are sending are frigging sex photos. I mean don't get me wrong, I like that too, but we can't have that on our network."

Gary and I are laughing

"So you guys are in that business, is there any way we can send you all the 'adult' ones? I mean somehow create more of a 'hook up' dating site and we can send all that kind of traffic to you. Like an adult version?"

OMG talk about just being given a massive bone! Did they really not understand that this was where all the money was, and they were just going to give it away? Apparently not.

"Yes, ABSOLUTELY." Gary and I both jumped in together.

Gary and I left, knowing that we had just been given an amazing cue, "Oh my God, can you believe this!!! I'll call my tech guys and get them working on this. Get your office to send over some starting pics."

That little meeting was worth attending times a hundred!!!

Back home, Gary and I are busy working on our amazing new project.

Then, as a natural outgrowth of the 900 lines, live chicks on-camera was invented. Gary had also been an investor in the phone industry and was on the cutting edge of the web. Several of us had invested in the dream of having guys be able to interact real time with a girl over a TV and now the computer. The race to take a girl live on the Internet was on. It was bigger than the Moon Race. We finally figured it out, and Gary's studio was the first one to actually go live. The technology was poor and the connection slow and choppy but the moment that frame went live, suddenly thousands of guys across the planet were tuned in. It was like Neil Armstrong, but it was one small step for man, one giant leap for Perv-kind.

The true story is it was set up to run twenty-four hours a day with these thousands of guys now glued to the screen. But after a few shifts of live Internet, the next girls didn't turn up. The poor naked model who had been there for twelve hours straight couldn't leave these guys with nothing. They kept going. Gary with his one nude model-naut. Finally, she had to eat, so the camera cropped out her head and zoomed in on her body while she secretly ate a sandwich. Then again as she took her cigarette breaks the guys stared close at her breasts, the only clue being the smoke seen drifting across frame. Then finally when she couldn't last any longer and fell asleep, naked with her legs spread, Gary zoomed the camera close up between her legs and no one noticed she was snoring away. Gary occasionally nudged her arm resting on her pussy, so the viewers thought she was pleasuring herself. She was actually sleeping! Nevertheless, the guys at home never noticed and the dollars poured in.

And so, the first live cam studio with girls twenty four hours a day was started.

The Internet was now a huge new outlet for my photos, but I was still creating an endless supply for the magazines as well. Plus, I had a few more of my own publications and some I was doing for Larry Flynt. All required a ton of content.

"Amateur Girls" was another great niche and we were going from town to town looking for fresh new talent. Swing clubs, I thought, might be a great place to meet uninhibited ladies who were more "real" looking and who might want to shoot for me.

The largest swingers' convention on Earth was The Lifestyles Convention held in Las Vegas each summer. So, back to Vegas and I set up a suite in the hotel as my "shooting location" and brought with me a team of photographers.

I took my boyfriend Gary and the plan was to peruse the pool area looking for potential couples whose pretty wives we could shoot. I had no problem holding myself out as bait. Arm in arm with Gary, I'd pretend we were just another swinging couple looking to hook up, so that they would flock to us.

Gary hated it, "All these guys are looking at you thinking they are going to get to screw you!"

He was intensely jealous and was not about to partake in anybody's partner getting hold of me.

I at this point had gone so far down the rabbit hole that it didn't faze me in the least. I was simply looking to make a buck and could care less if these were a bunch of swingers in a den of iniquity and if the husbands were fantasizing about screwing me.

It worked like a charm. I'd flirt and tell the couples, "Maybe later we can get together, but for now wondering if you would like to come and do a photo shoot for us."

Couples were all over us. In this way, I got about ten great girls a day coming back to our suite. I'd circle the event, flirt, pick up girls and bring them back to the suite, where I had three teams of photographers shooting. Meanwhile, Gary had gotten pissed off and was cooling off in our room and I was fresh bait all by myself. It was getting a little frustrating because every couple was trying to rip my clothes off on the way over to the room and I'd keep the lure dangling, "Maybe after we shoot."

Getting any work done around this sex-crazed bunch was proving difficult.

Now one of my assistants was a guy I sometimes used in LA. He'd come from the porno biz where he was well known as "Dick Nasty." To me he was just Richard the assistant photographer I could count on.

We are in the suite and I bring in this new couple who instantly recognize Richard. They both act like they've suddenly seen a movie star or something. So, I'm busy with another shoot and our model's swinger husband that is trying to rip my pants off as I am trying to direct his wife. My back is turned so I miss the conversation that went something like this:

Husband to Richard: "My wife and I are such big fans of yours. It would be such a great honor if you would let my wife suck your dick."

To which, Richard said, "Sure," dropped his trousers and his wife went to town, in the middle of the room completely not fazed by the twenty or so other people standing there.

I turned back to see what was going on, "What the HELL RICHARD! WHAT ARE YOU DOING?!!!"

Richard innocently replied shrugging his shoulders, "Well, she asked if she could! Just being polite!"

Her husband nodded in delight.

"Yes!" said the husband from the other couple, pulling at my pants, "Just let me lick your pussy."

Oh shit! This place is frigging crazy, and Gary is about to lose his mind!!!

The jealousy was killing us, still, Gary was a great business partner for me to finally get my websites up. He had a great team of top-notch programmers and designers and I laid out Gail's fantasy website world. So, his team took hard drives of my images and started to create. I had regular websites up and running, sure, a ton of them but I was designing my state-of-the-art interactive websites that at the time had never been done before. Programming that hadn't even been dreamed of. With pop-ups, cookies and tunnels that would take the guy on the absolutely perfect trip of his individual fantasy so that he'd be so hooked he'd never be able to leave. Coding that would individualize the guy without him even knowing but giving him exactly what he wanted to see and to literally make him come back over and over. And nobody, absolutely nobody could touch me with my vast library behind such sites. Gary had the technical expertise to pull this off.

Meanwhile, our dating site project and my sites were taking months longer than they should have, since Gary was also running sites for a big-time investor, Graham, who seemed to take priority. Gary's team kept being diverted off my sites onto some project for Graham and it was a constant bone of contention between us. They were going to be amazing when they were finally done but frustratingly, my sites were being built in Gary's "spare time."

Gary and I were away on one of our frequent romantic spa weekends and he's remotely checking in on his computer, when he gets suspicious that something's going on with his client Graham.

I'd met Graham a few times and we'd recently been over to dinner at his new Malibu mansion on the beach. A spectacular place that he did not hide the fact that he'd just paid twelve million cash for.

"We're pulling in three point five million this weekend," Graham quoted at dinner. And that weekend they hit exactly three and a half million in revenues.

Gary confided in me, "Something's going on. How can he know the exact figure? He's called and hit, his exact figure three weekends in a row. There is no way to do that. I've got a bad feeling about this."

Back from our spa weekend, it's Monday morning and Gary drives to Graham's Los Angeles office around ten AM as usual. As he is about to pull off the highway, he sees all the employees lined up in handcuffs outside the office. Gary keeps driving.

The next call I get is from Gary now in a panic. The FBI had frozen all Gary's assets including the hard drives with my fledgling websites and there was a full-blown investigation underway.

Gary's suspicions were correct and something not on the up-and-up had been going on. Graham apparently had some "friends" high up at the credit card processing bank. Most of the revenues on Graham's sites were not real customers, rather Graham and his friends were being investigated for pulling a hefty scale operation running customer credit cards for people that had never even had a whiff of his sites.

Ooops!

Gary was innocent but right now he was up shit's creek without a paddle. And because of these shenanigans, my brilliant genius sites all went into the trash. Luckily my sites were not up and running and weren't any part of this legal mess but all the designs, all the months of code that was being worked on, was all on the computer drives that were at Gary's office, never to be seen again. Months of work and effort down the drain. Once again, I was on the verge of millions, but it slipped me by.

CHAPTER TWENTY-FIVE

The Gold Rush

IT'S NINETEEN NINETY-NINE and the Adult Internet had become so massive there was now an industry just to support the industry. Forums and websites to support the website owners and pretty soon, an entire Las Vegas Convention!

Had every guy in America gone crazy looking at naked women on the Internet, every man in the world? Every day, new college tech geeks were coming on board as newbie webmasters to service the needs of this insatiable consumption. Every day new sites came up, new business models were launched. And all of these new website owners needed photos for their sites! They also needed affiliate programs, software, hardware, ways to process credit cards, ways to store their money and industry leaders were just as quickly coming up with ways for them to spend it.

I had a few ways myself. I was the go-to girl for photos, so I was licensing photos from discs to entire banks of hard drives, all fully loaded with delicious photos of naked chicks. But I was also selling domain names, turn key sites, fully loaded with my content and hooked up to live cams, chat rooms and traffic drivers. Services I couldn't provide were bundled with my friends' products, so a guy could be out the door with a complete site ready to drive traffic and collect the bucks!

There was a flood of high-tech college geeks starting websites and industry suppliers trying to capture their business with bigger, more dollars and higher-quality orgies of food, booze, drugs and of course sex.

The Adult Internet Expos were a great example of the lengths a company would go to get a slice of the market share. I was at one of these typical Las Vegas expos and the "business" had spilled over into the gaming lounges, the bars and the pool area where webmasters could be found doing "business" and hanging with hot chicks. Gary had decided that he couldn't handle other guys looking at me and well yes, that wasn't gonna work in my business, so we had parted ways and I was once more, free to mingle.

The expo floor was all pretty spectacular to anyone coming for the first time but to the regulars the envelope was just getting better and better.

Adult Check, akin to Porn Hub, offered a human snow globe, the snow being US dollar bills. The webmaster enclosed in the plexiglass tube, was blasted, leaf blower style, with wads of notes and they could grab as many handfuls as they could. It was a good analogy of what you'd experience if you were a webmaster at Adult Check. The whole industry was not unlike snowing dollar bills.

Its competitor spent two-hundred and fifty thousand on their "booth" which was a tour bus complete with rotating complementary bar and Jacuzzi stocked with Playmates.

The expo loud speaker announces, "CyberX webmaster of the month, Dave from Kansas City!!! Dave just won a paid vacation to the Bahamas for him and three friends, hot chicks included. And Dave is in for the webmaster of the year and a smoking hot RED VIPER!!! Fuck yeah." Some innocent looking part-Asian college kid walks up on stage. "Dave, congratulations, you're the man! Dave drop trou, our hot CyberX chick is going to give you a blowjob." And sure enough, some model pulls Dave's pants down, right there on the stage.

And if you wanted a break from the convention floor you could take one of the Erotica Cash helicopter, high adrenaline "buzz" rides up the Strip, which would surely scare the shit out of you, especially if you took their special pills beforehand, all complementary for webmasters, in hopes of gaining a slice of their pie.

And the after-hours parties were insane; coke, chicks, rock stars, you name it.

Companies offered more and more; "Buy our program technology and get a free cruise." or "Top webmaster of the month gets a free speed boat!" The offers got bigger and bigger.

I had a distinct advantage. No one had more access to the girls than I did and bottom line with all the goodies being offered, hot chicks were still a winner. I headed to the pool area to see if my logo'd chicks were out there.

I had my regular staff here but then I also had my stable of shit hot models.

Loud booming bass from the music blasted from the pool speakers and thumped the air in my chest making my heart flutter with excitement. The deejay encouraged the humping, grinding girls caught up in the frenzy, trying to out-perform each other on the makeshift dance floor. I was impressed at the quantity and quality of the chicks at this event, an indication that there appears to be no ceiling to our exponentially rising industry profits.

A large crowd of men was gathered at the edge of the pool. I could just make out what looked like four perfectly formed cute firm female butts, the curve of their bodies looking like the symphony string section of cellos, squatting naked with their backs towards me and their hands on their hips. There was some kind of contest going on and the poolside announcer in a straw fedora, Maui sunglasses and Hawaiian shirt was giving a running Howard Cosell commentary on the whole thing. Just what were they focused on? It was then I realized, the girls were squatting over beer bottles and the contest was to see who could pick up a bottle with only their Kegel muscles.

Oh, that is…awesome! I thought and made a mental note to self: *Must sponsor future beer bottle contests!* I mused absently as to whether the best placement of my logo would be on the bottle or if it could somehow be done with a stencil tattoo on those girls' perfect little asses.

But I couldn't spot my logo bikinis nor my staff at this particular moment. I presumed my Russian *Agent Provocateurs* were probably in the mix somewhere. I had a distinct advantage, here where I was able to use my Russian Mafia contact, Vladimir, or "Vlad the Impaler" which I never knew if that described some massive male member or if it was his Mafioso reputation. Vlad brought a continual stream of the hottest girls over from Russia.

He was introduced as a very high end "model agent" and he did indeed provide me with incredible, Victoria Secret grade babes to shoot for Penthouse and the likes. Later I discovered Vlad was bringing these smoking hot babes over from Russia to the US for possible marriage to men who were clearly rich but probably completely unattractive, social outcasts and were willing to pay Vlad a twenty K agency fee. These girls willingly signed up for the deal. In fact, they were often on Vlad's waiting list, begging him to bring them out. They came from abject poverty in Russia to this glorious land where streets were paved with gold, all intently looking to capture some deep pocket American to fall in love with them.

The girls were clearly thrilled to work at this event, with the opportunity to meet young wealthy guys. In return, I was getting a fantastic deal; insanely hot Russian women who make a great impression for my company.

Since I couldn't spot any of my girls, I was quite confident that they'd sought out my higher dollar value clients and were busy working it.

I went back through the expo floor and stopped by my booth to see how my new office manager, Julie was working out. My general staff at the ranch were pretty mainstream business hires. Certainly not models. Yes, we were dealing with some "out there" material but after a couple of months working for me it was pretty much like selling any other widget. Julie was my new assistant that I had great plans for and she did in fact end up working for me for years. But this was her first week out and I'd thrown her in the deep end by bringing her to an expo and having her manning our photo-disc selling at the booth.

"How's it going. Are you doing ok?" I inquired, checking in with her.

"No, great. Think I got everything covered…. But there was one guy asked if we have any pony stuff. I wasn't sure if that was just girls with horses in the background or something."

My mind flashed to my first visit to New York and the beat-up-guys club with the man who you could ride as a pony complete with saddle and the likes, otherwise I would have been just as clueless. "Oh, no, that's different. No, we don't have any of that kind of stuff."

She continued, "Really nice guy though. He's taking me to the spa this afternoon."

"Really! A webmaster taking you to the spa? Wow that's great!" I replied.

"Yeah he was telling me how he liked facials and I told him I LOVE to get facials. So, he's coming back later. I told him you wouldn't mind me leaving the booth for a few hours, right?"

"Oh my God!!! No!!! He's not taking you to the spa! He was talking about a different type of facial. As in, his yucky stuff all over your face!!!"

Her mouth dropped open as she realized just what this guy had in mind. "Oh my God!!! I feel so stupid. I never thought of that!"

I left Julie trying to navigate this new adult world and I went to check out some of the "business" suites and hang with the Industry Players.

I rode up in the elevator with a bunch of webmasters I knew. They acknowledged me, but no one acknowledged the couple already in there. The girl in the back corner was spread eagle along the polished brass handrail, her spiked heels lodged squarely along the side of each wall with a man's bare butt towards us, his Armani slacks and silk boxers around his ankles, rhythmically banging the shit out of her. His belt buckle clanked fast and faster like the tack on a horse going from a trot to a full gallop. I noticed the back of all the guys heads were tilted up, and I realized the elevator was mirrored, and we could all glance up and see every detail of the show. Still it seemed it was of minor interest to them. We started chatting about conversion rates and some new programs that were out. The attention of all the guys shifted and were focused on the business conversation. No one was distracted by the girl screaming in delight behind us and her bare bottom smacking the back of the elevator so hard it was rattling the whole thing. They were still guys, so they would certainly look, but it had become so blasé, such the norm that it was only worth a passing glance. Real biz and dollars to be made, was the real drive.

Just as the elevator arrived at our floor the girl came in a deafening crescendo, "AH-AHH-AHHHH — OOOOOO...." We continued to discuss some program as we left the elevator and the girl's orgasmic screaming was suddenly cut short by the closing doors.

We were all headed to one of the business suites. Opening to the main room, I saw it was sectioned like a school party with various stations that guests could sample. The most popular station was a line of guys getting some kind of cream pie treatment. One girl was on her knees clearly servicing the guy at the front of the line. There was another girl with a canister of whipped cream who appeared to be preparing the rest of the line. The guys standing there with their pants down around their ankles, their dicks covered in Reddi-Wip waiting their turn, like Cold Stone with cocks, all the while chatting business with each other. I knew most of them, but they usually had their pants on. I was mildly entertained as to how easy it was to please a group of businessmen. Such simple creatures. Like it wasn't even fair!

In another corner, one guy was partaking in some soft S & M stuff that was being offered. The hired dominatrix was an extremely tall, skinny flat chested black girl, with a square jaw, short hair and high cheek bones, looking, I thought quite hot, in only a pair of stockings and garters, not unlike I imagined Grace Jones on date night. The guest had been given a rubber mask and was stripped down to just his briefs, which were plain white overly washed and stretched yellowing jockey shorts. He was a rather overweight unattractive guy with rolls of white flab hanging out, who looked more like he was in a cheesy bank robber movie than some erotic sex slave scene. I couldn't quite tell but I was pretty sure he was a banker I knew and had done some offshore stuff with. I was slightly embarrassed for the guy.

There was also a self-serve bar where guests were helping themselves to not just drinks but to entire Tequila bottles. Left over bits of snacks covered the bar, some kind of crumbs, or maybe it was drugs…not really sure. I am offered a Quaalude from the executive drug stash by Monte, one of the higher ups in the company. His eyes look like he's had enough ludes to put down a mad horse. I gracefully decline.

I believe the sample corners were each supposed to be relevant to some product the company was selling and there were flat screens throughout playing various erotic scenes. One such set up did appear to be a legitimate live demonstration. Some girl was sat upright, her knees spread apart displaying a huge dildo sticking out of her pussy. The representative was instructing some interested buyer on how the remote-controlled dildo was supposed to work. Clearly it wasn't doing much for her as she sat eating a plate of sushi, oblivious to the sensuous love making the remote operator was providing. I mused that the average dude would likely think this contraption really worked and I could probably sell the shit out of it.

Many of the companies putting on these elaborate suites had been just an idea a year ago and were now in full swing as players of this little world making a killing. Little upstart sites still being run out of their parents' garages, were now bought and traded for millions.

The future of the Internet and how it conducts business today was all founded in adult. Hard to believe looking at this room full of guys half shit faced and the others with their pants down, that these were the tech gurus of our time. These guys would be responsible for our future. How credit cards could be processed, how advertising dollars could be spent, live chat, chat boxes, customer service, online banking, even how people could meet people… it was all created in the adult space first. The sex industry would create the Internet as we now know it.

I decided not much real business going on here and I'd headed back to the show floor to see my friend Mike and how our new venture was going.

On the way down I bumped into Greg, my extremely smart and forethinking attorney, whose specialty was copyright and patents. Early on I had met Greg and he revamped my model release to include the models turning over every right you could think of, including, "Rights of publicity" and "Synthespian Rights."

"What the hell are 'Synthespian rights?" I asked.

"Something you'll need in the future," he assured me.

Greg had turned my office into an organized machine, filling out patent applications on every program or business method I'd come up with.

Greg was the industry expert, go-to attorney in this new medium, advising all the top players.

And there was Mike, my friend with an impressive booth "Cyber Galleries."

Mike and I went way back. He was the guy that was my neighbor and we'd been friends from the Clive days when he first started repping some of my photos to Japan. We'd partnered on a bunch of projects over the years and had quite a lot of success together. Although there had been periods when he was gone for a few years, we had on and off been inseparable and were always some kind of soul mates. Even though there was nothing ever romantic, we adored each other. We had followed parallel paths and Mike was now back in California and big in the adult Internet. He had a booming web business and a successful talk radio show. Recently Mike had come up with an idea he proposed, using my images in galleries. A sort of ready-made gallery a site owner can use on his sites.

"Wow, very impressive!" I say, looking at his massive booth that looks more like a bar lounge with a bunch of webmasters hanging out. The booth walls were covered in huge blow up glossies of some of my best images.

"How are we doing?" I inquire.

"Gail this is fantastic, we've signed up at least a hundred sites already!"

"Really, wow!"

There were four or five Asian men in suits and black ties note pads in hand standing out like complete misfits next to the rest of the booth filled with web masters in jeans and Ts hanging out with a Cyber Gallery Beer in hand. I motioned to Mike with a questioned look.

"Big investors from China. We're talking about a massive deal together! Opening up China!!! They're gonna take the radio show huge and they're very interested in the galleries!!!"

"So how exactly do the galleries work?"

"Pretty simple. We've made a turn key gallery of your images that we host on our servers. The webmaster just plugs it into their sites. I'll upload your new content every month, but the site owner doesn't have to do anything. To the customer it looks like it's on their site, but the webmaster doesn't have to mess with the images or have any clue technically, they just plug us in!"

"How much does the site pay us?"

"It depends how many members they have. So, it starts at $200 a month and goes up to $2000 a month for unlimited members," Mike explains.

"And we've got one hundred websites that are going to be paying monthly?!!!"

"Yes. Hoping for five hundred," Mike say grinning.

"Shit, that's a great business model!"

CHAPTER TWENTY-SIX

Teaching Hollywood the Web

MAINSTREAM DOT COMMERS are now just coming online even though almost none of them were actually making money. At this junction they were just starting an Internet presence with an idea, a possibility of future revenue, but the only real revenue coming in was in adult websites and all eyes were upon the adult web profits. Our industry had developed every program, every platform, every mode of operation, to optimize the end users experience, and ultimately capture his wallet.

It was then that Hollywood invited me to speak to the movie industry on how to make money on the Internet. It had started out as a little seminar that was going to be put on by some Hollywood film guys. When I agreed to do it, I hadn't given it much thought but as it grew nearer I realized the idea of public speaking scared the crap out of me. I was starting to chicken out. I had been on many panels for the adult website industry, but they were all people I knew really well. A room full of Hollywood executives was way more daunting. Even worse, I learned some studio heads and serious players were planning to attend and now I'm totally intimidated.

I decided to ask some fellow website guys to join me to make a panel of four experts. I invited Mike, my best friend who I was doing the galleries with. Mike was also the host on his radio show, so he was not only knowledgeable, but he wasn't the slightest bit afraid of public speaking. All he did was talk!

Finally, the big night arrived. It was being held at a hotel in Santa Monica, California, sometime around nineteen ninety-nine. There was no real advertising, but the response was absolutely massive.

An hour before the event Mike and I arrive to a sea of people. *Oh my God, I thought this was going to be a LITTLE seminar!!!*

"Mike, I don't think I can do this. I'm just gonna wait in the car, you guys can handle it."

Mike laughed, "Come on Gail; you'll be great—it's you they wanna hear from."

I was dragged in by Mike, and I introduced him to Jamie and the event organizers who were completely overwhelmed. I was about having a heart attack realizing I was going to be scrutinized by Hollywood studio heads, when the program director runs in, "The ballroom fits almost a thousand people and it's pack jammed already. This is incredible! We're gonna be a few minutes 'cos we're setting up a video screen to transmit to the other ballroom and we can fit another thousand in there. Oh my God, this is huge! This is awesome!"

Great, I wanna throw up. I went weak at the knees and was visibly shaking. I excused myself to the bathroom. I was literally sitting on the bathroom floor wondering if I was going to faint or barf and more importantly trying to figure out how to get out of this, when Mike sends someone in to get me. He took my hand, "Don't worry, I'll lead, just imagine they are all naked. As soon as you're up there you'll be fine."

And he was so right. As soon as I started to talk about the various business models we'd learned in the Adult Internet space and how that could translate to Hollywood, I was in my element. You could have heard a pin drop.

Everything from membership models, free sites, advertising, affiliate programs, how to capture traffic, how to bill a person, copyrights, branding, how Hollywood could get eyeballs, to how they could deliver movies at high speed...the pros and the cons I had learned the hard way... Everything that was already old school, second nature to us in the adult web was on the cutting edge for everyone else. You have to remember at this time, for regular people, you'd still be asking, have you ever been on the Internet? Do you have an email address yet? Most people didn't.

The event went off brilliantly. That night in as hundreds lined up to talk to me afterwards, I realized just how far ahead the industry had gone and that we really were on the cutting edge of technology.

Every producer, every studio head in Hollywood wanted to know, how we were doing it. They listened in awe, at things that were just par for the course for me at this point. Even the Microsofts and the Yahoos didn't have the complete know-how that we'd had to develop out of the trenches for the simple need to deliver hot chicks to horny guys.

I talked about how studios could deliver movies to customers directly. How you didn't even need to be a studio and how on the web young upstarts had beat out established moguls. That it could be the same in movies. How to look to the future where our TVs would be computers and how movies would be viewed. That night myself and my panelists laid out the whole Netflix model.

I probably talked and answered questions for two hours straight... AND ABSOLUTELY LOVED IT!

A few days later, I am over at Mike's house just down the road from my office, picking up a nice check for our galleries. It's almost Halloween and I have to laugh at Mike's scary decorations, a half a body hanging over the front door.

Mike takes me up to a small hill behind his house, "This is my lookout point."

"Yeah nice view."

"Hah, well the real view starts at 11pm. Can set your clock by it."

I look confused.

"You can see my neighbors from here."

I look over and can see a curtained window.

"You won't believe this. Every night, I come up here and they open the window and this couple has sex right in front of the window! They totally know I'm watching! I like to come up here with a whisky and a cigar and just watch the show!"

I laugh at Mike, "So, how are the galleries going?"

"Amazing."

"Did you end up doing a deal with those guys from China?"

"Ah, I donno, they've turned out to be a total nightmare. In my office this morning, the guy's screaming his head off. I'm just gonna can that deal, it's not worth it."

The next day I'm sitting in my office when a webmaster friend calls.

"Did you hear about Mike?"

"What? No."

"He died."

"No!!! What are you talking about, I just saw him yesterday."

"Look on his site it says Mike R.I.P !"

I quickly typed in the URL to see what he was looking at.

"No, it's a joke. It's Mike. It's Halloween, it's just a joke I'm sure. Not funny though. Look I'm going to call his house."

I was in shock but knew it couldn't be true. I called his home and his wife answered.

"This is not true right? It's a Halloween joke right?"

"No Gail, he died."

"What!!! How!!!"

The blood rushed out of my head and I suddenly felt dizzy. I was in total shock and disbelief.

"We don't know, he was standing on this little hill behind the house and just fell down."

I almost dropped the phone, my body shaking in shock.

I don't remember driving over there and have no idea how I did, but I was at their house moments later. The door was open, and I passed under the gruesome Halloween body.

A few close friends and family were standing around in shock.

His wife was pretty together. I was losing it.

"They don't know what happened. He liked to go up there on that hill with a drink and he just never came to bed last night. Found him this morning on the ground. They said he was dead before he hit the ground but there is no sign of a heart attack or a stroke, they don't know."

"But he was so healthy, I just saw him yesterday!"

I was beyond devastated. Mike was my best friend. People always wondered why we'd never gotten married. I'd seen him through two marriages and he'd been around through mine, but we were always just very close friends. Our kids were friends, we'd go off on his boat for weekend get-aways, I adored him!

There was a massive turnout to his funeral. Everyone who was everyone in our industry. He was absolutely loved by all.

No one would ever know what really happened and it was written up as some kind of natural cause.

A few weeks later I was having lunch with my attorney Greg and a banker Ed, talking about a possible deal.

"I got offered a huge deal in Asia for processing, but I'm not sure about the investors," Ed explains, "I was over at this guy Mike's office from the KSEXY radio show, do you know him?" he looked at us, "The same investors were there and I'm not sure what was going on but shit, I thought they were going to kill him!!! The guy was so pissed off he was screaming his head off."

Greg and I look at each other and there is a long pause.

"You know Mike died like three weeks ago?" Greg says.

"No! Wow, had no idea."

The three of us sat in silence all wondering the same thing.

"But he died at his house, there was no sign of anything on the autopsy, there was no way anyone could have…" I wonder out loud looking at Greg.

"There are things they have they can slip in a drink or put on a cigar, with no trace…" Greg says.

We all shiver at the thought and my grief came running back.

The amazing galleries were disbanded, and Mike's company sold off in pieces. My heart was broken.

CHAPTER TWENTY-SEVEN

Scarlet Letters

A YEAR OR two had passed since my divorce, and from any outsider's point of view we had the most amicable arrangement and we were the best of friends. It was pretty-true, on most levels, until one day when a special lady came into his life. I was thrilled. Up until now it was obvious that he was holding out hope I would come back. Finally, he had met an attractive lady with kids and they planned to settle down together...What I didn't know was what was going on behind the scenes.

As I mentioned before, I was living a bit of a double life, sexy biz mogul on the one hand, respectable actress and now mainstream movie producer who was first and foremost raising kids single handedly. My girls went to an elementary school which carried a pretty high-end snobby reputation. Even though I was busy running my business, I still carved out time to be very actively involved with school, Girl Scouts, soccer mom, you name it. Juggling to make sure there were no nudie things going on when kids and friends were around and hiding anything adult in the office. None of the other parents had any clue about what I did for a living. That is until one day I got a call from the school principal to meet in her office.

"I'm not judging what you do. I'm just letting you know that you have a seriously crazy person after you and if I were you I would go right to the police. I got this letter in the mail today. ..... and I think a bunch of other parents got a copy too."

She opened the letter to reveal something that looked like an anonymous ransom note from some psychopathic murderer on a typical NYPD TV show. A letter purposely disguising the maker, being made up of separate words cut and pasted from newspapers. These strung together, mismatched, typefaces spelled out a note that was a WARNING to the reader. Its words saying something to the effect that I "was a disgusting porn star, luring young children for my pornographic magazines and that

I should not be allowed around any of their children." This along with some topless photo of me from a long-ago Page Three shoot in England.

"So sorry, Gail," the principal said as I stood staring in horror. "I would be very worried about this if I were you."

The principal, thank goodness for small favors, didn't seem to take the side of the writer. Still it was not a good impression.

She was right, many other parents got the same letter. Obviously, someone had access to private phone lists from the school activities of my daughters. Those parents were not so nice to me, nor my girls. I didn't get a chance to explain myself and honestly, I am not sure where I would have started anyway. Families that my girls had been friends with for years, simply would not even look in our direction. I was shunned by almost the entire community.

I can't tell you, how low I felt about myself and how ashamed I suddenly was about my life, my work. And most of all, I was devastated that it was hurting my daughters incredibly. Because of me and my work, my girls had to suffer such a horrible disgrace and they were too young to understand. They didn't know why, they just knew their mother was a bad person and they were not allowed to play with their friends anymore. Deep down I had created this business with the passion to create a wonderful life for my family, to be able to provide for my daughters and to be a powerful role model for them, and I had done quite the opposite and wrecked it. I felt like a lowlife scumbag. I was single and at this point I felt completely alone.

I suspected my ex-husband, Scott. But could even he stoop so low as to do something like this? If it was him, he had to know how much it would traumatize his own daughters.

Strangely enough I had just been randomly selected for an **IRS** audit that week as well. Luckily, the auditor was a pretty decent guy, and since he seemed to know a lot of telling questions to ask, I told him I suspected it was my ex-husband, who must have made some false report about me and this was why I was getting an audit. He wasn't allowed to say.

"Is there some kind of 'Freedom of Information Act' or something where I can find out if someone made a report on me?"

He said he'd check.

I took a long shot and guessed it was Scott so later that day, when I had reason to talk to him, I decided to mess with him a bit. "Yeah... they are going back five years, and they're asking all about the airplanes as a business write-off and they're asking, where they are now. Are you sure you don't have receipts for....," he was sweating buckets on the other end of the phone, I could tell.

I continued, "And he said there was this Freedom of Information Act and he's going to tell me who called this in...... I hope to God it wasn't you!!!?"

A little later that afternoon, my secretary takes a message which she relays to me; "This guy called from the IRS, said 'due to the Information Act...... blah blah', here is the number..."

It was Scott who turned me in!!!

I called the IRS auditor back and thanked him. But the auditor was confused, no one from his office had called.

"Who called from my office and said what? And how did you get that name and number?" the IRS auditor said most disturbed.

No more than twenty minutes go by and a team of Federal Agents break through our office door, handcuffs at the ready. It took me a few minutes to calm them down and convince them I really had gotten this call. Apparently, it's a serious offense to impersonate an IRS officer. So, who had called?

It was all unraveled when the Agents arrested Scott and his girlfriend for filing false claims with the IRS and there, in their house, were hundreds more hate letters all neatly pasted up and labelled, ready to mail out!!!

I have to believe that Scott was under great influence of a completely crazy woman. Still this was a scandal that would affect my family for years to come and a stark look at how the ADULT BUSINESS COULD BE VIEWED IN VERY DIFFERENT LIGHTS.

Scott left his crazy girlfriend, as a result of almost going to jail, and after that I forgave him, but still, I kept a friendly distance. We'd interact quite often about the girls and we'd talk pretty friendly on the surface, but I kept one wary eye open.

If you remember Scott had taken with him a very lucrative magazine *Hometown Girls*, which was a co-publishing deal with Larry Flynt. It was a turnkey operation for a nice fat check each month. Plus, there was a ton of profit on the photos as well. You would have thought, keep it in the family, and I would have been the one supplying all the photos. In reality, he went to extremes to find anybody else's photography to avoid ever throwing me a bone.

One day, Scott's over at my house, showing off to me, that he's getting promoted and they are going to be giving him an official management title at Flynt.

"Be careful," I warned. "I wrote a two-hundred-and-fifty-thousand-dollar buy-out clause in that contract. If they are trying to give you a new contract, make absolutely sure you keep that clause in."

He didn't listen. They gave him a new contract without the clause, and a month later they sold the magazine and he got nothing. He was hopping mad and nothing he could do.

Okay, now you are going to snigger at this one…couple of months down the line, I get a call from Lou, a publisher in New York, who I am producing a bunch of magazines for.

"Hi Gail, I just bought another magazine and I am wondering if you will package it for me. I bought it from Flynt. It's called *Hometown Girls.*"

Funny how karma works.

After the crazy girl incident, Scott decided to move to another state where he met a more normal lady and settled down. I was thrilled for him. Of course, the girls stayed with me and although they visited their dad once in a while they were always happy to be home with mom.

I was doing slightly better in the romance department….no crazy people like he was dating… At least I thought so…

Although my acting had been put on the back burner, there were occasional fun projects that came up, that would tempt me enough to carve out a little time. One such movie lure came from Film One and the owner Jalal, a dear friend of mine who produced independent action movies. I had teamed up with Film One as co-producer and I was also the starring love interest in these mostly male-cast, karate-fight-films. We were on the third in a series of these action movies entitled *The Circuit.* Film One was based in Toronto but we were shooting these in Los Angeles and movie base camp was pretty much my ranch. This time Jalal had brought with him a new producer from Canada, Lanz who he was grooming to take over his LA operations. Lanz would co-produce the movie with me.

Oh my God, Lanz was the most drop dead gorgeous man I think I had ever laid eyes on. Estonian chiseled features, set on a perfectly rippling six-foot-four, muscular body, he looked more like a Calvin Klein underwear model than a producer. And I'm going to work with this guy for six weeks on a movie!!! Apparently, he was equally impressed with my starring film presence, my beauty and charm. Or was it my connections in Hollywood and my apparently booming photo biz. Still didn't take much and as the film wrapped he moved from my guest house to my bedroom and we were officially a couple.

He was a total newbie to Hollywood and the movie business and relied on me to set him up and show him the ropes. Come to learn later, he had very little film experience at all and this young man from a small town in Canada had been "John" the odd job carpenter, until he arrived on the scene as Lanz, "the Producer." Still, his looks and presence were decidedly impressive, and he had all the air and ambition needed to be a Hollywood Producer.

Our relationship seemed to be going wonderfully. He was smooth, charming and attentive. I was still the bread-winner, so he was driving around in my cars and using my credit cards, 'til one of his movie projects took off. And I was the one introducing him to players in the film industry and helping work his career for him. But we were both in love and life was perfect.

Being Canadian he was a hockey player… of course, and I set him up to play scrimmages with Kiefer Sutherland's group and got him involved with the cool movie guys around town. Things were going great and we were quite the "Power Couple." Still I was running a very busy Internet business while trying to have the time to keep one foot in Hollywood with him.

He told me how amazing I was and how in love he was with me and how we made the perfect Hollywood Power Team. I was head over heels. I'd fallen deep and hard and was enjoying this perfect couple life.

My mother, who liked almost everyone, was not so impressed, "Just be cautious," she warned, "don't let him *use* you."

He tried to help. I had a lot more workload than him, but he pitched in occasionally, like one time I had this independent low budget movie shooting at my ranch and I was grateful Lanz offered to go back to the ranch daily and check on the film, so I could take meetings in town.

Then one day Lanz tells me he's going deer hunting in Orange County with a good friend of ours.

"Wow, never knew there was hunting or anything like that in Orange County." That was new to me. Apparently, it was not the best, they didn't catch anything and to boot, he'd gone in my old ranch pickup truck and it had broken down. He came back exhausted, dying to be back in my arms, and starving hungry.

A little later I had family in from England and we decided to take the kids to Disneyland. He hated the whole tourist park thing and had meetings, so he managed to get out of family day and stay home. Still life seemed like bliss.

We'd been together probably nine-months or a year and things were going really well, when he had to go back to Canada to visit family for a week or so and would be back right after. While he was gone, someone contacted him interested in a script of his. He called and asked if I would go in his closet, find this script and mail it out for him. He gave me pretty good instructions on which shelf and which box I would have to search.

So, I'm in his closet looking in the box he described and as I opened it, I notice on the very top, above all the scripts, is one of our photos from our day at Disneyland. *That's strange; what is the photo of me with my kids doing in his script box>* But on closer inspection, it wasn't a photo with me. It was a photo of him sitting next to a girl on a ride at Disneyland. But the date stamped on the bottom of the photo was the date I was in Disneyland a few weeks earlier, I remember the exact date because it was a birthday trip. I looked at it over and over, staring at the photo of Lanz on a ride with a girl appearing to be having a wonderful time on the very day that I went. *Huh?* I was totally confused. *How could this be?* A little twinge of concern hit me, *But there has to some kind of explanation. Besides everything was great between us, the year must be wrong on the photo stamp, there had to be some logical explanation.*

I tried to call him, but I didn't get a hold of him right away.

Meanwhile his good friend Simon, who he went hunting with, happened to call. I explained Lanz was out of town, but we chatted a bit about some other projects.

"Hey, I'm glad the truck broke down close to the Marina and not all the way down in Orange County," I said.

"What are you talking about? We never went to Orange; we only went to the Marina."

Turns out they'd never been hunting at all, they'd been out on a boat, a Hollywood party. Pressing a little, Simon was pretty honest with me.

"Why did he lie, Simon? Did he go off with some girl or something?"

"No, there were no girls on there, that we knew anyway. No, honestly, I think he feels you outshadow him sometimes, and he didn't want you to go cos you'd take the limelight. I mean actresses throw themselves at him for sure, but no, this was about him trying to pitch his movie. I know he's crazy about you, but you know, he's sorta jealous of you."

No, I didn't know. The whole thing was weird, pics at Disneyland the very day I had gone and lying about that trip.

I had never had much of a jealous streak in me and had never before considered doing anything like this, but that day I decided to rummage through my credit card bills. Then telephone bills…. Oh my God, there were calls to the same girls over and over and over. Dinner bills, tons of dinners. Spas and hotels when I was out of town. Dinners at exclusive romantic restaurants when he was supposedly playing hockey with the guys. Trails and trails on the credit cards. And sure enough, on the day in question, a ton of Disneyland bills.

Suddenly I couldn't catch my breath. It was like all the air went out of me, as if my stomach literally dropped and all the blood rushed away from my head. Dizzy, I laid on the couch my heart palpitating, wondering *Could this be true?* I'd never even thought to have looked at anything, I had no reason not to trust him. How could this be? There had to be an explanation.

I called my friend Jalal, who I was now unfairly, making somewhat responsible for bringing him down here in the first place and grilled him about Lanz.

Jalal answered innocently, "I don't know who the girl is in the photo but honestly, Gail, when you date someone that good looking, you're kinda setting yourself up?"

"What do you mean? Like I'm not good enough to date someone as good looking as him, like I'm chopped liver or something?" I spurted indignantly between the now gushing tears.

"No. I mean you're hot and all. I mean you're a Nine, yeah, err... probably a Ten when you're made up, but on the scale of one to ten, he's a Fifteen!"

Didn't help, now I am totally bawling.

Jalal continued, "And he's touting himself as a Producer. When you left him at the AFM (American Film Market), you were only gone a second and you should have seen the actresses all over him. God, thought they were going to spread right there on the show floor."

I'm now hyperventilating.

"I mean I've been in the business for twenty-five years and I can't tell you how many actresses have come on to me for a role in my movies. I'm happily married but for most producers in Hollywood, it's crazy easy. And he's strikingly handsome on top of it...I'm not dealing with him anymore, he's gotten too full of himself."

He continues trying to soften it somewhat, "Plus, don't know why you'd want to be with someone that good looking anyway. People that beautiful have had everything so easy their entire life, they are expectant, and they are never nice people.... You're an anomaly of course."

"Yeah, thanks for the compliment after first making me feel like crap."

Perhaps there was wisdom in Jalal's words and I remember seeing an episode of I think it was *Two and Half Men* where Alan, the not so attractive geeky guy is dating a hot girl and he says, "Look, don't want to ruin my chances here, but why are you dating ME?"

To which she replies, "Cos you're grateful."

There is certainly some truth to that and perhaps that was my lesson. I needed someone a little grateful.

My mind flashed to the many conversations I'd had with my friend Loretta Swit ("Hot Lips" Houlihan of *M*A*S*H* fame), who I shared a horse with. Loretta and her similar status girlfriends seemed to be constantly getting crapped on in relationships. I thought it was their fault for going for younger, handsome, film wannabes that everyone else could clearly see were using them. But this didn't apply to me, surely? I was the same age as Lanz and guys always went for my looks, not what I could do for them, that would be backwards?

Hours later, after stewing a great deal, I finally got ahold of Lanz and asked about the photo. I could barely get the question out, I had been practicing all day.

"Doll, there was nothing between us. She was a friend of mine and she had this rare blood disease and was dying, and she told me her final wish was for me to take her to Disneyland."

"You went in my car, on my credit card to Disneyland knowing that I was there with the family on the very same day.... Like you wanted to get caught!!!"

"No Doll, it's not like that, she had this disease and she was dying. You wouldn't have wanted me to deny her last dying wish. She's now dead and I'll send you the obituary from the paper if you don't believe me."

Could anyone say such a thing if it wasn't true? There had to be some truth to it surely? No one could be THAT bad. He had an answer for all the "business" dinners on my credit cards and I wanted to believe him so badly.

We talked about why he lied about the hunting trip and somehow, he turned it around on me; that I needed to be in the background more and support him more and not outshine him in public. Somehow, he had me almost feeling bad and that I needed to try harder. I got off the phone feeling, I needed to be better, I was the one who needed to change to fix the love of my life. *WHAT WAS I THINKING?!!!*

Still the next day, I started putting feelers out around my office to see if anyone had seen anything. Apparently, my staff were well aware of quite a lot, but had been keeping quiet, cos they knew I was in love and didn't want to spoil my bliss.

Still, since I asked, one of the guys was ready to spill the beans, "You know that day you found that rubber stuck on the hood of your car and nobody knew anything about it? Yes well, it was that day that Lanz came back to check on that film and he fucked I think every actress that was in that movie. There was like seven of them. He was showing off to us how easy actresses were. He even fucked one of them over the hood of your car!"

"What!!!"

I couldn't believe what I was hearing. I was literally sick to my stomach. Another guy that worked for me figured he might as well tell what he knew, "Yes he was telling us 'actresses in LA are crazy, as soon as you tell them you're a producer they all wanna fuck you,' and so he did! I'm gonna make a business card that says I'm a producer!"

"Yes, Gail. Said he was kinda shocked at first, that girls were *way* different where he was from. Said he was driving down the 405 (freeway) one day, stuck in traffic and some girl rolled down her window and asked if he'd have sex with her. So, they pulled off the freeway and he fucked her in the car at the side of the 405!"

"My car?!!!"

They both shrugged their shoulders, like, *Yeah I guess so, does that really matter whose car?*

I had heard enough, and I was devastated. It left a deep scar on my heart and I promised myself that never, ever, again would I ever date a guy that was THAT good looking. And never again any producer named Lanz.

My heart was broken and for weeks I cried myself to sleep.

A wise old Hollywood agent once said to me that the universe never allows you to have everything. You can have power, fame, money, family but then you can't have love. Or if you do have love then you're not allowed to have some other area of your life. I disagreed. "Look, in my business, those with the power, fame, money; Flynt, Hef, Guccione...oh, I see what you mean. But what about actresses that made it to the top that have fame and money, what about their love life...oh I see what you mean." Still I refused to believe it, you can have everything, I had to believe it!

Months later, I had just finally got him out of my head when he contacted me again, totally out of the blue.

"Listen Doll, I have this movie project and I need to raise thirty-five Mil. If you can raise the money for me, I'll give you an exec-producer title and three-percent of the back end."

Oh, wow. how generous, let me think about this for a minute, err.......
NO!!!...FUCK NO!!!!!!!!!!

CHAPTER TWENTY-EIGHT

An American Succexxx Story

I DECIDED I BETTER steer clear of Hollywood for a while, at least as far as prospective romantic partners were concerned. I had learned my lesson and I would remember it for future experiences. Right? In fact, wasn't that what having crappy relationships and getting your heart torn out and feeling excruciating pain was all about? So, you would learn and not repeat the mistake? That instinctual database that is created inside us that allows us to match and recognize that total bullshit artist, the bipolar rager, and that next complete user. The internal matching system that can sometimes turn middle aged women into neurotic psychopaths that project old fears onto every new relationship so that a new prospective is prejudged upon the laundry list of painful expectations from the past. Unfortunately, or fortunately, my matching system seemed broken or blindly superseded by my optimism for each new person and the blank slate I would naively give each new prospect entering my life. Which meant I could repeat these painful lessons several times in my life without ever learning or becoming jaded. This seemed to be the case for me in business as well.

Still, I was happily single for a split second and I threw myself into my sexy photo biz. I was not blind, deaf and dumb to the plain fact that I got a hefty chunk of my business because men really wanted to date me so being single for a while was great for my income. Men would much rather do business with my company than someone else and have a chance to spend time with me and I wasn't discouraging it.

Like Jack.

Jack had a massive, very successful web business. He didn't really need any photos for his particular business model, but he kept asking me to come over under the premise of wanting to buy images. I sold him a ton. In Jack's case, I was completely oblivious to the fact that he was really bringing me over with the intention of asking me out. He had full lush dark hair, big brown eyes and I thought quite dreamily handsome, but I saw pictures of his little daughter around his office and just presumed he was married. He wasn't. Anyway, it took him about four visits and probably over a hundred-thousand-dollars in photo purchases he really didn't need, before he finally plucked up the courage to ask, "Hey Gail, I was wondering if you'd like to have dinner with me."

I started dating Jack. I was thrilled and excited about him and truly fell head over heels. He had one of the all-time greatest start up stories. Totally penniless, he and his two roommates were electricians working on a warehouse that housed one of these adult sites. In reality, it was a company posing as a "child protection gateway" they called "Adult Check." Under the guise of making sure the kiddies weren't exposed to the shagadelic world of nakedness, the company took the credit card information and payments (and therefore supposedly verified a person was an adult) on behalf of thousands of sites. In reality it was just the conglomerate of literally thousands of adult sites in the vein of Porn Hub and they were making a shit load of money.

Jack and his roommates wanted a domain and inquired, "How do we get one of these adult sites set up?" The Boss Man grunted the charge was five-hundred dollars. Jack and the roommates all pooled together, each scrapping up literally their last dime from the cushions of their old smelly communal couch and a bean bag chair that doubled as a laundry hamper.

Then they waited and waited, pestering the owner until he finally blew up in their faces yelling, "I don't have time! We have too many orders! Here's your five-hundred back!" He pulled a wad of Benjamins out of his pocket and fingered five off the roll, then one extra hundred, holding it up with his thumb and forefinger dangling it in Jack's face.

"Go get a 'Websites for Dummies' book and do it yourself! It ain't THAT HARD!"

And they did. Not only did they build a site, they copied the entire gateway business they'd been watching for months. The first year they made thirty-five million! For years they were Adult Check's major competitor.

Jack picked me up in his yellow Ferrari for our first date. His smile made my heart sing. He said, "What restaurant would you like to go to? You choose." Not because he was being polite but because he'd never actually been to a "fancy restaurant" before. I thought he was joking but he wasn't. He'd barely had enough money to go to Denny's before now. He was a hi-fiving, hey dude, kinda laid back guy that had suddenly come into a fortune. Not to get me wrong. He was extremely street smart, just no training in social etiquette.

I took him to a Hollywood hot spot. He was very impressed with the restaurant and adjacent nightclub.

"Do you think this is a good business? This place I mean?"

I did, and so he bought it!

He bought houses for every relative.

The three roommates went from having absolutely nothing to more money than they knew how to spend. They bought a three million dollar "company" yacht. Then he crashed his Ferrari, he wasn't bothered. He said he'd wanted to get a red one anyway!

He was in the business of collecting credit cards and dealing with Visa/ Mastercard but they didn't always play fair.

"Screw them!" he thought, and he bought his own bank and opened his own credit card.

That's what many of the big players in the adult industry did. It was kind of a pattern. They'd first buy a collection of fast cars and a huge house. Then houses for everyone they knew, then yachts and toys, maybe a night club. Then a bank or two, and sometimes a casino. And what about a rap band? Yep quite a few invested in the music industry and bought themselves a rapper.

Jack and I had a great time together. We got along in all ways. I found him incredibly exciting and cool, yet sweet and amazing with my girls. He made one of the best dads ever. We got along fantastic in business and started strategizing together. Pretty soon we were designing programs and setting up web deals and building a business together and life was wonderful. We made great business partners and I was starting to throw in more and more with him until we were building our own web empire together. Jack had the funds and a building full of the hottest tech geeks, I had the content and some pretty stellar contacts and so I started hooking up the deals and we were taking over entire web operations for some pretty major companies.

Life was great, business and pleasure.

Except there was one small bone of contention; his heritage, or more specifically mine. He was Armenian, so even though his family liked me a lot, they would never approve of a marriage. Rather his family kept presenting him with seventeen-year-old, wide hipped, Armenian virgins for betrothal. You see in their tradition, you could have a hot sexy girlfriend on the side, but you had to have a good wife at home making babies. I actually fit both in Jack's eyes, I was the mommy and the sexy chick, but you couldn't have both in one, because your wife kissed your children with that mouth. They had to be separate which you could tell was a major dilemma for him. At first, I was the hot nightclub chick in his eyes and we went out all the time. But then he got to know me and loved how I was as a mom. "Let's stay in tonight babe and do something with the girls." He was happy to do things with my girls and he was so great with them. In fact, months would go by and he wouldn't want to go out, he just wanted to stay home and watch me being "mom." He had this internal dilemma cos he couldn't have the sexy chick be the wonderful mom.

Then he started begging me to have a baby with him, "Honey we'd make such beautiful kids together, please let's have a baby." I loved the idea. But then not to get married because I was not Armenian and his family would never accept that, "but baby, we could have an amazing family and life together," we just couldn't actually be married. I, on the other hand, wouldn't consider having a baby and not being married. We were at a stalemate.

Finally, he had to agree to his family's wishes and a nice Armenian baby machine.

I thought I had found the true love of my live, but it was only a year.

Once again, my heart was ripped open.

And of course, any business together, our online empire was now washed away.

Once again, I was on my own, sad and moping. Once again, I'd built a business with a man that was going to make us millions and it all just went away.

Still, an invite to a fancy webmaster event out of the country somewhere might take my mind off it.

CHAPTER TWENTY-NINE

Panama–Players & Hookers

I WAS BACK to being single again and apparently some of my staff were happily aware of it. I was clueless. I had a rough tough looking caretaker guy who lived on site, who was pretty good at taking care of the ranch doing manly stuff like running the back hoe and lifting heavy shit. I hadn't noticed that he'd taken to cutting down the grass exposing his bare chest, after all it was a hot summer. That is until drunk off his ass he showed up at my front door late one night.

"Look I know you must feel the same way about me. I watch you through the window taking a bubble bath at night and I can't stand it."

OMG, I did not feel the same way and he was doing WHAT!!!

"I can't live without you, if you don't want me, tell me now and I'll end it all tonight," he says down and out depressed swigging on a half empty bottle of cheap tequila.

I talked him off the ledge all night and when he was finally sober in the morning, I had to give him his packing orders.

I placed an ad in the local paper for a live-in ranch hand and a guy Edward shows up for the position. He's brought his friend Daniel along.

I'm walking them around the ranch showing Edward the various jobs.

"Er... we're a er... a couple.... Daniel and I."

"Great!" I said continuing to point things out.

"Daniel's a tech geek, does programming for...." Edward boasts.

"Oh, wow would you be interested in working too, in the office?" I ask Daniel.

"Yeah, great!" Daniel answered.

Daniel whispered off to Edward, "Do you think she understands we're a couple?"

Edward shrugs his shoulders, "She seems pretty cool about it."

Of course they had no idea how thrilled I was!!!

I had a new shit hot tech geek and a caretaker who had no interest in spying through my window.

Edward would become my best bud and sounding board.

And he'd take care of the place when I was out of town.

Even though I wasn't making as much as the real big boys, I was accepted as one of the major players in the industry and this meant invites to those exclusive webmaster retreats in places like Caruso, Panama, the Cayman Islands and the Seychelles. An opportunity for industry leaders to get together, plan and create business opportunities, as well as get totally blasted. I was finally RUNNING WITH THE WOLVES and loving it!

The Panama event was put on by Ivan, who obviously had international banking contacts there and wanted our billing, processing, investments and generally our US DOLLARS. We were treated like kings.

Ivan couldn't go back to North America due to creative billing practices that stretched the guys wallets and was a little in the grey zone. According to the FTC very much in the grey zone! He was continuing to operate the same business but now he would do his part from Panama where he had set up a massive support center.

We were treated to dinners, sightseeing and everything the area had to offer. Different companies would sponsor individual games and events, after which we would get the grand tour of Ivan's call center and the banks that were selling their services to semi-legally hide money.

Adult Bucks web master program was sponsoring the activity of feeding sharks. It was a fun group with a bunch of hyped up, drunken, half-drugged-out webmasters scuba diving in a shark filled water park. We were warned, "Keep your fingers out of the way because if you stick your finger in, the shark will take it off." It was awesome and as soon as we brought out our bait fish, a circle of massive sharks would come by. Then you would stick the fish out very carefully through a hole in the thin plexiglass and these massive monsters would come by, their mouths like vacuums, taking the fish right out of your hand in one quick sucking heartbeat.

This one particular drunken webmaster thought it would be funny to see what would happen if you stuck your finger out. He came out of the water, holding his hand high with blood squirting out everywhere, screaming, "My fucking finger!!!"

He spent the rest of the night in the hospital but was back with a hangover at breakfast with a half-reattached finger and quite a story to tell.

Then on to off-road ATVs sponsored by Maximum Cash. Once again, you had a bunch of hyped up webmasters racing ATVs across rough terrain. Remember these were not your usual athletic jocks, rather mostly "tech geeks" totally drunk off their asses, riding full speed going over bumps, rocks and trees. Several of them rolled their ATVs and a couple more ended up in the hospital.

It was a lot of macho guy stuff and a whole load of fun.

Then it was the tour of Ivan's call center. The idea was to get us interested in using his services, his billing and everything he had set up in Panama. He was a big hero there with the locals, employing tons of Panamanians and paying them equivalent of ten dollars an hour, when they were used to getting ten dollars a week. Anyone who could speak English was enlisted for the call center. He even had a whole free school teaching English to locals, getting them trained up as future operators. Plus, day care and The Full Monty, whatever they needed to get his staff working the phones. Everyone got a job and loved this guy.

Banks of locals were answering phone calls coming from the US and around the world. A line of young girls answering phone sex lines twenty-four hours a day. But they were also doing customer service lines, ticket booking lines, travel agency lines, you name it. They had computer screens in front of them telling them what they were supposed to be talking about. One girl was doing customer service for some kind for a mechanical parts business. Then she hung up and answered again this time in her sexy coy tone clearly talking phone sex. At the end of tour as we came back through the same girl was reading someone's Tarot cards. Ivan said, "This Tarot shit makes tons of money. And they keep calling back asking for the same girls, like, 'Oh my God, Lulu read my future and was totally accurate," he laughed and said these were just local girls who made this stuff up. I replied, "You just never know, maybe they are actually on to something."

Later that evening we are at a very exclusive club in Panama, where some other company sponsored a ridiculously priced, dressed to impress dinner that included Russian caviar and delicious temptations worthy of presidents, popes and kings.

Afterwards, we were guided to sit in an upscale bar lounge private to our group. One would have thought we were in some country club on the East Coast; a décor of overly lush leather couches with a warm inviting open fire. The only unusual amenity was a chorus line of about a dozen of the world's most stunning girls, each more beautiful than the last, came out from behind the bar to join us. Each made a direct line to one guy and asked what we would like to drink. *Wow this is very personal waitress service,* I thought. They were all dressed in very sophisticated evening attire, fitting to the setting. They mingled chatting and fairly aggressively "getting to know" each person. I was one of only two ladies from our group, the rest of about ten or so, were all men, but the young ladies made a point to equally mingle with us as well.

It was clear that for an additional sum, I figured probably a few thousand, they were quite happy to go home with you. In this group, a few thousand was like a cup of coffee, and the girls were working it!

I was quite impressed at how quickly each girl found their match. Our group started to leave pretty quickly, two by two, in taxis. I had planned to go back in a taxi with John who was a website owner I knew very well. Just as we are about to get in the cab, a leggy blonde gets in with us.

"Did you get one, John?" I whispered to him.

"Yeah, of course," he answered grinning cheekily.

John is on his phone most of the ride back to the hotel and I chat with the girl a bit. I'm shocked that a girl this drop dead gorgeous would actually be hooking. She had natural platinum blonde shoulder length hair, piercing sky blue eyes, eye lashes to die for and a body to kill for. She looked Nordic, but it turns out she was Czech and spoke perfect English with a slight sexy exotic Eastern European accent. I told her that she was stunningly beautiful.

"You're stunning yourself!" she remarks.

As we arrive back to the hotel, I have some things to get from John's room, so I plan to walk them back, get my things and then leave them to whatever they have planned for the evening! We're back in John's suite and he's about to get me something I need off his laptop when his phone rings again. John is engrossed in conversation and the hooker and I are left sitting on the bed making small talk. I figured I'd be polite and have a bit of a chin wag with her until John got off the phone and I could get my stuff and leave.

I started with; "I must ask you. You are so beautiful. Why would you do this kind of work?" I said, asking the question I had been dying to know all night.

"Cos, I am lazy," she replied in a very matter of fact way.

"What do you mean?" I continued.

"I don't want to actually work. I'm lazy," she replied.

I was quite taken by how she made no bones about it. There was no poor little girl with a terrible upbringing being forced into this. She wanted to do it! She loved it.

"I like handbags, I like shoes," she continues. I had noticed her three thousand-dollar Hermès bag, and her equally expensive strappy heels. "I go out a couple of nights here and there, when I feel like it, going to clubs and parties and being around men, who I do really love, and I make ten grand a week. What other kind of job could you make that? Plus," she tossed a strand of platinum hair out of one perfect blue eye, "I like sex." She smiled and laughed to herself, "And men pay me to let them pleasure me."

This twenty-four-year-old bombshell was a seasoned woman of the world. We both looked over at John who was still on his call, talking in the corner, crouched over his phone, waiving his free hand in the air.

She looked at me again, up and down with those limpid crystal blue eyes, like azure glaciers, licking her frosted lips and there was a moment of awkward silence. Then she says, "I'm being paid to have sex," she tilts her head and nuzzles towards me. "He looks pretty busy; do you want me to go down on you?"

I'm partially shocked but a rush of adrenaline runs through me at this stunning woman wanting me, and the word just leaves my mouth:

"Sure."

She was sitting next to me, but in one lithe, fluid motion, she slid off the bed and got down on her knees in front of me. Like a cat opening a door, she pushed her head between my knees. She put one hand up my dress and under my butt and started squeezing with a soft but firm pulse, like a heartbeat. With her free hand she gently pushed me down onto the bed and lifted my dress carefully to expose me from my naked breasts down. There was no kissing or foreplay. She looked up at me once and smiled, then dove into the triangle between my legs.

I had a second thought and my hands reached down to her glowing blonde hair to try and stop her, as my legs squeezed her temples. She moved my panties to one side with her tongue.

"UHHHHHHNNNNNNNN!"

I let out a loud, involuntary moan of sheer ecstasy as my hands snapped back up to my mouth and my back arched. I pushed my mons pubis deeper into her worshipful ministrations. She just very gently and sweetly started softly sucking on me. I remember thinking, *God this woman's a fucking expert! Never felt*..."UNNNNHHHHNNN."

She pulled back, put my legs together in the air, and in one fell swoop, did away with my panties all together, tossed them at John, where they landed on his head. Without even turning around he pulled them off and tossed them on a chair.   As I released myself to the extreme divine pleasure this earthly goddess was capable of inflicting, it was like she could feel my energy, she could feel all my bodily cues. Soft, firm, hard, cruel… then backing off just as each threshold was reached.

I'm moaning and groaning in total release and she is riding the waves with me, pushing closer and stronger as she feels my body speeding up to grand finale.´

At this point John looks up and sees I've stolen his hooker. It's enough for him to finally decide his phone call is not that important after all and he quickly finishes up. Truth be told, John would have probably done anything to get me in bed, and he was incredibly sexy, but I hadn't wanted to ruin any business we were doing. Yet here his fantasy is unfolding in duplicate before him. He seizes the moment and my inability to care about anything while at the mercy of this sex queen, John jumps on the bed ripping open his shirt to join the steamy action, already in full swing. John kisses me wildly while the other girl pulls down his pants and exposes his massive throbbing cock. *Oh my God, John has an amazing body!* I thought.

I wanted it. For a night I decided to throw caution to the wind.

CHAPTER THIRTY

An Insane Valuation

IT'S THE BEGINNING of a new millennium, and with it, the year two thousand brought in an exciting Internet era. Mainstream websites were now being formed and the adult sites are coming to me in droves to license images. Even if they had already licensed images from me for their magazine, this only gave them the rights to print the photos one time. So, if they wanted to use the images on a website, they needed to pay me an additional fee to use them on the web.

One of the first people to use my company's photos on the web was someone that didn't want to pay for them. He had purchased rights from me for his mail order catalog, but I insisted this didn't give him any rights to open up a completely unrelated adult site charging a fee to view my images. Even when caught outright, red-handed, up to his elbow in the cookie jar, and rightfully and righteously caught, he still wouldn't pay.

This brought me to file the first ever Federal Internet copyright infringement lawsuit. I filed in Florida where the company was based. There weren't any Internet laws on copyright at the time. But now it was time to set some cold hard precedents on what exactly Internet rights consisted of.

My steadfast Los Angeles attorney Greg wished me luck but told me at the very best I might get a pittance of just a few thousand dollars which would not even be worth my trouble or time. It certainly wasn't worth his and he found me local representation in Florida.

But on the plane ride cross-country I started to fantasize about how one would argue the value of any image in this new arena. There was a copyright law for print use that stated an award for damages in the amount of one hundred and fifty thousand dollars per infringement. But how could that play out in an area of the law where there were no rules yet? I scribbled down some figures.

The next morning, I arrived at the court steps in my tight little perfectly pressed suit and patent heels, where I met with my local counsel for the first time and explained the case. I outlined the new argument I had come up with on my way over. He wasn't totally up to speed, but he had the law degree so together we'd wing it.

The federal judge was a testy old New Yorker down for the season in Florida. He probably should have retired twenty years ago and at the ripe old age of I'm guessing about ninety, I worried he might not be on the cutting edge of the technology wave.

Still there was plenty of life in that old cat, who took an immediate dislike to the defendant and an equal dislike to my local attorney.

This is Federal Court and it appeared way more serious and strict than I had seen before and the Judge has little patience for any waffling.

"Counsel you are not making any sense!" the judge snapped at my attorney, scrunching up his face in displeasure.

Then his demeanor completely did a one-eighty as he turns to me, "I'd like to hear what Ms. Thackray has to say." He smiles invitingly for me to explain all this in my own words. He is patiently listening as I use this opportunity to rattle off what I had come up with on the plane.

"Well, your Honor, we are really pioneers here, in this whole new world, an undiscovered country that has not yet been explored. We've seen in the press just last week that an Internet company called AOL has bought out the mogul of all broadcasting companies, Time Warner."

I am a little nervous to start but as I launch into my mental notes I am genuinely excited about the future of the Internet.

The judge let me ramble on.

"If the Internet becomes as widely adapted as many experts believe, the future value of an image on the Internet could be astronomical…"

The judge seemed captivated and mesmerized by my spunk and sheer gall.

"These handful of photos could in this new medium be downloaded thousands of times. Each download, of each image, could constitute, under the current precedent for print infringements, an award of one hundred and fifty thousand dollars in damages, per image, for copyright infringement," I continued.

I finished with a big breath and waited for the reaction.

The judge smiled at me impressed, "I agree we don't know where the Internet will go, but it could very well revolutionize the world. Very well argued, thank you."

After a short break the Judge came back with a decision. Looking directly at me, he said, "I have taken your testimony into consideration and I am going to agree with you," he said with a serious but warm tone, "We need to consider that the Internet is fast becoming a very serious medium and, in the future, could well overshadow more traditional forms."

He is still very directly addressing me.

"Now I'm going to give you the full one point eight million. However… I am going to reduce the number of images."

I wanted to smile from ear to ear back to him, but held back in this more serious setting.

Wow is he really awarding me one point eight million dollars for a handful of images!!! I thought, *And did he realize that by reducing the number of images, the per image amount is actually even more! He is awarding me even more than I asked!!!*

"Thank you, Your Honor!" I said trying to contain my massive grin.

And that set the law for copyright infringement on the Internet!!!

These mail-order people had very few assets, and I knew I would probably never collect and honestly didn't even bother. Still, I had exactly what I wanted, a piece of paper putting a dollar value on each of my images. A massive dollar value!!!

I returned back to LA to tell my attorney Greg the amazing news, "You'll never guess what the judge awarded me," I said excitedly.

"What, you didn't actually get close to the seventy thousand you were going to ask for, did you?"

"No! Actually, I changed my mind on the plane and decided to ask for one point eight million. And guess what? He agreed and that's what he awarded me!!!"

"What?!!! That's incredible!!!" Greg said in amazement. "Do you realize what we can do now with that judgement? That means we have precedence for copyright infringement on the Internet!!!"

He thought for a second, the dollar signs moving across his eye lids.

"Do you realize that for anyone using your images without a license, this is a slam dunk!"

Now there was two ways to do business, those that licensed images and paid me, and those that stole images, who were served with a demand for one hundred and fifty thousand dollars, per image, and then they paid me.

There was a new sheriff in town and my business model changed overnight from selling images to hoping people would steal them!

The Silicon Valley dot com boom was just starting and venture capital, IPOs and the value of every web based company was hot news.

With all the press about my lawsuit that rocked the Internet world, a legitimate analytical data company, Forester Research, became interested in looking into our operations. Their head analyst flew down to evaluate my company.

They spent a few days at my office going through files, pouring over spread sheets and typing notes. Then based on the number of images, the projected use and the new legal precedent, Forester Research placed a value on my company of

FIFTY MILLION DOLLARS!!!

And they happened to mention this all over mainstream press!

Walt Disney used to say, "Never forget. It all started with a mouse."

For me, it all started in a trashcan!

CHAPTER THIRTY-ONE

Costa Rica Casino Money

ONE OF THE Internet inner circle of players was a friend of mine, Natan. He owned a dating website that was taking off huge. He'd started a bunch of adult sites where he made a ton of dough, but this one was dwarfed the others by comparison and was now his flagship mainstream dating site. Like many guys starting out, his partner Darrel had come to me ages before and made a deal. Instead of paying to license images from me, I'd provide the images, in return for a third ownership of their site. Their site, had in this case been rolled into the dating site, and I technically owned a third of it.

Natan and I had become friends. He was cute, extremely smart, and there was for sure an attraction between us. He did me a huge favor and introduced me to two major execs at Yahoo, Anthony and Josh, the heads of advertising, so as a result I thought it only fair I didn't hold him over a barrel on the contract I had.

Natan and I arranged to have a business dinner while I was in New York, and I'm sitting at the restaurant waiting for him, when a rather hot, unknown, young guy arrives and introduces himself.

"Hi, you must be Gail, I'm Mark. Sorry, Natan couldn't make it, so he asked if I'd take care of you for the evening. Take you to dinner and show you around."

"Err…. Ok," I said, eyeing this young stud, muscular abs only slightly concealed by his ever so handsome New Yorker Armani business attire.

I thought it was a little strange and felt a little hurt that he obviously wasn't as interested as I thought but standing in front of me is a drop-dead gorgeous young Paul Newman look-alike, shit hot and driving a Ferrari!

"Boy, he said you were beautiful, but you're really, really hot!" Mark said looking me over.

Mark is on a call with Natan and he hands over the phone. Natan apologizes profusely, "So sorry I got tied up, really couldn't get out of it but Mark will take care of you."

I was a little thrown at the replacement, but decided might as well have a nice dinner and he was certainly attractive company.

Mark was twenty-eight. A little young for me, but fun and hot as all hell. Dinner ran into drinks, then a club and more drinks and by this time we were getting very well acquainted. And as the night went on, as promised, he took great care of me! After a wild night out on the town, we finally ended up back at his apartment in central Manhattan full on making out. Didn't go all the way, cos I wasn't that type of girl, but I was pretty wound up I must say, and I was a split hair away.

He had a beautiful apartment that overlooked Central Park, thought it strange for someone so young.

Thought it even more strange when I went to the bathroom and as I'm sitting on the toilet, I'm staring through the shower curtains into the bathtub where there is a file box, overflowing with money. I mean wads of US DOLLARS; TWENTIES, FIFTIES, AND ONE HUNDRED DOLLAR BILLS. Some with bits of duct tape hanging off them. I thought, *Wow, that's crazy!* But I figured I better not ask anything and admit to snooping.

I asked what he did.

"I have a few companies; a travel agency, a parts company, some other things…" and finally, I managed to get out of him that he and his brother owned casinos in Costa Rica.

We had an awesome time. As he dropped me off at my hotel, he promised to visit me in LA "really soon." Honestly, I thought I'd never see him again, and would have been a bit disappointed. But the next day he called and asked if it was ok if he booked a flight to LA at the weekend.

Sure enough, three days later, I was picking him up at LAX, my heart excited like a teenager. He'd booked us into the Four Seasons for a few days and was planning to pamper me like crazy. Wow, this young kid has class.

We arrive at our five-star hotel room and we barely get through the door and we're ripping each other's clothes off. He picks me up in his huge muscular arms and I wrap my thighs around his waist as he carries me directly to the bed.

"God, I've missed you, I'm so crazy about you!" he declares, kissing me passionately pushing his jeans with a huge hard cock against my crotch.

This guy has a body to die for, like the Abercrombie & Fitch models; smooth, lean, tanned, muscles.... I'd held off for three days, I couldn't hold out any longer!

He rips off my remaining panties and goes to kiss me all over.

We barely came up for air that weekend and don't think we ever left the room. He was cut, sexy and had stamina like a Kenyan runner. And so, started a hot wild love affair. Passion-filled trips back and forth, New York–LA every week. Luckily, one of his companies was a travel agency and so there was no end to first class tickets.

Natan was apparently quite upset and sent Mark an email that read; "What the fuck?!!! I told you to take her out to dinner. I didn't know you were going to start dating her!"

But I was really falling for Mark and he was making regular trips to see me.

My gay friend Edward was not complaining about the presence of some hot shit boyfriend around the ranch. "Gail this is a hot one, be careful, but go for it!"

Mark seems to have a fantastic business with the Casino in Costa Rica and we are talking about creating an online casino together.

"Look, I'd love to do a casino on the web, but I've heard it's very sketchy on whether online gaming is legal yet," I say.

"Oh, it is! There are tons of people doing it. You just have to bill offshore. You'll figure it out babe."

I tell him what I know so far, "I've been looking into this for a while. It's just the laws are not clear yet. It seems you can do Sports Book gaming or games of skill but straight out slot machine type gambling online which is where all the money is, seems to be very much in a grey area and anyone doing transactions that are US based could get into serious trouble with the FBI," I explain.

"Can't we run it all offshore? We have banks in Costa Rica we can run it through," Mark suggests.

"We can't bill US customers is the main problem and that's of course the bulk of the money!" I said but I'm seriously digging into this, determined to figure it out and contacting everyone I know doing it or trying to do it. A week or so later I think I might have a solution, "Mark, it seems there are ways around it. We can create a club with tokens. Honestly Mark there is so much money in this it's way bigger than adult, I gotta figure this out."

Things were going great with Mark, or so I thought. He's back in LA again and we're in some super nice hotel, when I'm in the bathroom and I notice there's a leather badge of some kind on the counter top. I open it to discover it's a full-on sheriff's ID badge. It had his photo, his name, his badge ID *Oh my God who is he? What is going on?* My heart suddenly drops. *Was this love affair all some kind of farce? Is this online casino business a trap?* I also notice a date of birth that clearly makes him twenty-six, not twenty-eight!

I stormed back into the bedroom, "What the fuck! Are you tracking me! Are you a fucking undercover cop?!" My mind is spinning wondering what I've mentioned about the casino business, off-shore accounts, webmaster programs anything that might not be one hundred percent kosher, sharing merchant accounts…

"No, don't be crazy! It's just a fake thing we have in New York. You donate a hundred-grand to some cop-widow foundation thing and you become like a cop friend. You get a badge. It's not a real badge but I can park my car anywhere and not get tickets. Everyone who gets a Ferrari, gets one."

I'm greatly relieved but not quite done, "Well…Okay. But also, this birthdate makes you twenty-six, not twenty-eight!"

"Err… well…. Come on babe, I didn't want you to think I was too young for you, Okay, I'm twenty-six. But I'm a mature twenty-six!"

I'm not happy but satisfied and glad I don't need to dump him.

"Come here babe and kiss me…" he begs sweetly.

I am once again caught up in the bliss of being in lust.

A little while later I'm off to Europe for some very important business meetings. Mark offers to get me the flights, "Call my office at the travel agency. Here's the number. Barbara will book you First Class everywhere."

"Wow, thanks babe."

A few days later I talked to Barbara who comped me first class, strangely she didn't know her boss by the name Mark, she mentioned a different name.

"Yeah, they just use my Jewish name that's all," he later explained. Okay that made sense.

On my return from Europe I thanked him for the flights.

He replies flippantly, "Oh great, glad they worked!"

"What do you mean, 'glad they worked?' Are you telling me these were not real tickets?!!!"

"Well they worked, didn't they?"

"Oh my God, I've just travelled all over Europe to some very important business meetings, on some kind of phony First Class tickets!!!"

I'm a little taken aback that his travel agency doesn't seem to be all on the up and up, but after some coaxing, I write it off as these promo tickets he explained he gets occasionally.

Still, I am getting slightly suspicious and when I happen to notice his driver's license hanging out of his wallet at the bedside, I decide to check it. OMG, it was clearly his ID with his headshot, but it had yet another name! And it showed his age was twenty-four. Now I'm pissed.

"Look, what's your real name? Why do you have different names?"

Of course, he had an explanation about a middle name and a given name and ….

"You're lying to me. What's going on here? And you told me you were twenty-eight, then twenty-six, but you're really only twenty-four!"

He confessed that yes, he was only twenty-four, but swore that this was his full legal name. Still I wanted more, I needed answers to who he really was.

Finally, he comes clean. Turns out he's taking private planes down to Costa Rica every week or so, with different friends, partying and having fun, but each coming back with shit loads of cash duct-taped to their bodies.

"Look babe, it's just a way of moving the cash. It's legit money but we just have to get some of it moved out. I mean, I suppose we'd have a problem if they ever searched us but they're not going to do that, not on a private plane," he explains.

"Come with me this week. You'll love the casino, it's right on the beach, prime spot and absolutely stunning. You'll have an amazing time. We can stay in one of our houses in the jungle. You've never seen anything like it! Plus, I really want you to sit down with my brother and figure out how we can do this online Casino."

I'm very tempted to get into a business that is obviously an inane money maker, but this is not adding up, and I'm thinking something's not legal here. I mean my industry is a little in the grey zone, but anything that has a real threat of jail time I'm not about to do.

Next, Mark asks if we can just run a few Mil of "clean transactions" though my merchant accounts.

Okay, now it has all become too much and this is not something I am willing to do. I'm getting really worried wondering who he really is and I'm not about to put my entire business on the line.

Then all shit breaks loose. Mark has to make an emergency flight to Costa Rica, and their whole operation is on the run within hours. Millions-of-dollars-worth of properties left abandoned, while they are running from the FBI. And something about some local gangsters who turned them in to take their properties. Through crackling throw-away cell phones, I'm getting, I know, only half a story.

"Babe, I've got this frigging awesome deal we're going to make shit loads of money with. I'm going to book you on a flight down to Panama tomorrow. I'll meet you there the next day…"

I'm really head over heels on Mark and he's crazy fun and crazy sexy, but crazy dangerous. I have enough crazy in my life, do I really need a crazy guy too?

Finally, I decide I'm going to have to give up this wonderful romance no matter how hard it is, it's not worth risking everything.

But before I have the chance to fully end this chapter, back home the shit suddenly hits my own fan…

CHAPTER THIRTY-TWO

A Very Big
Banking "Error"

I'D MADE SO many webmasters rich, helping them start a website and advising them on what content would and would not fly, setting them up with everything they needed from billing to live girls, and giving them an instant-get-rich education. But, finally, I was going to make my own huge splash.

Like the Beatles said, it'd been a "Long and Winding Road" to get my own sites up and running. I had helped so many little start-ups, why couldn't I get my own launched? Probably because I'd wanted the biggest and the best and had grand ideas of massive sites with state of the art programming with multiple spiraling tunnels of revenue capture. Yes, I had some little ordinary sites, but now I was going to launch the real deal!

My first attempt at these awe-inspiring sites was back in like ninety-four believe it or not, when my first husband decided he was the computer-knowledgeable one in the house and would liaise with the website designers I'd hired… yeah that was the kiss of death. Then I almost had them right there with Gary's expert team, but just as they were about to be completed, they were thwarted. Remember, my boyfriend, who was developing them, was raided by the FBI. His boss was arrested and all his assets frozen and everything went in the tanker. I mean, luckily, I hadn't been any part of that but all the hard drives with all the work was all gone.

I had rebuilt sites with tech companies I thought would create the most amazing back end that ended up simply not working. It went on and on, until I had finally removed myself from all connections with all my old boyfriends and took the reins myself.

Anyway, it had taken way longer than I had thought, but I finally had the sites I'd dreamed of; that showed off my massive content, had all the bells and whistles and smoking hot technology. All set to conquer and capture the minds, bodies and wallets of men's libidos around the globe.

We hooked up the processing bank and that night we flicked the on switch. We waited in anticipation to see if subscriptions would roll in.

I was about to be the QUEEN OF THE WORLD!

The next day my office staff show up to a barrage of phone calls. As I walked in, my girls were in a flustered panic. I was greeted with:

"Oh my God, Gail, the calls are crazy!"

Oh my God! I thought, *My sites have hit HUGE!!!* This was way bigger than I had ever hoped. I would be the first person in history to officially BREAK THE INTERNET!

I had three girls answering the calls and they couldn't get to the end of them. Thousands, literally thousands of people were trying to call. It was like a radio station announced a million dollars to the first twenty callers, the phones were beyond jammed. What was happening? Had our sites really hit that big? I was bursting with excitement.

But the callers seemed to be all complaints. Now, one would expect a small number of chargebacks, so that was no big deal, but if this was the small amount of complaints then my sites had gone HUGE.

Strange though, callers were saying we had billed their credit cards odd amounts that wasn't even our price, but on their statements, in black and white, pointed the finger at me. "Falcon Foto" had done this. It said so on their statement.

They'd never heard of Falcon Foto and were clearly very upset that I had taken $59.95, five times, out of their credit card this morning!

More importantly, the bigger question was, did I have millions of dollars in my bank account?!!! I was crazy with excitement.

Then I checked our account. It appeared that a small amount of money had been deposited from our sites, maybe two or three thousand dollars but the bank had already sucked it out immediately to cover the hundred thousand we had in chargeback complaints so far. What the what? Clearly this was just not possible. How could I have made two thousand in sales and have so many people claiming they wanted their money back that I owed one-hundred thousand in returns? I had more refunds than the actual sales!!!

Had the bank made some huge mix-up? Were my sites confused with someone else's? Something had gone majorly wrong. But even if something had been mixed up, where was all the money? On its way to me? I wasn't sure at first if I should make a big fuss or just keep quiet. Perhaps I had millions of dollars en route to me and if I kept quiet maybe nobody would notice, and I could just slink off with it into the sunset.

A bit more digging and unfortunately it seemed the money, had, indeed, quite magically disappeared into thin air. Abracadabra! My heart sank, my bubble was burst. If the money wasn't coming to me, why was I getting all the complaints? That would mean I was the victim of the biggest frame job in the very brief history of the web. So where did the money go?

At this point we couldn't do any business at all. It was all hands-on deck battening down the hatches and trimming the jib sails as we tried to figure out what these callers were talking about. Asking the callers if they ever visited adult sites, didn't always give us the answer as many wives were calling in, who handled their family banking and they appeared to be clueless that their husband had as much as peeked at a porn site.

I called Greg, my attorney.

Now, my office has been turned into an emergency call center and my company's name had gone from hot shit on a silver platter to cold crap on a paper plate. You could find my name online under "complete scammers" and "this site charged my credit card blah-blah de *blaaaaaaah!*" My dream of finally launching the most brilliant sites on Earth had just been squelched. No customer would want anything to do with us after this! My Five Star Solid Gold company, just valued at fifty million, was now dirt.

Within a day, boxes of mail arrived. Complaints! Literally boxes that filled the entire postal truck. Back in those days, a hard copy retrieval notice came in the mail.

Looking through these notices, I recognized the name of a processing company, owned by my friend Chris. He couldn't believe his eyes. Thousands of these transactions, had gone through his company. We all came to the same conclusion. Either this was a seriously massive mix-up, or this was ingenious billing tampering on a massive scale.

Switching of bank codes would have to be done at a very high-level bank with an international scope and grasp—who could have done this? This was Joker teams with the Riddler super villain kind of stuff. I didn't need a lawyer, I needed Batman.

Don't get me wrong, I admired the ingenuity and dazzling brilliance of what appeared to be the perfect crime. A brilliant scheme. Just upset I wasn't in on it.

My attorney took immediate action and filed against the one main bank for ruining our reputation.

It was then that this bank admitted that it was "their fault" and there had been a "banking error." You see, by mistake, their bank had placed my company name and phone number on all billings that came through. Supposedly, the computer stuck at our name and placed our name on every transaction. Thousands of them.

Also, my office phone number was on the statements not my eight hundred customer service line — "Oh that must have been another banking error."

And sometimes my company name was spelled correctly and sometimes misspelled, as if it had been hand entered "Oh that was another banking error." The bank declared.

Then some people were billed three or five times instead of once, and, again "That was another banking error."

What were the odds that the computer had made this many multiple banking errors randomly at the same time? And that these multiple banking errors would cause tens of millions of dollars to disappear...into thin air? In a magic trick that would have made Doug Henning and David Copperfield beam with pride?

My banking friend guesstimated approximately five-hundred thousand people were being billed collectively sixty-million a month. It was absolutely massive. I was getting the mess from all of this, but where was the money going?

Even though the bank declared it was an error they didn't run to immediately fix it, as one would presume. Visa/Mastercard was informed, every bank in the loop was informed, but no one ran to fix it, nor slowly crawled to fix it. They just blew me off and placated me saying they were working on it, while the massive flood of Niagara Falls continued. This mess went on for months and shut down my entire operation. The "error" continued on.

Why wouldn't Visa/Mastercard step in and shut it off. Well you have to understand, every time a person makes a charge-back, Visa/Mastercard charges an additional fee. And if that merchant goes over his chargeback limit, Visa/Mastercard charges an overage fee, dreaded throughout the industry as that fee can be millions of dollars! Visa/Mastercard were actually making more money on this "error" than anyone!!!

Meanwhile at my office the picture was becoming clearer that there was a huge "mix-up."

Why had my name been attached to this whole event? Had that part, been an error or had someone purposely tied all four of my arms and legs to the horses and yelled, "YAAA!"

My attorney advised me to only have discussions in person, for "safety reasons."

Are you fucking serious?!!!

He was.

"Call me from a phone booth somewhere," he insisted.

"Make three copies of all the paperwork, bank retrievals, anything being delivered to the office, the faxes, all the notes the operators have, everything!!!"

"What, all of them? It's like twenty storage boxes so far and it's coming daily!"

"Yes, and send one copy to my office in a car that's not yours and then two to storage places. Be very careful who knows where the storage places are. Don't tell anyone on the phone, don't get followed. Pay by cash...."

"I'm going to inform the banks that you have made three copies just in case someone wants to knock you off, they'll know there are other copies of the evidence."

KNOCK ME…..??

Holy Shit! Is he for real?

By now the FBI had caught wind of something and showed up at my office demanding answers. It appeared like I was pulling in millions of dollars and ripping off complaining customers in the tune of hundreds of thousands. Scared shitless, I explained we had already contacted the bank and they explained it was a banking error. The agent wanted to see any paperwork. I called my attorney and was told, "Just send them down to us and we'll deal with them." My attorney made it perfectly clear, the bank had admitted error and I was innocent in all of this.

My team of temps were handling the phone lines, trying to clear my name and pointing the customers to the actual site they had really paid for. The big site owners around town were eternally grateful.

Then something strange started to happen. All the phone calls to my office were suddenly being diverted. In other words, the phone would ring once, there would be a strange click and the phone would go back to a dial tone. Immediately another call would ring once and again click and back to dial tone. The lines were an ongoing one ring, click, one ring, click. Someone was now hijacking all calls to my office and diverting them elsewhere.

But where? And why? Who could do this?

My local phone company came out to see if I had problems on my lines and if I had any taps on my phones. After working for a few hours, the technician was a bit flustered.

"Anything?" I asked.

"Err... yeah. Yes…. a lot. You have taps on all your office lines and all your house lines are tapped as well. But don't ask, cuz I'm not allowed to tell you. I'm not allowed to even tell you what I just did."

"Why? Are these government agencies like the FBI? Or some private person that tapped me? Can you tell?"

"Oh yeah! They're different, I can tell. Both. Yes, all of it. Or none of it. I don't know. I'm not allowed to say. They're all off now."

Still the call switching continued.

There were a couple of plain black Mercedes with smoky windows seen passing my gate, over and over, in an area where there is very little traffic at all and certainly not a high-grade sedan like these. Perhaps I was being paranoid. My attorney was even more paranoid.

Shortly after, we went to the deposition with the bank who had the "error." My one attorney and I on the one hand; a row of attorneys against us. "I represent processing company x", "I represent bank x" "I represent bank y", "I represent bank z" "I represent ...." .... And on it went. We'd only sued one bank but clearly every bank in the chain was concerned. This was way bigger than we thought. I was terrified.

My attorney was taken into a back room for a private discussion with the other attorneys. When he came out he looked ashen and completely terrified as he took me to the side.

"You need to settle this, and I mean right now, or we are both going to get killed, and, Gail, believe me when I tell you we are not speaking figuratively," he said, white as a ghost and visibly shaking.

They were offering a pittance. "This is not fair, this is ridiculous. I'm not settling for that."

I wasn't sure whether my attorney was angry at my response, distraught or scared shitless, probably all three.

"I am going to New York to sell some photos. I am going to need some time to think about this," I said firmly. "I need to sleep on it."

"SLEEP ON IT!" he yelled, the last bolt in is wagon coming unscrewed. "Well, while you sleep on it we might just BOTH wake up DEAD!"

———◦◦◦———

A few days later I was in New York when my attorney called.

"Grab a *New York Times*."

I stood staring at the front-page headline in shock which read:

A famous New York mob family had been caught in the largest money-making scheme in history. The headline said they were making sixty million a month. The article described how they had made multiple millions in the audiotext, phone sex industry. And there on the front page was Micky!!!

I couldn't believe it. Micky, one of my phone sex guys from New York!!! He was taking the rap for the whole thing and twelve years!!! It said he had been the largest money earner ever for the mob family and had made it in the phone sex business. My life passed before my eyes. All those ads I had created. Running around Europe setting up phone lines… really? Had those all been for mob?! I had never ever suspected this and was completely clueless, and there I sit staring at the newspaper reading for the first time, who he was. I know I was English and I know I was young, but these guys looked totally normal! They had offices in a high rent district, running what looked like normal companies with a ton of employees, who were just as clueless. But what about those "investors" I'd met?

I felt dizzy vertigo.

Thank God, the only business I had ever done with them was through the ad agency and was always straight up business. Yes, they had made a ton of money, but it was all on the up and up. Luckily I never had any kind of partnership or revenue share.

And that had been many years earlier.

After we had parted ways, years later I knew Micky had gone on to build a massive website company. I'd seen him at several web events and we were always very friendly, just never discussed the old phone sex biz. But their sites were legitimate legal sites, so were they also running credit cards like the article said? This I had no knowledge of.

And this "banking error," that had just happened to me—was this the money the newspaper was talking about or was this a total coincidence?

And even if this was them, was my name really "stuck" that day by a computer glitch at the bank or had my company been specifically chosen, because this was pay back? All these years later? Because now they weren't my *"Friends"*? Thankfully, I'll never know.

CHAPTER THIRTY-THREE
Time to Sell

IT TOOK A while for my company to recover with customer complaints still hogging the phone lines for months after. Thank God the FBI never suspected us as part of the multimillion dollar shenanigans, but still, this "banking error," had ruined our name with consumers. Even though our sites had nothing to do with it, we had to shut them down for a while until things blew over and then redo them all with a different look. Meanwhile our core business of licensing images to other companies was still going strong.

The new millennium had just begun, and the Internet had gone crazy. New sites were popping up daily, all needing to license images. Then there were those that just stole them. This is where my attorney Greg came in.

Remember, I had a piece of paper from a federal judge that said we were to be awarded one-hundred-and-fifty-thousand-dollars per pirated image. This was a clear path to sue anyone that used our images without payment. The penalty for not paying a fifty-dollar licensing fee led to a one-hundred-and-fifty-thousand-dollar charge per infringement. This of course switched my business model from selling pictures to enforcing copyrights.

We set up a complicated system of matching and pulling photos from the web. If someone had our photo on their site, our computer geeks would find it, pull it, match it, and check if that the website owner had an official license agreement. If no agreement was found, websites were noted and the pictures documented and that was our ticket to collect. We had hit the jackpot! Our potential income looked outstanding.

Forester Research had quoted in the newspaper that the value of Falcon Foto was worth fifty-million-dollars. *Really? I'd be happy if someone gave me thirty million!*

The dot com was starting to boom, and these new dot com companies were being sold for millions on an idea and potential. I had that, but I had something else that most other companies couldn't offer, and everyone wanted: a hard asset—*the library*. Now was definitely the right time to sell.

I hired a wealth management company that specialized in selling high-net-worth companies. The firm had an appraisal completed on the library and created an impressive perspective for Falcon Foto. We placed the company's selling price at the bargain price of thirty million dollars.

Within a week of Falcon Foto going on the market, we had a public company from Spain show interest. When the company contacted our sales representative they said, "If Gail would consider ten million for the company have her fly to Spain on Monday." I was on the next plane. It was a great match. They were offering part cash, part stock; not a bad deal. It would appear to be a match made in heaven. As we were finalizing the terms and I was basking in my excitement of this arrangement my banker called and said, "Get your ass back on the next flight." Playboy had called and was willing to pay the entire THIRTY MIL!

So, I did.

Playboy wanted to acquire my library. The due diligence was intense because the Playboy organization was huge and there were so many layers to the review.

Larry Lux was the president of Playboy.com. He hadn't been there long, but then the entire Playboy.com Internet presence had only recently been formed. Larry was impressed with my business prospective that would enable Playboy to expand to all areas of the adult web, as well as the opportunity to acquire my physical library, which together with theirs would enable them to control almost all the sexy pictures on the web. Not just the Playboy style photography but all styles, tastes and niches. Obviously, they would want me to stay on for some period of time to see this through. I would have been quite happy to take the cash and walk away but they wanted two years of me.

It was agreed. I would start working with Larry Lux while they did all their reviewing. Hopefully this due-diligence would only take a couple of months and then I would get a big paycheck for Thirty Mil. Meanwhile, I figured I would knock their socks off with what I could do. My enthusiasm was renewed, and I was excited at the possibilities to grow a brand such as Playboy to finally dominate the industry, as it should have.

Larry Lux and I got on like a house on fire. Larry's last position had been VP of *National Geographic*, so he openly admitted he had a lot to learn about the adult web business. There again, most people in mainstream dot com had nowhere near the depth of knowledge as those of us who had grown up in the adult web. I gave him the expedited version of how to make money on the Internet and he was mesmerized as I lay out a strategy of Playboy-branded niche sites, free-traffic-driving sites and every which way Playboy could propagate their brand and collect a dollar.

Playboy.com was based in New York and one of the first things I did was walk Larry around the corner to my friends Anthony and Josh at Yahoo. Yahoo was at the time the biggest player, known as the "go-to" search engine. New York was where they handled all the keyword searches and the ad buys for those valuable links. Still they were getting tons of searches for sex, boobs, girls, hot and horny... you get the picture. But Yahoo were really trying to hide this kind of sleazy side of their business. They were trying to do what?! Had they really no idea how valuable those adult search terms could be? No, apparently, they hadn't or rather they didn't care. The bigger picture was Yahoo's brand and reputation. A huge opportunity was staring me in the face. A multi-million dollar opportunity!

Sitting in the Yahoo office in the giant Alice in Wonderland–looking velvet chairs of bright purple and yellow Yahoo fame, I make a proposal; "Let's say a person types in a sexy word like "boobs" into your search engine box. You redirect them seamlessly to our page," I explain, sketching a rough flow chart on one of their white boards they have laying on the coffee table, "The consumer sees a list of search results just as they would on Yahoo, but the search mechanism is actually powered by our guys in LA, Search ABC."

Anthony raises a very interested eyebrow, "Hmm, so Yahoo would no longer be doing anything with the adult traffic? We wouldn't take the ads or handle adult in any way, we just send the traffic to you, and we are not in the adult business?"

"Correct! And on top of the page, instead of your logo, the header will be branded Playboy.com." I pull out a mock up I've made of a potential search results page, with the Playboy banner across the top. Lux looks on, impressed, the first time he is seeing this, and he really has no idea of the scope we were about to pull off.

"It would look something like this, with Playboy at the top, a brand that everyone perceives as sexy but not sleazy! But it will really be powered by a search engine, Search ABC."

And for the final buzz words they need to hear; "So, we give Yahoo a cut of every ad dollar that comes in, but Yahoo is completely out of the adult business!" At this point I am seeing major dollar signs and I realize neither Yahoo nor my guy from Playboy have any idea just how massive this is.

The Yahoo execs are impressed. "This is great! How soon can you be ready to do a test?" Josh says.

Playboy and the search engine group had just been handed the deal of a lifetime. I now made the call to my friends in LA.

"Hi Dick, you are going to absolutely LOVE me!"

"Hi Gail, what's up?"

"How much traffic can your search company really handle?"

"Massive. We have banks of servers and back-up banks! More than anyone."

"What if I was to get you Yahoo's entire adult traffic?"

"What? Are you fucking kidding!!! How the hell did you pull that off?"

...And the Yahoo deal worked like a dream.

Playboy was working through their mountain of diligence; meanwhile Lux and I were full steam ahead. I had now created a bunch of Playboy niche sites that were working great. I was back and forth to the Playboy. com office in New York where Christie Hefner and Larry Lux ran the dot com. Playboy the magazine was based in Los Angeles.

Larry called me, "You know we have a huge Playboy building in Beverly Hills and there is a lot of space. We've decided since you are based in LA and have a bunch of techies out there, we'll put your library there and have you run an LA version of Playboy.com out of there. I'll stay in New York, but I'll be back and forth."

So, Lux and I began the move to the Beverly Hills office. We were nicely greeted by Marty the head honcho there and the staff, who showed us around this lavish building of plush carpet and classic erotica art from the fifties. We were welcomed and shown a good third of the building that was to be our new offices. Everyone seemed excited about the new Playboy. com venture moving in. All the websites and the running of the Internet ventures was to be handled out of LA and Lux and I started interviewing potential Internet heads.

It was about seven pm one evening at this beautiful Playboy office, the sun was finally setting through the beautiful double windows revealing an impressive LA skyline. It had been a long day for me, talking with potential web guys and general furniture rearranging. Lux had flown back to New York and almost everyone had left for the day, with the exception of a few cleaning crew, security, and Marty the VP of Playboy, who called me into his executive suite for a little chat.

He shut the door behind us and invited me to sit on his couch. He was seated facing me in a comfy chair, and I noticed there were years of vintage Playboy magazines, neatly displayed on his coffee table to the side of us.

"So, your intention is to come in here with your photos and make millions of dollars on the Internet is it?"

"Well yes, I hope so, that is the plan," I say with a proud smile.

He leans in, his face now inches from mine and not in a sexual way but a rather intimidating way. His voice and demeanor change drastically.

"Now let's get one thing straight," he growled, his voice in a low demonic tone, "I have stock in Playboy not Playboy.com!!! So, you think you're gonna come in here with your big library and start making shit loads of money?!!! Well let me tell you, every dollar that you bring in for dot com, as far as I'm concerned, is a dollar out of my pocket. Understaaaaaand?!!!"

Yes, I understood. Playboy was a fucked-up company!

I immediately called Larry.

"Wow, I don't get it! That's unbelievable," Larry gasped in shock. Larry had clearly not experienced anything like this during his years as VP of National Geographic and he really did have the naive mentality of "We're all in this together to grow the company, as-a-whole."

"You need to talk to Christie, she needs to unite the company somehow, this is really bad."

"I'm going to talk to Christie, this is ridiculous," was all he could say.

But clearly this problem ran way deeper. Marty was going to do anything he could to sabotage the web progress and keep the dot com from making money and affecting his bottom line. Within a few weeks, Marty's team had somehow undermined Larry's existence and he was suddenly and drastically shafted. Out on his ass with no warning and little reasoning. Marty had won.

A new president was brought in to dot com probably under some control of Marty and who appeared or pretended to have no idea about my deal.

I called Lux at home, "Where does this leave us Larry."

"Gail, I have no idea, I'm as shocked as you are! I'm out! There's nothing I can do."

I contacted the new President of dot com.

"Where do we stand on the deal to buy out my library?"

"Oh, I don't know anything about it. If you want to send me your proposal, I can look at it."

"Look at it?!!!" I explained just how far down the line we were, and the new President pretended to be very interested but said still, he'd have to look at it all. I had the naive hope that he would be excited when he saw all the merits of the deal.

Not more than a few days go by and I received a cease and desist letter for the sites I was doing with Playboy that were running off my servers.

"What do you mean I am infringing on the Playboy logo? These are sites I built for Playboy!" I said to the new president honestly confused.

"Well, until we've made a decision you need to take the Playboy name off everything."

"But they are making money! Did you look at the emails I forwarded you with all the site designs and revenue flows and the correspondence between Larry and I?"

"I haven't had a chance, meanwhile you need to take those sites down," he said coldly.

"And what about the Yahoo deal I put together?" I asked

"Er… the Yahoo deal? That was a deal Larry Lux brought in."

"Actually, that was a deal I put together," I said firmly and indignantly.

"Well, that contract is between Playboy, Yahoo and Search ABC, you're not a party to the contract."

"Yes, because I was supposed to be part of the Playboy party!!!"

"Look, you'll have to take that up with Larry."

So that was it, I would receive not a penny on the massive Yahoo deal, not from Playboy, not from the search engine guys.

Within weeks, my set up, my systems, my websites I built for Playboy were ripped off, almost word for word with a new tech company that was in their back pocket. And to boot they were even infringing on my images!!!

I could have sued them, should have sued them, but in the end, I figured my time was better spent not going backwards.

Fuck 'em. I'll take my library back and do it myself! Fuck Playboy. Why create a mega business for a company that doesn't even know a gift horse if they're looking it straight in the mouth? I'll do this, and I'll do it for myself!

CHAPTER THIRTY-FOUR

Yahoo Clubs
They Didn't Want!

AND I SAY I KEPT my acting and photo business separate but there were times when I took advantage of mixing the two. Like the Cannes Film Festival…

Any self-respecting actress must attend Cannes. I had three roles there. One, of course, as an actress, to hang out at the Cannes'-Hollywood parties and be seen. Two, I had actually produced a low budget movie and was there with my distributor to not only smile and look pretty when the foreign buyers came around, but to close the deals! And third, I could shoot a couple of girly layouts on the side.

Screenings and meetings by day, Hollywood parties by night and then the occasional girly shoot on the side. In Cannes this was all fun and games. Like the half-naked girl in just stockings and heels we put on the back of a motor-bike and tore through the streets of Cannes. Shots of the crowds, rubber necking at our girl streaking the festival, were more impressive than the girl herself, and the pics sold like hot cakes.

These things seemed to mix well. The mainstream Hollywood players were intrigued by *Private's Porn Boat*, the exclusive yacht moored offshore that Gail could get them on. The porn stars wanted to be introduced to the real Hollywood producers, and the Hollywood producers wanted to be introduced to some porn chicks. I could take my foreign buyers as my guests to the big Hollywood parties and afterwards to the Private's Boat, where they could meet naked girls, which is where I could really close my business deals with them.

All mainstream guys seemed to be intrigued by our adult web world and wanted a little sneak peak behind the red curtain. There happened to be an Adult-Con Expo going on in Las Vegas and I invited the guys from

Yahoo to come on down and see how the other-half lives. Walking round the main red-carpeted floor, looking at almost naked girls giving away everything from t-shirts to cars, these guys were like kids in a proverbial Candy Store. That night I took them to a private VIP webmaster party in the MGM Presidential suite.

It was heavy security; only highest-level, Very Important Persons were allowed. I enter with my three Yahoo guys in tow, each totally out of place in a suit and tie. In first sight was the Sushi Bar. This consisted of a row of naked girls laid out on slabs covered in slices of sushi that the guests were enjoying eating off. There was a sunken Jacuzzi where Snoop Dogg was hanging out with a bunch of naked babes.

We were ushered over to meet some of the sponsors who immediately offered my guys a selection of one-hundred-year-old scotches and Cuban cigars. As I introduced my guests to the big-cheese website owners, they were drooling at the mouth, honing-in on my Yahoo traffic gods and worshiping the ground I walked on for bringing them. This was gonna be huge brownie points for me, and the site owners were tripping over themselves trying to close a deal with my guests. However, Anthony and Josh were having a hard time concentrating on talk of keywords and hits, while acts of complete debauchery were clearly going on all around them. They were shell shocked, as naked porn-chicks passed by and slipped hors d'oeuvres in their mouth, or occasionally something even more tasty. Certainly, this was something far different from their usual business dinners, but they were quite happy to have a new experience and it didn't take long for them to be drawn into the whole spirit of the thing. It was a loud, completely crazy party that involved things being smashed and sprayed with champagne. I heard the room cleanup bill alone was ten thousand!

A week later, I was back in New York and the Yahoo guys had about gotten over their hangovers. Now they had a new dilemma. You see they had these new things called Yahoo Clubs. Online communities, like knitting clubs and fishing clubs, but yes, they were out of control with the sexy clubs. "We just can't stop these people putting up these sexy clubs and we know most of the images are stolen so it's a real liability. How can we get them to purchase your images instead?" Anthony asks.

Oh my God!! Did an Angel just descend from heaven and land in my lap? Here I am to the rescue. I had a better idea. A much grander scheme.

"Let's create a central database of images so all adult traffic driven by these clubs goes through a series of sites, which of course I'll create."

My webmasters built a massive web of sites, in a flat second before my Yahoo guys could change their mind. The switch was flicked and OH MY GOD, unbelievable! I had truly hit the jackpot.

Wow, views were coming in the millions. Millions of guys clamoring to see my pics. The main issue was back up–to back up hosting in order to handle literally millions of hits an hour.

For a few weeks I was higher than a kite.

The massive insane traffic coming in was more than anyone could possibly handle. We couldn't get enough servers to keep the amount of end users happy or handle their business. Whole warehouses filled with banks of hosting computers were crashing because of massive overload. We had officially been the first company to BREAK THE INTERNET.

Then a story broke in the *LA Times* that anyone could build a Yahoo store and that stores on Yahoo could be adult. Meaning you could buy porn DVDs on Yahoo! So what? Everyone knew that! But this was damaging to the Yahoo squeaky clean image. The head honcho decided to cut off all ties with anything adult.

What????

Noooooo!

This was nothing to do with me! We were not running a shop, we were running the clubs and we weren't porn!

"Sorry, Gail. Yahoo's new policy. Bad luck, eh?"

And like that, the light switch was turned off.

CHAPTER THIRTY-FIVE

Flirting with Investment

MY OLD TIME Hollywood friend and Manager extraordinaire, Michael, introduced me to one of the most brilliant entertainment attorneys Hollywood has ever seen. Mr. Big Shot Hollywood Attorney, Dayton graduated top of his Ivy League class and with his razor's edge street smarts he saw immediate potential in my business and decided to introduce me to his movie mogul client, Jay. Jay was a massive name in the film biz, churning out several blockbuster movies a year. Still, Jay might be interested in learning about other investment opportunities such as mine...

Dayton arranged for Jay and me to meet over lunch. An hour later, I was riveted by Jay. The feeling was mutual, and this impressive man was so captivated by me, he was ready to go all in, and with a little due diligence of course, invest mega millions for a share of the company.

It was then that Jay and I started spending every moment together. We spent the first few months poring over my books, showing him how the biz works and bringing him up to speed. I introduced him to the mainstream tech guys I was dealing with and brought Jay in on a lot of the deals.

Things were going great and I was excited Jay was going to be my partner. He was a shrewd businessman who had built his empire from the ground up. He'd started from less than nothing and worked his way to the top. Working at the docks, he'd been able to secure the exclusive rights on imports, which he sold in the seventies, for hundreds of millions. He took that money and turned it over and over in the film biz until he was literally worth billions. Street smart and ballsy. There was a lot I could learn from him and I was suitably impressed.

Yet, here is this man, I admired greatly, gushing over me and how brilliant he thinks I am. Constantly complimenting me on my business savvy and my entrepreneurial spirit, but also as a person, as a mother. When you are admired by someone it feels wonderful, but when it comes from someone of Jay's stature, it was an incredible compliment. He had a mega enterprise to run, yet he seemed like he had all the time in the world for me. Many men have given me compliments about my business sense, but it doesn't have the same impact until you truly have mutual respect.

Jay's excitement was focused on my business and what we were doing together, while his movies with massive stars…, well that was par for the course. Right now, his attention was on me and how we were going to run the world together. I had met my business match. Turned out our stars were really aligned with the exact same birthday, and though decades apart, we were like two peas in a pod. Couldn't have been more in sync and more excited about working together.

Then one day after an exciting meeting, we were back at his penthouse suite, poring over the paperwork together and he's leaning over my shoulder looking at the figures, when he leans in a little further and takes this perfect opportunity, kissing me square on the lips. A long incredible kiss. Wow, was I completely blind to the fact that for the last three months Jay had been falling in love with me and this was way more than business? And had I too, without realizing it, been enamored by more than just his business sense? I kissed him back with shock but equal zest.

He was a lot older than me, by maybe twenty-five years, I was scared to know exactly how many, but at this moment, I didn't care, I knew that this felt so right.

…And so, started our amazing romance.

Now as a couple, our pursuit of business together was just as exciting, if not more so, and he constantly brought me into his world genuinely seeking my advice on the movies he was doing. Working at his office, on the studio lot, asking my advice on this star or that. We could be a mega power team. Still, he pampered my ego in business, and it was all about Gail as he gushed for me both in business and pleasure, pulling out all the stops to romance me.

I confessed to my friend, Michael the manager, who had been the beginning of the introduction chain and kept abreast of the progress, that well, things with Jay and I, had, well….it had turned a little romantic.

Michael hit the roof, "Oh my God Gail, you're going to ruin a multi-million-dollar investment! Why is he going to invest now! Of course he's hot for you! Couldn't you have strung him along? WHY IS HE GOING TO BUY THE COW, WHEN HE'S GOT THE MILK FOR FREE?!!!!!!" He shook his head in disgust, "Oh my God, women! They fall in love and they don't listen!!!"

I'd known Michael for years, from probably when I first stepped off the boat, at least before, during and after my marriage. He had long been my sounding board in Hollywood affairs as well as occasionally romantic matters. He'd represented a star cast of women in Hollywood and was well versed in the pitfalls of women in love.

I assured Michael this was true love and it was mutual.

"This is not going to affect me financially, I'm still going to get the investment. It's going to be even better!" I tried to assure him that I was totally in control of my feelings.

Michael rolled his eyes.

I had insisted that Michael get a finder's fee when this was closed and now I swore that it wasn't going to be affected. But Michael, I honestly believe, had first and foremost, my interest in mind. He had seen way too many deals get screwed up when romance got involved.

We are in love! This is going to work out between us! Well it was done anyway, we were dating so there was no going back, so hopefully it would work.

And it did work, we started this beautiful relationship and Jay brought me more and more into his movie world and wanted me to be by his side. He was also just as great with my girls, who loved him, and he was just charming to Mom.

He wasn't your typical producer.

"Jay, you must have every actress in LA chasing you," I'd asked early on.

"I don't go down that road. Have plenty of producer friends who are star fuckers, not me. You think it's bad enough having some celebrity prima donna on your movie, imagine if you're sleeping with her! I'm not interested in women who want me because of what I can do for their film career. I steer clear of the casting sessions and never meet with an actress alone.

I'm interested in women who actually want to have a real relationship with me." He turns to me holding my face lovingly, "Besides, Gail, no one holds a candle to you."

It's now about nine months down the road and things were going well, so well that in one of our romantic moments, Jay turns to me, kissing me softly, "You know what I admire about you the most?" Jay says lovingly, "Yes, you're smart, you're beautiful and you have a business spirit like mine, but the thing I admire most about you is you're an amazing mother."

I am just stunned by how sweet and loving he is.

He continues, "I'm so in love with you, I want to have a baby together. I've never felt so strongly like this. Have a baby with me."

I was a little shocked. I already had two girls, he had children of his own too, but over the next few weeks he became more and more persuasive. Telling me he loved me as a mother and spending time with me and my girls. At first, I was reluctant, but then I started thinking, *Well, I'm still young enough...*

We are alone in our hotel suite and he's arranged the most romantic candle lit dinner for two on the patio. Watching the setting sun, he leans in kissing my hand and asks again, "Can you imagine the most amazing child the two of us would create? I love you Gail, please be the mother of my child."

Finally, my heart gave in, "I love you too and it would be wonderful."

I agreed to having a baby! I smiled basking in the sweet loving moment and he leaned in, kissing me like he was the happiest guy in the world.

There was a long loving moment as we both realized that we were making the most special commitment to each other.

"Let's start trying tonight!" he said and we both laughed, kissing wildly.

"But seriously, I want to be married first before we really start trying. I don't want to get pregnant and not be married," I said, stating the obvious and quite sure he would want the same thing.

But here seemed to be a problem. There was a long pause before he finally confessed that, well... err... he couldn't because you see, he'd ....err...........never actually gotten divorced!!!!!!!

"What!!!!!!! And you're telling me this now!"

I was furious. I was heartbroken. I was in total disbelief.

"You're asking me to have a baby with you, and you're married?!!!"

"Darling, I'm technically married but not really. I'm a Catholic, and my wealth, it's complicated, it's too difficult. But, we're not really married, just on paper. She lives back East on the estate."

You see, he had an extraordinary fortune and obviously had decided divorce was not a financial option.

I thought about all the times we were supposed to stay at his estate back East but it hadn't worked out.

"It's a six-hundred-acre estate, she lives in the main house, when I'm there I stay in the guest house, there's like a mile between them!"

He tried to reason with me, "Why do you care? We can live in the Bel Air house, we can live at your ranch, we can buy whatever place you want, we can still be together."

I left heartbroken. I didn't know what to think. Meanwhile Jay lit up my phone over and over, begging me to reconsider, sending me flowers every day and pulling at my heartstrings. I told Jay we were definitely through, but in my heart, I was still torn.

I'm at home crying when my caretaker Edward comes over to console me. I couldn't get over the fact that I was and would be someone's mistress!

"I just want to have a normal relationship with a normal guy and we get married like normal people and love each other, not this Hollywood shit…" I sobbed. I wanted the "fairy tale."

"Oh my God, Gail. Just have a baby with the guy. It's like a fifty-million-dollar baby!" Edward said, being practical.

I think it was that very moment that sealed the deal for me, "Wow, oh my God, is that what people think of me? Like I'm dating him because of his money! Oh my God, cos he's older, people think I'm like Anna Nicole Smith or something?!!!"

All of a sudden, I started questioning myself. Why was I really attracted to him? Was it really his power and his money? *Be honest with yourself Gail, if he was homeless would you still want to be with him? Of course not! Obviously not…… Is that a bad thing to be attracted to someone's power? And that we got along so amazingly well?* But there was no convincing myself.

"But I have my own money anyway!" I snorted through the tears.

Edward tried to lighten the mood by joking, "…and you do kinda look a bit like Anna Nicole Smith."

Not what I wanted to hear. Here was Edward trying to convince me I should go ahead with Jay, but what he'd actually done was make me take a deep hard look at myself and I didn't like what I saw. In that instant, I knew, no matter how successful I would be, it would never be a shadow of what Jay had and people would always think I was a bimbo, gold-digger. And crazy as it sounds to me today, that was a huge deal.

I had a dinner planned with the attorney Dayton who didn't really know what had transpired, so I went along for the meeting as if nothing was amiss. I hadn't told him that Jay and I were dating up until then and I didn't really tell him the entire extent but confessed some little snippets…. That Jay and I had been kinda romantic….and I told him we'd had this conversation about Jay not being divorced but living separately from his wife.

"I've stayed at Jay's estate and his wife was there. They were in the same house, I mean they looked pretty married to me…," he offers up.

I almost choked on my anger and sadness all at the same time but didn't tell him what was going on inside. Still that little bit of information really was the final piece to make my decision.

Now whether Dayton innocently dropped this clanger, which is how I took it at the time, or whether he very strategically and cunningly placed this clanger, I am not sure. For later that evening one thing led to another and at the end of the dinner, several glasses of wine down, I was confessing my broken heart and he was consoling me. I was telling him how hurt I was and how I wanted a real man, an available man to love and adore me. He wholeheartedly agreed, telling me I deserved the best, I could have any man I wanted.

And in that moment, Mr. Hollywood Attorney grabs me and kisses me passionately, "I am so crazy about you," he confesses.

Okay, this brilliant man is incredibly attractive. A high-powered attorney and probably the smartest guy I know, and I must say an insane kisser. I kissed him back equally as passionate, totally carried away in the moment.

Oh my God, I can't do this. What am I doing?!!!

I peel myself away from the situation before I was about to get myself in even more of a pickle.

I dust myself off and try to reclaim an air of professionalism.

In the end, I decide it best to close that chapter in my life and made the final decision to cut it off with Jay. The decision to end it with him, also meant the decision to blow the investment. A massive investment and a massive blow. Michael was right, as always!

CHAPTER THIRTY-SIX

The Suing Machine

AFTER I ESTABLISHED COPYRIGHT law and order in the Wild, Wild West, I set up an impressive suing machine. You see, I licensed discs of images to webmasters to use on their sites, but once these images were published on the web officially, thousands of unofficial sites would just download the images, essentially stealing them.

Yes, this would be your little back street amateur site, but believe it or not, it was also the guys bringing in the big bucks. The big sites usually had some lower level web guy who probably hadn't given much thought to licensing images and had really just stolen them by "mistake." It was near impossible for a site owner to make sure he had licenses on absolutely everything. Plus, his marketing structure would probably include thousands of feeder sites under his umbrella, many of which were some college student who had also just downloaded my images. So basically, my pretty little pictures were pretty much everywhere.

I set up a vigilant campaign to take down infringing images. But not really, as I was secretly hoping they would steal them because I could make more money threatening to sue them, than they would have ever paid for a license.

I hired programmers who developed image matching software for me. With this, I could upload an image to my matching system and it would literally crawl the web, like a trained spider, bringing back images that were a duplicate. I even had a turnkey suing program where it would match the image, pull up the infringing site, double check there was no actual license and fill out the lawsuit!!!

I had a bullpen of guys whose sole job was to crawl the web looking at nude photos trying to see who might have stolen our images. I was literally paying college kids to look at naked girls all day!

Then it was pretty simple; with legal precedent set, one infringed image was worth one-hundred-and-fifty-thousand-dollars! I had a piece of paper that allowed me to plunder and pillage. So, some poor website owner who happened to get caught with a handful of my unlicensed images was likely to get slapped with a multimillion dollar lawsuit. Which I would be willing to settle out of court for a fraction.

Much of this had become a full-time preoccupation of Greg and my team of attorneys, whom I was keeping quite busy.

It was around two thousand and one, and "Napster" was all in the press. I wondered how I could use the proliferation of my images on the web and turn it into some kind of Adult-Napster. I was the content provider but, unlike the music industry, I actually wanted a Napster to get my images out on the web. Plus, I had stamped my company URL in the corner of each image, so these stolen images were great little advertisers driving traffic back to my sites. Now what if I could find a way to embed something in the image that would bring the customer back to me? Then I would do everything I could to encourage clients to "steal" my photos. Then they would be promoting my sites by stealing more of my photos and I would be stealing their customers right back to me. Yes, please come steal my photos!!!

It hadn't been a secret that a year earlier Forester Research had valued my company at fifty million and, even if there was some hot air there, I let everyone know that I was in a flurry of excitement. In light of this, I garnered a whole new level of respect as a major player.

It was right about this time when I was invited to another of those all-expense-paid exclusive webmaster gatherings, and enter a new potential love interest. In retrospect, looking for true love, with a new net worth stamped on my forehead, wasn't the best timing. But still men flopped at my feet because of my looks, and personality, right? Surely, money was not a driving factor.

And let's be honest, what I was looking for in a mate was a business partner. Someone who could live in the excitement of this industry with me. Someone dashing and brilliant who could rule the world by my side. Or at least someone I believed could.

We were enjoying an evening cocktail mixer on the candle lit patio of an incredible sprawling villa right on the sand somewhere on the beautiful Mexican Riviera. A private party put on by some web company where we could hangout, look cool and strategize the newest technologies that would drive the future economy of the entire planet.

Jason is obviously the organizer of this particular private gathering. I watch him moving around, impressively holding court with the big guys, commanding attention as he directs the evening events. He's dark, handsome and fiercely intense. I find myself captivated watching his presence.

I discover he has just appeared on the scene, having worked as a tech genius at Microsoft.

Wow, hot, sophisticated and SMART.

I had to meet him!

We were instantly enthralled, staring eye to eye talking about business, while the rest of the party seemed to disappear from our awareness.

"Yeah, I was developing, DRM (Digital Rights Management) technology. Have you heard of it? It's a way of wrapping images, invisible to the end user," Jason explains.

I asked, summarizing his explanation, "In other words, you can take an image, wrap it in some invisible code, propagate it on the web and then at some point, when you choose, you can use that code to instantly pop up another site, sell the viewer something or make him do something else….?" my mind already wandering to how we could use this to wrap my images.

"Yeah exactly! Brilliant, right?"

Oh my God! A way to send out every image with a homing device that will bring them home whenever I want!!!

Now this was sexy! I was sold. I hired him and his team.

As he was creating master programming, I was falling in love. Sparks were flying, and fireworks were going off. At only twenty-eight, Jason was nine years younger than I. Not my ideal age, and a complete swing in the other direction as far as romantic age difference, but Jason was successful, confident, mature and a genius tech geek with edgy, entrepreneurial ambition.

He swept me off my feet with lavish spa weekends, Beverly Hills dinners and the hottest parties in town, but most importantly with his expertise and the deals he had brewing on the web. Was this attraction true love or was I in love with the potential, the excitement of the dream to run the world with a partner who gets it?

He was dynamic and charming and extremely good at convincing most people of anything, especially me, and in a short time, I was smitten and invited him into my life. Jason became husband number two, and my partner in crime.

We threw in a fun little snippet in our wedding vows; he agreed to endure my expensive horse hobby and in return, I agreed to not talk to him before ten AM. He was a night owl.

The vows should have read not to speak to him before one in the afternoon, as that was the earliest he ever woke up. Or should I say before two, give him time to get some Starbucks down him before he was able to be coherent. Really, he wasn't getting going until he'd had enough uppers late in the afternoon and more at his prime when he hit the coke in the evening. Actually, he was at his best, late at night when the drugs had really kicked in, then he was a hell of a business machine. Great for a business partner who you can go out to events with and shoot the shit. Not sure it was so great for any kind of real marriage. But that's what I wanted, right? A business partner! So, no need to worry that a ring would change our experience and as most observed, I continued to be a single mom in my daily activities and my marriage was more like a young hot-shit late-night boyfriend relationship and a business partner to rule the Internet with.

On a personal level, Jason and I got along very well. We went out constantly to all the best restaurants around town and every industry who's-who event. Always five-star, since he had an allergy to anything less than first class. He took hours longer than me to get ready and was all about looking good in the social arena. I was his arm candy, especially in this industry where everyone knew me and that would surely raise his coolness factor.

Edward was not complaining about the hot new husband around the place who was happily taking charge.

Jason didn't have a whole lot of interaction as a family man, that was my department. He got along fine with my daughters who were now a couple of pre-teens he could relate to more on a friend level, but that was fine, and probably the only way they would have wanted it. After all they had me as a parent and we had a very close relationship. My husband was in their eyes "whatever makes mom happy."

He did however want to have another baby of his own, I was ready, and I thought this would probably make him more of a family man. I was wrong.

He jumped two feet first into all the business and all the exciting deals I had going on, and my head was spinning with the ideas he had to take us to the next level. With my library and my clout, and his tech savvy enthusiasm, we were about to take over the Internet!

He had an impressive grasp of technology and everyone was excited to do deals with us.

His "hobby" of "volunteer" work was equally as impressive. Jason described himself as "The highest ranking non-paid person in disaster communications in the Los Angeles County." This meant that he was part of the Sherriff's Department, held a Sherriff's badge and would go out on night "ride-alongs" in the hood, for fun, just to "beat up bad guys."

What!!! He was a hero too!

He was even more involved with the FBI and the DEA. He'd built their private sector "Citizen's Academy" websites and was their go-to tech guy. This entitled him to field agent badges, official emails, and more uniforms than would fit in an entire walk in closet. Our living room walls were plastered with certificates from Law Enforcement, the FBI and DEA and even the Mayor of Los Angeles, many of which were presented to him at various dinners in his honor, some I even attended. Kinda ironic he was in the DEA when he was himself partying like a rock star and probably putting away more drugs than most dealers they were trying to take down.

But my husband was connected for sure.

His car was equipped with full on police sirens and flashy Mars Venus lights that he used often, if he just wanted to get somewhere quicker, drive down the emergency lane in traffic, or "scare the shit out of some asshole driver."

Our house was installed with high tech radio equipment and he would be pinged and paged whenever there was a hint of an earthquake, fire, riot or other disaster. He was ready and on call with an arsenal; pistols, automatics, semi-automatics, SWAT gear, and enough bullet proof vests to protect an army.

Being in the know came in really useful for collecting from these legal suits I'd filed, and Jason took a personal passion in pursuing this. After filing a lawsuit, Jason would start with an email that just happened to come from his official DEA email with his signature DEA field agent ID number. And if this didn't totally scare the crap out of them, he'd follow up with a settlement meeting where he'd dress in his FBI agent attire, carrying his official leather briefcase with the embossed gold letters, "FBI" and his FBI pin and cufflinks, for an added subtle touch.

During his regular visits to the DEA Jason would hop on the high security computers and run info. With just a name and very limited information on some target website owner, he'd come back with a personal rap sheet; a spreadsheet of their assets, and any skeletons he could use to twist their arm.

Jason came running into my office on an extreme high with news on the latest guy we'd filed against, "I got him! Three companies out of Idaho," he says showing me a stack of print outs, "Got an aerial of the house, zoomed in on the car in his drive and ran the license plate. His sixty-foot yacht is in mother-in-law's name. He's out of the US a lot but he's back each month for visitation rights. I'm gonna serve him in Florida the moment he steps off the boat to meet his kid!!!" Jason's jumping up and down with excitement. "Oh, and he's got a tax issue, too, so he's not gonna want that dug up. Sneaky shit. I'm taking the Beemer and he's gonna roll over the house when I threaten him with the tax shit!" ... and this is how he would track down the money.

CHAPTER THIRTY-SEVEN

Celebrity Sex Tape

I HAD PRETTY much retired from acting. I was simply making too much money and didn't have the time to be lured away to Hollywood. I still rented out my ranch from time to time for Hollywood friends. It was then that a movie starring Tom Sizemore arrived at my ranch for a month-long shoot.

Sizemore was well known for his action roles in movies like *HEAT* with his friend De Niro. He was also known to be uninsurable for his out of control "Tom side." Tom was a fucked up, higher than a kite, crazy cokehead, but he also had that loveable, irresistible-guy side. He loved my ranch and when the movie was over he didn't want to leave. This is how I somehow adopted Tom Sizemore and he came to live in my guesthouse.

He loved the whole adult Internet, money making things going on at the ranch and the occasional chickie-honey he'd get to meet. Tom brought a whole new dimension to the goings on at the ranch. His hanging-out celebrity friends, who also wanted me to introduce them to this whole adult Internet world. He got on well with the family. Liked to hang out with my husband who was not opposed to joining in on the coke. He got on well with my mom, though he tried to get a smile out of her occasionally by walking around in only a shirt, letting it all hang out in the breeze. And he would have liked to get along with my oldest daughter Rachel who was only seventeen at the time! He must have had a premonition that she'd follow Mom's footsteps and become a model and Playmate.

Having a guest like this was always full of surprises, like coming home to mega star Jack standing on your bridge with Tom doing lines of white stuff. And sometimes when Tom knew there was a shoot going on, he'd invite over Charlie and other famous actor friends and I'd come home to a bunch of guys watching the show. Yeah, pull up a lawn chair, grab a beer and watch the nudie shoots being filmed!

Tom and my husband were now hang-out late night partying buddies and Tom told him he could have the role of his "manager." My husband loved this and had a newfound interest in trying to book Tom gigs. This also meant booking Tom at the most luxurious accommodations for his court ordered rehab. Tom at this point was on a first name basis with the staff at a nearby very exclusive rehab center. Probably Jason could have done to check in there too, but somehow, he presented himself as the sober representative.

I pulled in the driveway one evening and I'm headed inside when there's a huge gunshot noise coming right from our house. I rushed upstairs to find Tom lazing on the bed with a pair of sound muffling headphones watching a video and my husband shooting off live ammo over the balcony.

"Oh, my God, you can't just shoot out of the window!!!"

"Fucking awesome!!!" Jason screams not noticing me at first, with his ears covered. And then he sees my pissed off face, "Oh relax! I know what I'm doing. I'm shooting up the stream. I can hit a target from a thousand feet you know!"

"Fucking buzz kill," he mumbles under his breath, unloading the remainder of the bullets.

Tom's watching the famous celebrity porn tape of Pamela Anderson

"Why don't I have something like that?" Tom complained. "I can fuck like a fucking CHAMP! People would LOVE to watch me fuck....um... somebody!"

"Hey that's a great idea, we should shoot it and pretend Heidi leaked it," my husband said.

Our young lad Tom was far from innocent. Remember Tom was dating Heidi Fleiss when the whole celebrity Black Book Affair came out revealing major stars that were booking her call girls. Most of the ones in there were his friends and I wouldn't be surprised if he wasn't helping with the business arrangements.

It was then that we came up with a scheme. To shoot the "Tom Sizemore Sex Tapes."

We were talking about my company producing a full on porno, so it was crossing my line a little, but my husband was more than excited to oversee this little project. Fine by me. All on you sweetie.

Where better to shoot than a suite at the Chateau Marmont Hotel. Hollywood's most notorious hotel for star stalkers and celebrity sleuths. They check in for the night. My husband, Tom, their director, my camera man Mark and a couple of new, unknown porn chicks.

The following morning, I get a call from my hubbie. "Ok, well it went well," he said, sounding exhausted, "Well not really, it was like pulling teeth, but we finally got it in the can."

He explained a little more, "Tom was as usual coked to the gills, took all night to shoot what was supposed to be some quick amateur little orgy thing. We ended up going through those girls and some others, trying to get the coke to ware off so Tom's unit would stay up. Anyway, we got it finally!" I learned years later that my husband had actually jumped in as stunt cock at the end for the money shot. I would have been furious at the time, but I suppose he was just "taking one of the team" to get the job done.

He put Tom on the phone for a different prospective. "Gail, it was AWESOME!" Nothing with Tom was EVER less that AWESOME! "This shit is gonna sell!"

Tom sounded somewhat sober at least. My husband said they were just packing up and would be home in a few hours.

Not more than twenty minutes went by when I got another call from my husband. This time screaming and frantic:

"Oh my God! Oh my God! I think…I think… Tom's dead…!"

Pause as I could hear frantic commotion in the background.

"He took a breath!" someone else shouted

"…Err, no he's not dead, think he's breathing but it's bad. It's really bad. I don't know what to do."

"What?!!! How did this happen? He sounded fine a few minutes ago?"

"Everything was fine, until Tom invited over a couple of his hooker girlfriends to join us for breakfast. We went back to the room to pack up and next second there is huge bang and Tom's flat on his face."

My husband turns to the girls;

"What the hell happened?"

The one girl replies, obviously guilty, "I think he drank my GHP, by mistake, it was in a water bottle." She holds up the empty bottle.

"What?!!! How could someone drink a whole bottle of GHP! It tastes like fucking gasoline! And he thought it was a bottle of... WATER!?"

She just shrugged her shoulders, "He just drank the whole thing!" the girl said close to tears now.

By this time the other girl is holding a spoon of brown-sugar-looking stuff with a lighter underneath, wafting the smoke into Tom's nostrils. She is apparently trying to wake him with just a little hit of METH.

"What the FUCK are you doing?!!! NO!!! Both of you. Get the hell out of here!"

At this point my husband and Mark are left alone in the room with a non-responsive Tom Sizemore. My husband is keeping me on the phone. I think, mainly to have someone else, to share the liability.

"Well the other thing is the manager keeps calling and calling. They've got some other celebrity booked in this suite and they're downstairs covered in paparazzi, going nuts. The manager is having a fit."

Now this is all happening in the very same suite that John Belushi died in! *Something in the Feng Shui,* I thought.

Jason goes over the options, "I figure we have three choices. I call an ambulance and save his life but if I do then he's breaking probation and that's two years in jail; the paparazzi's gonna have a field day and Tom's gonna kill me. OR I don't call an ambulance and there's a good chance he might die."

For all his faults, Tom was a loveable character and I didn't want anything to happen to him. I was truly worried about him.

"So, what's the third option?"

"Just tell the paparazzi what's going on and charge them to film the whole thing."

"Where is he now?" I ask, trying to weigh up the situation.

"We've got him laying naked in the bathtub. We threw a bucket of ice on him but that didn't seem to do anything."

"Is he breathing?"

"Kinda..."

"Kind...of....?"

There was no clear option. We loved Tom and wanted the best for him, but this was a tricky situation.

"Are you shooting all this at least?" I ask.

"Hell, Yeah!"

Our conversation is cut short by an angry manager at the door. Jason has to come clean; "Ok, look, let's be honest, we have a little situation here right now," he explains, letting the manager finally squeeze through the door. "Look we have Tom Sizemore OD'ing in your bathtub. So, either help me carry him out to another room or you're going have to figure out a way to buy us some more time."

The manager, seeing naked Tom on ice in the tub, went white as a ghost and called to the lobby explaining Mr. Sizemore would be needing a little more time to vacate the room.

It was hours and hours on the phone, hours of touch and go. Was he going to make it? And hours of angry celebrity reps trying to get their Penthouse Suite and hours of dodging paparazzi. All of whom had no clue what was really going on.

Four hours later Tom Sizemore sat straight up like nothing had happened. He was ready to rock and roll again.

"Where did the girls go? My cock wants to ROCK! AWESOME!"

The Tom Sizemore Sex Tapes was released as a sneaked out celebrity sex tape.

It was a Massive Success for my company!

Of course, no one knew we were behind it and somewhere in the bowels of my company lay the tapes of Tom, on ice, drooling in the bathtub.

CHAPTER THIRTY-EIGHT

Joining Flynt & Dishwasher Dildo

GOOD OL' BOY Larry Flynt and I went way back. Remember, I'd done *Barely Legal* magazine for him, followed by a couple of other major successes, as well as licensing photos to his company for years. Actually, Larry and I really didn't go way back; I knew him as well as someone could at that time. But there had been years when he was on such strong prescription drugs he didn't know what the hell was going on. This, a result of the shooting that left him paralyzed and sitting in his solid gold wheelchair. So, I had mostly dealt with his corporate president.

Today, Larry himself called me into his office because after more than twenty-five years, Larry had fired his president. Larry had miraculously found a treatment that didn't involve debilitating drugs and was, after years of mental absence, back at the helm.

Stepping off the elevator it looked more like an antique store with lavish Victorian décor. This was the same furniture that had been piled up at his mansion, as a result of his fling with the attractive art dealer. Such furniture had ended up overflowing the house and was the reason he opened the short-lived Larry Flynt's antique shop in Beverly Hills. A strange place with few visitors, though you could often spot Michael Jackson in costume, which consisted of a baseball cap and a pair of buck teeth (like that's going to do it!). It seemed, after the store closed, all of those beautiful antiques had now been distributed lavishly around Larry's impressive executive offices.

"I asked you to meet with me today, because as you may know, I fired my president," Larry explained in his long drawl. I was waiting to see where this was going before I reacted.

He continued, "Now, you have done some wonderful things for my company over the years and I want to talk to you about a future at Larry Flynt Publications."

Wow, Larry was trying to hire me to run his company!

I was shocked—mostly that Larry seemed to actually know through the fog his brain had come out of, that I had been behind *Barely Legal* and so many of the other deals I'd brought him.

As flattering and exciting a proposal as this was, I was too independent, too busy running my own little empire and frankly too successful to want to do that. Though having the power and control of Flynt Enterprises was an interesting proposition. It wasn't just the magazine now. It was merchandise stores, clubs and most importantly casinos. A brand and an empire in every aspect of the word. I smiled slyly at him as I considered how I could make this work.

I proposed an agreement where I could still run his company, still have the power and control, but I wouldn't have to sit in the golden office every day.

"I tell you what Larry, I'll agree to do everything you're talking about but as an 'Independent Consultant."

Larry's listening intently, "And to prove to you how good I am, I'll do it for just a small retainer, but a percentage of everything I bring in. And I mean the real net profits on what I do, so you're only paying me if I actually make you money!"

Larry was grinning from ear to ear, he loved a good deal. I of course was banking on it working out to be far more than any salary he would ever consider. We agreed, six percent.

Thus, started a year and a half long, extraordinary relationship with Larry Flynt.

I ran home to tell my husband Jason. He thought this was hot shit, "You're the fucking hottest sexiest woman alive!!! And do you know the things we can pull off with you in there?!!!" We started to brainstorm on the ways the Hustler brand could make shit loads of money and the leverage and prestige that would give us.

While the fat cat Larry had been "away," so to speak, the rats had clearly come out to play. He was loved or hated, actually reviled, by most of his staff, who were almost all intimidated in his presence. His office was intentionally set up that way with the hundred-foot-long walk from his door to his desk, across the red and gold carpet, passing the carved statues to arrive at his massive black lacquer, ornate desk. Or perhaps it was the way he had his little Victorian guest chairs set up in front of his desk. Visitors would sink into his dainty antique, soft velvet cushioned chairs that shrunk you so low down you'd have to lift your chin to even get eye level with the surface of his desk and peer up to look up at the larger than life, looming Larry Flynt.

Never would an executive dare tell Larry they disagreed with him, they'd simply nod and say yes. Larry had inadvertently created a bunch of "Yes" men.

I didn't feel the same. Perhaps because I knew I was not "staff" and could care less if he didn't like what I had to say. I would march into his office, go directly to his side of the desk, park my butt on the corner and converse with him, tits to eye level.

Larry was a brilliant man, but he wasn't always right. He wasn't out there in the trenches and couldn't possibly be up on the latest who's who and what's what of the industry. If I didn't like what Larry suggested or didn't think it would work, I would tell him straight up. That was probably a first for him and he respected that. For some reason, I felt at total ease with Larry right from the start. I felt like I could tell him just about anything.

I would soon find out there were layers, upon layers of side deals and kickbacks going on throughout his company and most everyone he did business with.

The first little distraction in Larry's life, at the time, was this conniving secretary and I say that in the nicest of terms. This woman had come to work at Hustler Publications and had the honor of working on the Tenth Floor. The floor that held Larry's palatial gold office as well as a few additional prestigious board rooms, my new office, VPs and others at the helm.

After working at Hustler Publications for a very short while she emptied the dishwasher in Larry's personal office. It was there she found something so terrible, so shocking, so gruesomely horrible, that it caused her poor gentle virgin psyche irreparable damage and harm! Scarring her for life. It was there that this poor innocent child, as pure as the driven snow… Oh My God… found a dildo in the dishwasher! How horrible it must have been!

I mean, come on! She's taken a job at Hustler Fucking Magazine, where she walks past the photo room everyday with huge blow up photos of spread pink pussy and big dicks and she is devastated by a rubber penis in the dishwasher! I don't know who I was most pissed off about, the money-grubbing bitch who purposely took a job there, so she could file a sexual harassment case, or the "justice" system that thought it worth awarding her one million dollars!!! To me this was deeming to all women who have legitimately experienced real sexual harassment.

The damage was already done by the time I entered Larry's life, but it was enough to trigger all my tiger mom instincts to protect and serve, against all who try such bullshit on my watch. I would be Larry's White Knight and champion, the defender of the golden throne (or wheelchair).

First order of business was not only to protect and serve but I must admit a little personal satisfaction of my own: Larry's websites.

You see, right at the beginning of the Internet, being on the forefront of the wave, and also having a supreme track record with my ideas, I had persuaded the then-president of Hustler that I could create and run a Hustler Magazine website. My package comprised of several players including a Web company in the valley. The owner, Dick, was a good friend of mine and had bought my photos for years. You may remember I'd already thrown him a massive bone of a deal for his company SearchABC with Yahoo, and Playboy and I'd not gotten a penny from them in return and I'd been cut out of the deal in all directions. Well later I had pitched them as the backbone to start websites for Flynt. I'd done such a good job on selling them to the President, that the President did a deal directly cutting both me and my other partners out. I'd seen these guys later at the shows touting their new Hustler site deal as well as their deal with Yahoo. Never did I get an explanation or even a "thank you" and certainly never a dime. So here I was, the Flynt president now fired, and I've been hired by

Larry to revamp whatever areas of his business needed revamping and the first thing he wants me to look into are his sites!

To my shock, the websites were not really making money at all! Really? Come-on; Larry Flynt's websites?! Now I was doubly pissed.

Larry called them directly to let them know that I was coming over to go through their records and that they better cooperate fully. I was sent by Larry on a full shit sniffing safari. Now, one would have fully expected at that time they might have apologized for kicking me to the curb. I figured they might even try to offer me a few dollars and I'd like to say that I would have been honorable enough to turn it down, but I don't know. A "sorry" would have certainly helped. After all, we went way back. But I was not taken aside by Dick nor did he even try to sweet talk me.

I started to go through some of my initial findings, "The credit card processing company… now isn't this one of your other companies, Dick?"

"Well yes but the rates are standard, we provide top quality service."

"And the hosting is that done through a different company that is yours too?" I say looking at the spread sheet, "Wow, this is huge, one hundred thousand a month, why so much?"

"Well, er… it's 'farm bandwidth.'" I looked confused but didn't want to say I'd never heard of it. He continued, "Well that's when you have multiple users."

I took detailed notes and left with a lot of data my geek husband was excited to pore through.

"What's 'farm bandwidth'?" I asked my husband. "They said it's like multiple users."

"No idea. A meg of data is a meg of data. Sounds like something they made up. It's like a sixty-watt light bulb; it doesn't matter how many people are sitting under it, it's still a sixty-watt bulb."

Within hours, Jason had pinned servers and accessed databases and printed out exactly where they were skimming and screwing up. He went a step further and with access to DEA and FBI computers he uncovered all kinds of juicy information about partners who were connected to other companies and deals, including those with Trent.

Trent was a Flynt "in-house" executive, in charge of overseeing the website operation but seemed to be awfully good friends with them. He was well bent out of shape.

The next day I went to see Larry.

"Well if you think I'm paying too much for hosting on my sites, then you need to prove it. I need quotes from other people. Get me three quotes from reputable companies."

A few days later I had the highest bidder coming in to pitch Larry.

"They've requested to land on the helicopter pad." I was kind of embarrassed but suggested an explanation, "They're from San Fran, a big tech company."

"Okay, here we go!" Larry rolled his eyes, "Sure let's see these big shot arseholes!"

The team came in laying out the full dog and pony show, as expected.

The CEO is heavily pitching, "I know we might not be the cheapest, but we're the best. We're quality and you get what you pay for."

Larry looks at me not impressed, "Okay, how much are we talking here?"

"Well, you have a lot of sites and all in, with full service... it's going to be ten thousand a month."

Larry shoots me a look. Remember he's paying a hundred k a month, "Er...ten thousand a month all in? No additional fees?" Larry makes sure he's heard correct.

"Yep!"

"What about 'farm bandwidth'?" Larry asks.

"What's that?" the CEO asks.

"Well, I dunno; if there are several people using it," Larry continues.

The CEO looks confused, "It's like a sixty-watt light bulb; it doesn't matter how many people are using it."

Larry thanked them and as soon as his office door was closed, he slammed his fists down on the desk buzzing through to his secretary, "GET ME THOSE FUCKING WEB ARSEHOLES ON THE PHONE!!!"

And so, we started piece by piece uncovering the workings of Larry Flynt's sites.

Trent happened to be in his office at Flynt's for once and called me in for a meeting. He appeared fairly friendly as he shut his office door, strangely enough locking it behind us. Then he turned, grabbed my arm forcefully pulling me close to him, and planting his face inches from mine, looming over me within spitting distance.

"Now listen here bitch! You fucking get me fired and you're fucking dead! Do you hear me?! DEAD! You do not know who you are FUCKING with!"

I was genuinely scared and looked to smooth things over quickly, "Look I'm not coming in to try to get anyone fired, I just want to get the sites running a profit for Larry and the best thing we can do it put our heads together to get these things turned around."

Finally, he calmed down a little and released me from his grip.

The more Larry learned about his web sites, the more pissed he was with Trent and pretty soon, Trent was fired, and Larry Flynt Publications saved themselves a hefty salary they were paying for nothing. I was quite happy to absorb his job, take the power, and control and oversee the website operations myself for no extra fees.

Soon after that we had a new team in place and the sites were finally rolling in the dough.

Unfortunately, I found that almost every division at Larry Flynt's seemed to be run in a similar way and thus started my long rampage at the Flynt house to turn this cesspool into a money churning machine.

CHAPTER THIRTY-NINE

Celebrity Sleuth

SEVERAL SCANTILY CLAD girls hidden in the bowels of my photo library had popped up as mini celebrities over the years. You have to remember I'd shot everyone and anyone in the biz and after they were exhausted I'd stooped to my Hollywood starlet contacts. Plus, I had bought every other photographer's work, from as early as the decade of Marilyn Chambers. So my library had become dotted with girls such as Stormy Daniels and the likes.

But one particular newbie had worked her way up the food chain to becoming a prominent semi-political figure. If you didn't know her name, you would at least know her as the girl married to a certain Mr. Mega Famous News Billionaire.

So, Mr. Billionaire's wife was lodged deep inside the lower intestines of my erotic photo library. I contemplated what I should do with these photos. Since my library was technically still up for sale, I wondered if I should tell any potential buyer who this little amateur model had turned out to be, or if I should keep my mouth shut. One look at the model release database would be a dead giveaway. Any buyer doing their due diligence would not be able to miss this. Then should I remove all the images of this one celebrity? Well that was another issue, since originals had been used, mixed up, renamed, sorted and remixed up again as different staff came in and messed up my less than perfect filing system. In addition, there were ads and electronic scans and versions out at various publications. I could never be sure to take down all the photos of her if I tried.

At this point in her life, she was hated by so many, there was no end of adversaries that would pay top dollar for these pics. Some would like to expose them in print and make the worst scandal they could, others had equally nasty intentions. Not least was Larry Flynt, who despised her and her husband and would have given everything to run her in his political venting section "Asshole of the Month." Between people she'd screwed over in business or personally to family members who wanted to get back their inheritance, I was offered top dollar for these.

There was only one real choice. Do the right thing and offer the photos to her. However, she would have to buy the whole damn library to ensure she had them all. Does this sound like blackmail? Well sort of. But there again I wish I'd had the opportunity to buy back every dumb shower scene I'd done for some Showtime movie or some stupid nude photo I'd done when I was young. I convinced myself I was doing the "right thing."

Plus, I knew this girl. Even when I met her as a young upstart she was a ball busting, money obsessed gold-digger, who would have steamrolled her own mother to get in bed with the next guy with deeper pockets.

At the time I shot these photos, Veronica was dating my friend, Randy. She was a not so innocent twenty-four-year-old and Randy about forty years her senior, so clearly she was with him for true love. She had him wrapped around her little finger, tantalizing him into buying her cars, clothes and her every whim. But on a much bigger scale, she had, according to him, got him sending money overseas and giving other pretty big sums for investments, and in particular he had sent sixty thousand dollars to China on a deal.

Randy told me she had been sponsored from China as a poor young teen, adopted through the church to a couple who raised her but then later basically abandoned her, and that she was now living in an abusive relationship with a guy who was trying to get her to marry him. What Randy didn't know until way later, was the other half of the story he later shared with a now different view of her—that apparently, she seduced the husband of the couple who adopted her, destroying thirty years of marriage. Shortly after she'd dumped him for a richer guy, until someone with more money came along who she was currently with when Randy came on the scene. The current guy wasn't abusive at all, rather also paying for everything and she was actually married to him for a Green Card. Randy was the new guy on the side who was shelling out the dough. Still, it didn't take long before Randy was dumped for a richer guy, on and on until she got the main prize –Mr. well known Billionaire.

According to a now jaded Randy, she never looked back and never returned the money she borrowed from him. All in all, I didn't really have much empathy for her. She appeared to have none for anyone else. Plus, Randy had become a dear friend and it irked him madly, looking through old love letters that she had given him, knowing that cutting him a check for his loan would have been a cuppa coffee to her and she never cut him the check. Randy urged me several times to let him do something with the pics and get his money back.

I am sure Veronica remembered that she had done a bunch of phone sex ads for me and one of those "Ooow, ah" sexy phone recordings. You know those heavy breathing, "I'm a little slut and I'm desperate to suck your dick" confession tapes. She had actually been pretty popular, and we'd run a "Win a date with Veronica" contest, for which thousands of guys had paid to record their naughty fantasies for Veronica in an effort to win the big prize. I had a shelf full of audio-clips guys had made on the nastiest things they wanted to do to her.

After much pressure from Randy, I had an attorney make the call. I wish I had been a fly on the wall on that day.

It didn't take long. Within a few hours, the head attorney of Veronica's firm was sitting across the table from my attorney. The conversation went something like this:

"Well, how do I know that this signature on this model release is actually Veronica's?" was his absurd opening gambit, arms folded, acting decidedly cool and smug about the whole situation.

My attorney passed over copies of her driver's license and college ID as proof of identification. The attorney looked a little more concerned.

"Hum. Well this doesn't give any rights to reprint the photos."

To which my attorney read from the release the parts that said something to the effect of "can use real or fake name in any publication including those of a sexually explicit nature, even in a defamatory manner…"

"Ok, err, well how bad are these photos? I heard they were not that bad."

My attorney slides some phone sex ads across the table. They show Veronica on the phone in a sexy pose. The pictures were not particularly sexy at all but in this context, it didn't look good. Veronica's attorney read the copy;

"Hooker from Bangkok will suck you dry!"

In a horrified, shocked and shaky voice, with complete disbelief he spat out, "But she's not even from Bangkok!"

Veronica's attorney looked visibly upset, like he might actually cry for a second and my attorney said he had a hard time keeping a straight face at that point.

Veronica's attorney recomposed himself, "There are other girls in some of the photos. Witnesses or accomplices, I suppose?"

That didn't really help them any. Three had gone pro and were household name porn stars and one, a porn director, who just happened to have "recently won BEST DIRECTOR IN A BLOW JOB SCENE according to Adult Video News," my attorney noted and flashed him the AVN cover article.

The expression on the attorney's face was now complete shock, "Well, where did these run? We would need copies."

My attorney explained that they were worldwide and to contact all the magazines would be a huge endeavor. Regardless, it might not be wise to let the magazines know they had a celebrity somewhere in their archives. It would be better just to keep the publications in the dark.

Veronica's attorney was clearly disturbed by the ads, but then regaining his not so poker face he said, "I would need to see the ORIGINAL ads."

To which my attorney replied, "Ah…well here's the problem. You see the originals were with a guy who is now in the state pen doing twelve years."

"What do you mean?"

My attorney was of course referring to my ad guys in New York who I had later discovered from the cover of the *New York Times* had some dubious connections. He slipped an indictment across the table he had retrieved from the Internet.

It read; "The crime family, consisting of the Captains and the Made Men…in the business of audiotext…millions of dollars…."

Veronica's attorney now grasped the severity of the situation. He took a long deep pause…

"You mean to tell me these phone sex ads that Veronica did, ended up in ads that were for the mob?!!!"

He held his head in his hands, "Oh, this is way worse than we thought…"

When all was said and done I was truly trying to do Veronica a favor by giving her the first option. I owned the rights to all of it. I could sell them all to the highest bidder and have every right in the world to do so. She was cavorting with some of the richest men in the world, and I gave her first shot to literally buy back her past for peanuts in her world, and she could go on being the high faluting lady she imagined herself to be.

After the meeting I received a response to my generous offer, a letter from her that read something like, "Don't you dare do anything with those photos or else…" My phones were tapped, cars following me everywhere and threats that indicated Veronica very much wanted to kill me.

Randy called me more than freaked out, "I don't want to talk on the phone, come over."

When I got to his house a black Mercedes was just leaving, he told me an attorney from Veronica's office had just left, "Listen he was a nice guy and we had a talk and I've decided just to forget about the whole thing."

I am dumb founded at his complete turn-around. "Did he pay you the "loan" back?"

"Er…no, I just decided to drop it. I mean I still liked Veronica."

It didn't make sense. He'd been pushing me for years to do something with the photos and he was more than irked about what she had done to him.

"I just thought about it and it's a long time ago and it's not worth worrying about."

No matter what I did he would never tell me anything different.

He was an older guy and unfortunately a few months later I got the call that he had taken a fall and died.

I may never know the complete truth.

So, what did I end up doing with the images? I gave it serious consideration but struggling with my conscience, in the end, I did nothing with them and they remain tucked away in the bowels of my archives.

Shortly after, Mr. Billionaire divorced his wife.

CHAPTER FORTY

Larry Flynt's
Ace in the Hole

I WAS JASON'S ultimate trophy wife but not because he wanted to take me home and bang the shit out of me, but because he thought I made him look good. He's out with me on his arm, "You look hot tonight, honey!" He didn't really care, but thought other guys were going to stare at me and he loved that.

At home, it was hard to get him to sleep with me. I had to find that perfect time, a small slither of a window of opportunity. You know, based on what drugs were in his system. "No honey, I can't have sex at night, you know I have insomnia and it keeps me awake afterwards!"

I'd get up at six AM to get the girls ready and he'd be just coming to bed. Ships passing in the night.

I'd try climbing back in bed in the middle of the day to get lucky, "Not when I'm sleeping. I'm being rapped! You don't care about my feelings! I'm being violated!" he'd complain bitterly.

Sex was pretty good on the rare occasion when I hit the timing right. Most of the time I was frustrated eye candy.

Working for Larry and going to meetings dressed in tight slinky business attire was definitely a boost to my husband's attraction to me, or was it the power and control of the Flynt empire that excited him. Either way we had managed to conceive, and I was expecting my third child.

Didn't slow me down. Once again, the ball busting hormones were in full force.

I was busy with Larry. Larry was probably the most uncouth man I have ever dealt with. Didn't bother me much. Certainly, after all my experiences as a model and the whole Hollywood actress casting couch scene, I didn't seem to have much in the way of boundaries in the shock department.

Larry and I were meeting at the *Four Seasons* in Beverly Hills for lunch. This was our regular meeting spot, Tuesdays, Wednesdays and Fridays. Larry had his own table to hold court, and for three or more hours, this would be our office.

As I arrived and sat down, Larry held up his index finger and middle finger together running them under his nose and taking in a deep sniff.

"Hummmm, Ah, yes," he sighed deeply with a huge grin from ear to ear. "Not gonna ever wash these fingers. That was some good pussy licking!" he proudly announced.

There were lots of rumors that since Larry's accident and the old pecker not really working, he'd amuse himself by occasionally spreading one of his models over his desk and pulling up his gold wheelchair for a nice afternoon snack.

I rolled my eyes and sat down.

At this point I'm a few months pregnant and my breasts noticeably swollen.

"How are you? How's those milking titties coming along?" he remarked, changing the subject. "Sure would like to get a suck on those fuckers!"

I shake my head, but he doesn't let up and continues, "God your husband must have a big dick to keep you happy!!!"

"Does he? ...Well? Does he have a big dick?"

Despite his crudeness I was mildly amused by his shock value talk but passed it off as one of his usual comments that didn't require a response. "Ok, Larry, I have good news. Now we have to talk about getting you that Nevada gaming license."

"Great!!! We need that. So how big is it?"

"It's average. So, I think we need to meet with my guys in Vegas, but we're looking at starting a smaller one first to get the license somewhere like Pahrump."

"Average. Fuck that! Average! There is no chance, pussy like you. God a man would give one of his balls to land you."

"It's average. Now let's look at dates for Vegas."

And this was how our typical lunch conversation would start.

Surprisingly enough, a lot of the Hustler empire was in the red and I was still rooting out all the people who'd been screwing Larry. I was uncovering one thing after another, and people were being fired left and right. I was worried that there wouldn't be anyone left. I knew Larry wasn't the most lovable person to begin with, but some of his supposed loyal staff, who had been there for ten, even twenty years, held such a grudge that they were justifying it as their right to rip Larry off.

Everything at Larry Flynt's was fear based. At the head of the Gestapo was Lydia Helmen, who I'm pretty sure was a reincarnation of Stalin. Lydia was the head of Human Resources and she hated me right from the start, since Larry hired me directly and I was well in his ear and out of her supervision. Lydia ran an intimidating and oppressive ship, everyone afraid of getting fired. I didn't understand why they didn't just walk out. They seemed to put up with the abuse for years, like some horrible repressive relationship they longed to leave but fear of the outside made them stay.

About six months after I arrived, Larry hired a new VP with an impressive resume, at the top of which, was the shining glory of Executive at Disney. He was given a very nice salary of four-hundred and fifty thousand, a year. Larry had hired him based on Lydia's insistence because of her faith in him or her probable side deal kickback. She convinced Larry it was a prestigious move and he was expecting this guy to be "The Shit."

I was instructed to "Teach Ian everything you know about the adult business." Ian was clueless. Good business concepts, but knew nothing about the Internet, phone sex, or what sex shit guys wanted on their videos. And some of the things that worked at Disney simply wouldn't work here.

He picked my brain and I gave him the accelerated education of the sex biz and how to stretch a guy's wallet ten days from Sunday.

Most of the time he acted vaguely interested in my valuable education and then tried to take credit for my work. I would present something to Larry, and Larry would ask me as a courtesy to explain it to the VP to keep him in the loop. Only then the VP would come back to Larry with the same thing, passing it to Larry as "his" new ideas. Down to titles, spread sheets, research, complete layouts, I'd already given Larry.

"Fucking moron!" Larry would say to me over lunch at the Four Seasons. "What am I paying this fucking asshole for?"

You think Larry would have just told him outright that he was on to him, but for some reason he didn't. Larry would continue to vent to me, "He was in here today with the whole Internet layout, like it was some new idea of his, and he's saving me a bunch of money with these deals! Can't this ass contribute anything of his own?" Larry was getting more and more pissed off. I didn't quite know if he was hoping to salvage this guy, due to the high up-front fees he'd paid for him, or whether he was just saving up the revenge. My bet was on the latter.

Dustin Flynt, Larry's nephew, had just gotten on board and was stationed in the video division. Larry had a few family members, like Dustin, Junior and Theresa, working in his company and where they lacked experience, they far exceeded in loyalty. Dustin was the spitting image of his uncle, with curly strawberry blonde hair and piercing blue eyes. He had drive, ambition, and a real desire for the Flynt Enterprise to make money.

Larry called me in, "Okay. I've told this guy from Disney he's running the video division."

"Okay," I replied.

"Now I want you to go work with Dustin. Dustin thinks Ian's a moron, so he's going to ignore him. I want you to instruct Dustin and tell him the way you really want it run."

"Larry, you are setting us up for a bad situation. Do you want me to help Ian, or work against him?"

"Yeah I can see it's going to be a big cock fight! I live to watch a good scrap. My Ace-in-the-Hole against the Disney asshole. My money's on you!"

And that sums up Larry.

So, I set about revamping the video division.

I wandered around the warehouse with Dustin, shelves and shelves of Hustler's video titles. I picked up one and examined it, "Hum, *Hometown Girls* presents…" a video series obviously based on my magazine creation of the same name. "What the hell, Dustin, this girl on the cover clearly has fake boobs and she's all professionally shot with a ton of make up on…" I look closely, "Starring Brandi Rage and Candy Cupps'…OMG, these are not amateur chicks. No guy who wants to see real amateurs is ever going to buy this!"

I pick up another title, "Big Top Sex."

"That was one of our really big budget features," Dustin says.

"Who the hell thinks guys want to see sex at a circus? If it's big budget, we need to compete with Vivid. We need to find the most incredible girl and we need it shot ultra-high end. That's where the money needs to go, not to some stupid clowns in the background!"

"Yeah totally makes sense," Dustin agreed nodding. "Clowns don't turn me on."

"Plus, if it's that big budget we need to shoot a version that we can sell to cable, so we can make some real money," I said, my wheels turning.

"You have any contacts there?" Dustin asks.

"Yeah absolutely, I've produced mainstream low budget movies and I've done quite a few sales with those guys." I'm now thinking about much bigger possibilities as I continue walking down the aisles.

"Oh, look at this line, 'Mega Tit Coeds' with a bunch of thirty-year-old fake boobs in pigtails, ok that's just wrong."

"Yeah they don't do much in sales," Dustin confirmed. "For someone who says she's never watched a porn movie, you seem to know an awful lot," Dustin laughs.

"Yeah…don't ask."

A day in the archives and I could understand why they were losing money.

"Okay, Dustin, let's set up production meetings with all your top directors."

In Dustin's office I sat with the crew that had been shooting the Barely Legal videos.

"Okay, enough of this high budget location stuff. We care about the girl. No more of these shoots in the Bahamas of some well-known porn star.

We want eighteen, nineteen, twenty max, in real settings. And absolutely no fake boobs."

Within a few weeks, I'd revamped the whole library, killed off the failures, and Dustin had a humming machine under him. We even had deals set up with cable companies. I dropped a copy of the progress reports, the new titles and the revenue increases on Ian's desk to keep him in the loop.

It was job well done and video division now in the black. Larry was suitably impressed, and Ian thought he took the credit for it.

That is until Ian decided he should ask Larry for a bonus.

"Well, since I made such an impact on the video division and we now have cable deals," Ian explains.

"Oh really." Larry says, listening.

Ian presents Larry with my spread sheets, "My new titles were really what made the difference. I knew when I first went through our library. I had a lot of ideas and I thought that..."

"YOU thought?!!!!" Larry could no longer restrain himself, "I'll tell you what kind of bonus you need. A bonus out of here!!!"

Larry figured the pawn in his Chess game was not worth the money and Ian was fired.

It didn't seem to have an impact on the company either way, except, unfortunately, this moved Craig up the totem pole; Craig was one of Larry's execs who pretended to be extremely nice to me in front of Larry but was one of Lydia's implants and clearly had his fingers in every cookie jar.

Luckily, I had a great relationship with Larry's financial department. His CFO, Jerry, and I spent many evenings, well after hours, going through the books, examining the bad deals and how we could fix them. He was thrilled, "This is great. We're making so much progress. No one has ever done anything like this!"

Paul was another member of Larry's team I loved. Paul had been Larry's main attorney since the days of the mob. When Larry's magazine Hustler first went on the newsstand in the seventies, the mob said, "Hey, we collect money for the magazines and you are going to pay us for every issue that goes on the stands."

Larry said to Paul, "Go tell them I'm not fucking paying them." So, Paul was the guy who had to tell the mob, Larry wasn't going to pay them!!!

When I spoke to Larry about who shot him, he just said, he knew who it was, and it was taken care of. My guess is that it was mob related.

While I was cleaning house, Lydia was still hoping to sweep me out. And she was sure baby number three would buy her some time to figure out how. She called to arrange my maternity leave.

"I'm not taking maternity leave, Lydia, so you can forget about it!"

"But you NEED to, and Larry is willing to work out payments for the time you're gone."

"Tell Larry not to worry, I'm not going to be gone."

"Huh!" she puffed and hung up.

I had made enemies who would have done anything to get me out and I knew I couldn't be away for a second. I was planning to drop the baby in the boardroom if I had to. When the birthing day finally came, I was on a conference call with my valuable client and one of Larry's execs, Craig, when I went into labor. I knew this squirmy bastard was trying to steal my client and change the deal, so I rode the call all the way to the hospital delivery room. Finally, in agony, I had to admit I was about to have a baby and needed to get off the phone. I had baby number three over the weekend and sure enough, Flynt Junior called to inform me that this sneaky shit had indeed set up a meeting Monday with my client with the probable intention to screw me over.

Imagine when I walked in Monday morning in my business suit, minus baby bump. Baby was in the car with Mom waiting downstairs.

"So why didn't anyone tell me about the meeting this morning?" I exclaimed as I strutted in, catching Craig red-handed.

I didn't miss a beat and was right back to work. It's been a year now and the Flynt Company was finally returning to its glory! The video side was making money and the Internet division was making even more but the biggest moneymaker for Flynt was gaming. Larry had The Hustler Casino in Gardena, California and we were about to take that to a whole new level. Branding the Hustler name to shops, Casinos, night clubs, even hotels.

I introduced Larry Flynt to Mr. Wild, who ran MGM and put Flynt's Nevada gaming license in play. Then on to setting up Hustler Night Clubs in Macau. Getting Flynt's company back in the black was one thing, but the gaming potential and the new branding opportunities were way more exciting. We sat at the conference table in Flynt's Vegas suite, crowded with Hollywood Players and Nevada Moguls. Flynt looked around the room at Wild and the old-time backers that were behind the real casinos on the strip. Larry said, "Gentlemen, for once, I'm the little fish in the room!" Flynt was in his element and I was in my element pushing his dreams.

CHAPTER FORTY-ONE

Royally Screwed

I'M JUGGLING WORKING with Flynt, trying to keep up with my own business and being a parent of two teenage girls at the same time. I think I'm doing a pretty good job of hiding the naked pics from the girls and making sure there are no shoots going on while they're around. Of course, teens are much more resourceful than I imagined and my office full of naked photos is just too tempting for their high school guy friends. The "Keep Out" signs were making the library area way more intriguing, and our place was apparently the most cool hang out of all their friends.

The open studio was a great place for them to throw parties, which I didn't mind, and my daughter Kyla decides to have her birthday party there. I'm over at the house on the other side of my ranch pretending to be chill, and trying to keep a discreet but watchful eye, when I look out from my balcony in horror to a never-ending line of cars entering my property and already a stadium size crowd is forming. It's an hour before the party is due to start and partiers are arriving in droves. *Kyla is very popular, but what the hell?*!!! Within minutes, there are hundreds of drunken teenagers grinding to the blasting DJ music echoing throughout the canyon like a full-on raver. I'm panicked as I see the massive crowd spilling out like the lava of Pompeii about to descend on my office. Kyla came running over freaked out that the party was clearly out of control.

I have never been so relieved to hear Sirens screeching up the canyon and surrounding my house. Thankfully it was a team of cop cars here to shut this down.

"There's five hundred people on your property but there's probably five thousand trying to get here. The whole area is blocked for miles with traffic backed up to the freeway!" one of the many police officers said flustered, as he tried to break up the party.

The teens were finally turned away.

"What the hell happened?" I grilled my daughter.

"I dunno. It was this DJ friend of mine from high school, he was just playing at this concert thing they started *Cochella* and I guess he posted it on this new site called *FaceBook*. I had no idea it was that popular!" Kyla confessed, shaken herself.

She was grounded for a month.

At that moment I realized the impact the Internet was about to have on our new generation. It was no longer just for adult entertainment, the Internet was about to change our lives in all ways.

Actually, my teens were pretty easy. My husband on the other hand was like a very difficult teenager.

Jason had just gotten back from Langley on some training camp for DEA agents and came through the door totally revved up, "OMG Gail! You won't believe this!" He opens his briefcase and in a carefully placed plastic baggie he brings out a tiny plastic see-through thing that looks like a finger nail.

"The latest in spy technology! This tiny little device is an audio transmitter. Nano technology! Can place this anywhere and get conversations downloaded to a computer. Fucking awesome, right!"

"Yeah, wow." I respond, wondering why on earth we would care. Not like we were going to bug anyone.

Jason was getting more and more paranoid, and more and more into weird cop shit. I told him he needed to cut back on the drugs, so now he has various "prescription drugs" as replacements.

While my attention is on Larry Flynt, my husband is taking care of the business at home and he has a ton of major schemes in the works, but we also seemed to be suing people more and more.

"You can't file against Dave and Janet, they're friends of ours. We've been to their house a bunch of times," I tried to reason with my husband who was rummaging through his medicine cabinet.

"Well, they shouldn't have infringed on our stuff," he says downing a handful of pills. "Shit, this stuff is awesome, take ten of these; who needs cocaine? Have you seen my black dress pants?"

I check out the bottle, a bit concerned, "It says 'take one as needed.'"

"Well I fucking NEED it!!!" he screams at me, "Has the fucking maid put my pants somewhere again?" he says frantically pulling open drawers.

"Maybe they're at the dry cleaners."

"No, they are not at the fucking dry cleaners!!! Do you think I don't know what's at the fucking dry cleaners?!!!' He's now pulling violently at the bathroom door, "God Fucking Dam it!!!" he screams kicking it and then launches his fist entirely through the door.

"Oh great!" I say, throwing my hands up, looking at the hole in the door.

He rips back his hand which is now in shreds and blood dripping all over the floor. This is a pretty regular occurrence, so I'm just pissed about the door, "Oh did that make you feel better? Well you better get that door fixed!"

"Arghhh..." he pulls the door completely off its hinges. Walks it across the bedroom and out on to the balcony, launching it onto the driveway below with a crashing bang. Edward happens to be walking by and it misses him by inches.

"Edward, Gail says we need a new door. When you get the chance, please!"

I decide best just stay out of his way for a while and take off to do errands and leave him fuming. Later that evening, I come back with a bunch of groceries. I notice Edward's rehung the door and there is a small wooden picture hanging over the hole.

Jason is lounging in the living room in a state that is a complete one eighty. As I'm putting the groceries away, he comes over with his phone set on record and with the screen two inches from my face is following me around the kitchen. He's clearly taken ten of his downer pills.

"Look who's all wound up now..." he turns the screen to his own face and continues recording, "Look at me, total calm and relaxed..." he switches back to me getting in my way as I am trying to get to the fridge.

"Jason, stop recording everyone like this, it's annoying."

He's clearly off his head.

At least things were a little more sane at the Flynt office.

For the last year, things with Larry and I were fantastic. He couldn't have been happier. He'd introduce me as his "Ace in the Hole," Singing my praises; "Everything this girl brings me is a Slam-dunk winner!" or "This fucking chick has a sixth sense that can crawl up an ass and bring out a gold nugget!"

Larry would put his money where his mouth was. If I told him we needed two mil because we were going to turn it into four mil, the money would be there the next day. Don't get me wrong, he was a cheap bastard. He didn't want to tip the valet and would get irritated with me when he caught me slipping them a few bucks. He wouldn't part with twenty dollars unless he was getting his money's worth. But he'd pay twenty million for something if I convinced him it was a stellar deal. I was batting ten for ten and not one of my deals had gone south yet.

In a way, Larry and I had become so close we were like inseparable lovers without the lovers part. There is something truly exciting, almost erotic, about the art of the deal and that ecstatic excitement two people share when they are juiced up, in the chase and the celebration you share, especially when that ends in ultimate success. Larry and I had it. Deal after deal was rolling in and we were on a high.

I really did feel comfortable enough to tell him everything and he certainly held nothing back from me. I looked forward to seeing him and was always excited to share whatever news I had. He called me constantly, late in the evening, which I didn't mind at all, in fact I got a pang of excitement when the phone rang.

Larry was ecstatic about me. The rest of the company who'd been shaken upside down—well, not so much. Larry had become so attached to me, that he would not do anything without first checking it with me. Many of his staff were well bent out of shape that he'd "need to show it to Gail first," and his wife, I had to believe was getting rather peeved about it too.

A few years earlier Larry had married his caregiver, Liz. Liz had an office down the hall from Larry's and some title to justify her presence. Her office mimicked her husband's, on a much smaller scale. A huge ornate oversized gold chair at the one end, more resembled a throne where this tiny little Filipino lady sat, her feet dangling too short to touch the ground and enough gold chain around her neck to sink a ship, in a vision that looked like Cleopatra's fortune in a scene from "Honey I Shrunk the Kid."

She may not have been a Harvard Business major but to her credit she tried, was hardworking and fiercely protective.

She hired almost everyone in her large extended family, none particularly skilled but hardworking and happy to do various mundane tasks around the office.

Larry asks my advice, "Liz wants to hire her cousin to work in the documentation department. What do you think? Will they be able to do that without any qualifications?"

"Look, it's your wife's family, just give them the stupid ten dollar an hour job. Why are you even asking? Just throw her a bone and keep her happy."

I made a big effort to be nice to Liz and encourage her and an equal effort to convince Larry to pay attention to her and keep the family politics at bay. Still, every single decision at this point was either "to be talked about with Gail at the Four Seasons" or he would call me. Almost every night I was getting these phone calls, sometimes about silly little stuff which I am sure was just an opportunity to hear my voice.

The phone would ring at like eleven PM;

"Gail it's Laaaaarrrrry…"

Like I couldn't tell from the drawling deep crackly, toad-like voice.

"Liz has this deal and it's about these websites she wants me to get."

"How much is it?" I asked half asleep wondering why he wasn't calling about the nightclub deal in Macau or something of real significance.

"How much are they, honey?" I heard off to the side. *Oh, this was not good.*

"Twenty-five hundred," he came back with.

"Twenty-five hundred?! Are you fucking kidding me! Who gives a shit if it works, just give it to her. It's your wife!"

Asking me about every business deal but also antiques he was looking at, the color of the carpet Liz wanted him to install.

My instincts told me that his wife had to be jealous of our relationship, even if, obviously there was nothing romantic going on. Dustin confided in me that at the Flynt Mansion, this was absolutely the case and Liz was getting "More than a little cheesed off."

Luckily, I was out of the Beverly Hills picture for a couple of weeks. I'd been over in Europe running around setting up mobile phone deals for Larry working with phone carriers to allow aps on phones where end users all over the world could now view naked Hustler chicks on their mobile devices.

Larry had a contract with an agent who handled these rights, *GM Mobile* who worked with some carriers over there. But GM's contract was coming to an end and new carriers were popping up, offering much better deals. Plus, if we knew how to work with them directly there was no need to pay an agent their fifty percent. My job was to cut these new deals. After a very successful trip, I'd come back with advances of ten million dollars for Flynt and more than triple the projected revenue to start at the end of the month when GM's contract ended.

My butt is perched at the end of Flynt's desk when I give him the good news.

"My Fucking Ace in the Hole!" he exclaims, grinning from ear to ear.

"You have to give notice to GM you're not going to renew within the thirty days. Make sure Craig does it."

I popped in to see Jerry the CFO who informed me of another little issue that had come up while I was gone, "Our sites suddenly got hit with a ton of returns. A big German bank. They're holding five hundred thousand dollars, which they're saying are customer chargebacks and fines. Anyway, the account is frozen, so we have to sign off on it to get our account running."

I am looking over the paperwork with Jerry, when I notice something,

"Wait a minute, look at the date here, this is from years ago."

"Yes, I know, they go way back."

My alarm bells suddenly go off!

"Wow…I can't believe they would do this…" I say scanning the paperwork, "Oh my God, I bet they did!"

"What?" Jerry asks

"Well, this is really a fluke coincidence that I know this, but a few years ago there was this bank error… Listen give me a copy of these sheets I need to check the codes."

I went to my storage to look at the retrieval notices from the bank error a few years earlier. As I pored over the papers, I realized, *"Holy shit!" These really aren't Larry's chargebacks!*

"Larry, these are not even your customers," I say presenting Larry the evidence.

"What? Why do you think that?"

"Years ago there was a bank error, well not sure it was an error, anyway millions of dollars went missing. The money never showed up but some of the customers got refunded. So, we were pretty sure the banks just spread these refunds over the major players. I can't believe that they would do this, from so long ago, but it looks like they've just assigned some of these to you. The codes on the customer chargebacks don't match any of your members. Meaning these people never even went to your sites and I'm pretty sure I can prove it."

"What the fuck!!! They can't do that!!! You need to talk to my attorneys over there in Germany."

"I did already, they think I'm right."

A few days later, documents in hand, I was to turn right back around and fly to Germany to get Larry's money rightfully returned to him.

Before leaving, I asked Larry for my six-percent commission that had been accumulating.

"Yes, Larry, I've been paid some of it, but I haven't been paid my percentage on any of the recent deals."

"Yes, we'll get to it when you get back from Germany," Larry said assuring me.

"I was hoping to get it before I left, I've had the spreads into your accounting for weeks now."

"They're working on it but we're going through a big audit right now, so they're really busy and they're going to need some time to work out all your commissions."

"Well can you at least give me my percentage on the ten mil. You got your money in the bank, there are no expenses against that, it's clean. You can figure the rest out later, but pay me the six-hundred thousand at least."

"Don't worry we'll sort it out as soon as you get back," Larry said with a genuine look.

I was a little frustrated that they didn't seem to have enough time to sort out this little thing before I left but I wasn't that concerned. Larry and I were tight, right? Plus, I was about to clear him of five hundred thousand.

On the way to the airport, all excited for my trip to Europe armed to fight the big flight for Larry Flynt, I get a call from Lydia at Larry's office.

"Gail..."

"It's Lydia."

The last person I would have expected to hear from and she sounds mighty pleased with herself.

She continues, "I have been praying for this day for a long time...."

Then she says slowly and loudly for emphasis:

"TODAY... IS... YOUR... LAST... DAY...!!!"

"Excuse me? What the hell?!!!" I replied in complete shock. I swerved my car and pulled over to the side of the freeway, wondering if I had heard this correctly.

"Larry has decided that you no longer work for us," she said smugly.

"WHAT!!! I AM ABOUT TO GET ON A FLIGHT. WHAT DO YOU MEAN?!!!"

"Gail, you know you have made a lot of enemies here and I must tell you, it was such a great pleasure to be able to make this call."

"I AM ABOUT TO GET ON A FUCKING FLIGHT TO GET LARRY FIVE HUNDRED THOUSAND DOLLARS. WHAT THE FUCK DO YOU MEAN?!!!

"That's up to you, but as of today you no longer work for Larry Flynt's Operations."

"I NEED TO TALK TO LARRY!!!"

"He's not available right now."

"PUT LARRY ON THE FUCKING PHONE NOW."

"He doesn't want to talk to you. Bye Gail."

And with that she hung up.

I'm sitting at the side of the freeway, beyond furious. I wasn't totally convinced that he even knew about this, *Did Lydia make this up. Did Larry really give this order? Did he forget I was going to Germany?*

I lit up his executive office and his home number. Over and over.

"Sorry Gail, Mr. Flynt is not available can I take a message?"

"TELL HIM IF HE WANTS HIS FIVE HUNDRED K HE BETTER PICK UP THE FUCKING PHONE RIGHT NOW!!!"

He wouldn't get on the phone, he wouldn't return my calls.

Finally, I turned around and drove home in complete disbelief.

He never got his money back from Germany.

But he was certainly about to get something else....

CHAPTER FORTY-TWO

Larry Gets His Comeuppance

A COUPLE DAYS go by and I had been officially fired. Lydia, I am sure with great delight, wrote the letter herself. I can imagine her typing with satisfaction,

"Mr. Flynt has made the decision that he shall no longer be retaining your services…"

I was sure this was the most aroused she'd been in thirty years.

I called the CFO Jerry who I'd worked so closely with, who was not only shocked, but devastated.

"Gail, I don't know what to tell you. This is absolutely crazy. It doesn't make sense."

"Yes, well just because I no longer work for him doesn't mean he doesn't owe me the six percent of every deal I brought in. So, when am I going to get my accounting?"

"Gail honestly we have your spreads, he just has to authorize everything."

"So, when can I get payment?"

"Er… I'll have to talk to him and get back to you."

I was pissed with Larry but also very sad. I'd actually grown to love Larry and all his crass ways. Plus, all that potential, all those amazing deals that were just coming to fruition. I was sure he didn't want rid of me. I knew it was pressure from his staff and even his wife. But a certain part of me knew that he'd also done it to try to get out of paying me the commission. How could he want to screw me over like this, after all we have done and gone through together? just couldn't believe it! I didn't want to believe it.

As fate would have it, a few days later, I was sitting in my home office when I get served a court subpoena; all my records and me to appear in a week's time on a mobile phone case.

GM Mobile was suing Larry Flynt for thirty million dollars.

Apparently, the day he fired me, Larry decided to take another two-million-dollar advance from these people. Cashed the check then waited three days and sent them a notice that he was no longer doing business with them!!!

He did what?!!! Yeah, Larry blatantly screwed them over!

I was stunned. I sat looking at the subpoena in total disbelief. *Why would Larry do this?* I figured it had to be Craig; Larry knew better.

Obviously, I had no choice but to go to court and of course I had to tell the truth, but my personal feeling was Flynt had totally screwed these poor guys and it was not going to bode well if I was being screwed too.

Fresh back from Europe, I was the only one with all the relevant information; Larry and his staff had nothing.

My attorney calls up Larry Flynt's office and talks to the CFO; "Gail's been subpoenaed to appear in court next week and to bring all her documents pertaining to this case. I am wondering if you will be requesting a copy of the documents."

"What do you mean documents? How many documents does she have?" he said rather confused.

"We have six hundred and twenty-three documents," my attorney stated in a matter of fact attorney way.

The CFO went silent. My attorney continued, "Also Gail tells me she is still owed commissions and I think it might be in everyone's best interest to get that resolved."

Larry Flynt's office seemed extremely concerned and there was a sudden flurry to work out my commission. No more than a few hours later a messenger arrived at my office with an envelope. It contained a check. I was nicely surprised. Then I opened it. It was for fifteen thousand!!! Reimbursement for some Vegas expenses Larry had put on my credit card.

I called the CFO a bit confused; "Jerry, thanks for the fifteen thousand for Larry's hotel bill, but what about the hundreds of thousands in commissions he owes me?!!!"

"Err... we're still going over that..."

"You can at least pay me the six hundred K on the ten mil deal. You can work out the rest later, but that money doesn't need 'going over.'"

"Gail, look, I totally get it, but er…you know what he's like. I'll talk to him again."

"I have to go to court on Tuesday morning; if he doesn't pay me before Tuesday morning, I'm going to go to court with a very bad taste in my mouth."

Finally, a meeting was set up for me to get a check at the Flynt office on the Monday. But Monday morning came, and they canceled the meeting at the last minute.

"Larry is really sorry, something came up, but we have the check ready. Larry said that we will for sure meet on Wednesday and we will have the payment for you then."

"NO WEDNESDAY IS NOT GOING TO WORK!!! If you have a check then I'll come right now and get it."

They promised and promised to deliver the check, "It is being messengered over," "Coming now," until it was Tuesday, no check and I was on the court steps.

I went to court!

Larry had two of his in-house attorneys there. Not Paul. I presumed because Paul and I had great mutual respect and he was shocked and upset at me being fired. He also knew I had all the information on the mobile case and Larry's group were completely clueless.

Larry's attorneys kept looking at their computers and didn't know what questions to ask me because they had absolutely no idea about the business.

The prosecuting attorney started in aggressively, "If you choose to hide information on behalf of Larry Flynt, we can and will file charges against you personally…" They had subpoenaed me as the most knowledgeable person on behalf of Larry Flynt's company and presumed I would go to great extremes to protect him. They had no idea I was actually sympathetic to their cause and was ready to tell the truth of course and volunteer any other information they might find useful.

As the prosecuting attorney asked her questions, I was happy to elaborate.

A question came up about a staff member at Flynt's who had been fired. Clearly, I knew it was to hide information about the mobile deals from GM. I was asked what exactly did Larry say in his office about firing this person.

The prosecutor reiterated the question, "Do you recall what Larry Flynt said?"

The judge smiled patiently, "Just give your best recollection of what Larry said in that meeting."

"Well, your honor, I don't recall the specific words, but it was something like...WHO DOES THAT LITTLE FUCKER THINK HE WORKS FOR?!!! EITHER HE SHUTS HIS MOUTH OR FIND SOME FUCKING EXCUSE TO FIRE HIS ASS!"

The judge couldn't help but let out a tiny little smile.

Larry's attorneys put their heads in their hands and sank into their chairs in defeat.

Larry lost the Thirty-Million-dollar case.

Wednesday's meeting was cancelled. I inquired again about my promised check, but it never showed up.

A few days later, I'm sitting in my office when some other attorney calls me up, completely out of the blue, "I'm calling you as a witness and subpoenaing you in a case against Larry Flynt. And I am just calling to see if you are willing to accept service?"

I mean this is a totally different case, not related at all? What are the odds? And again, I am the only one with any information. Inside I'm laughing a little.

I said, "Yeah. Okay. Sure."

And then he continued,

"OFF THE RECORD, WHAT THE FUCK DID YOU DO TO LARRY?"

"What do you mean?"

"I put your name down on the witness list and they freaked the fuck out."

I told him there had been another case from the previous week and to look it up.

I called Larry's office to see if they had put together my check yet and to let them know I was being called to a second case.

Still no payment arrived.

A week or so later, I go to the deposition for this second case and it was Larry's same two attorneys sitting there. They wilted when they saw me.

It appeared it was a deal Craig had back doored as soon as I left. I was happy to be as helpful as possible in the deposition.

That day Larry settled with the people for a very large amount and the case was closed.

I was still calling Larry's office asking if he would pay me my commission but was still getting the run around. When a third attorney called me, out of the blue, completely unrelated…. No, I am not making this up, complete coincidence. Three lawsuits in the space of about ten days!

"We just filed a lawsuit against Larry Flynt and I am going to subpoena you as a witness."

This time, I didn't even get to a give my two cents. Larry settled with them before I could even set foot in the deposition.

Still no check from Larry and at this point it had cost him way more than he ever owed me.

I was so sad. I loved Larry. Our closeness, our friendship, everything I'd done for him. But that was Larry. He'd fight to the last before willingly pay a penny and in the end, he'd screw himself.

━━◦/◦/◦━━

A little later I saw Larry at a social event. I kinda purposely went there and was not avoiding him at all. He rolled over in his wheelchair.

He scowled at me and I shrugged my shoulders with a look of, "Well you deserved it." I wasn't going to just let him roll all over me. As he came closer, getting in my face, I said in a whisper, "You met your match."

He smiled sarcastically, in a half pissed off, half admiration sort of way, "Okay, I'll give you that one. Respect, yes, BITCH!"

I thought about suing Larry for my commission but decided I really didn't want to get into years of a legal battle with him.

But above all else, I missed the bastard. I'd had a blast with Larry. Our eighteen months together had been some of the most fun times of my life and after all was said and done, I actually cared about him.

It's about six months later. Things had changed in my life and I decided life was too short to hold a grudge. I got the urge to make amends. I called his executive office to ask if he was available and thirty seconds later he was on the line. An hour later, I strutted into his office wearing my sexiest business suit and high heels. The same two attorneys were sitting nervously at the foot of his desk, sunk down in those fancy chairs, note pads out and ready. I walked straight by them, went up to Larry's side of the desk, perched my butt on the corner, like I always did, and gave him a huge kiss and a hug.

Grinning from ear to ear, he turned to his attorneys and said,

"AH, I LOVE THIS GIRL. THIS IS MY ACE IN THE HOLE."

So, we've made amends…but still he never paid me.

CHAPTER FORTY-THREE

Fall of an Empire

THE PHOTO WORLD had really started to decline. To compete with the web, magazines were going harder. There had always been a distinction between porn videos and the much softer magazines. To me, I drew a really big line between them and those lines were now getting more blurred. My husband was happily pushing that envelope.

In the old days, a shoot was a pretty big set up, with professional lighting, makeup artists and a crew. I had photographers, who were really good at their craft, working with chrome film and large format. Now, with the advent of digital cameras, any amateur could take a snap shot of his girlfriend and compete with my high-end images. More and more amateur sites, and total free porn sites were popping up, so the industry was rapidly changing.

Back home, my husband was really taking the suing business by the balls, but he was just steamrolling through everyone and making enemies left and right and I was getting revenge lawsuits back for whatever BS they could come up with.

I came in one afternoon pretty furious and Jason was just back from Starbucks, his eyes red and heavy, like he hadn't quite woken up from the half a bottle of downers he'd taken to wear the edge off. I shoved a paper in front of him, "I was talking with Brian about refinancing today and turns out I have a six-hundred-thousand-dollar judgement on the back of my ranch!!! EFI entertainment!!! Any idea who that is?"

"Er…Oh that was those guys from San Fran, we took them down remember and we got all their websites."

"So, what is this about?"

"Oh, I remember, yeah, that was some officer's loan in the agreement, we were supposed to pay it out of the sales."

"So, you knew about this!!!"

"Well I didn't think they'd put a judgement on you. They filled some kind of lawsuit and cos we didn't answer it in time, I guess we lost."

"What the fuck! Why didn't we answer it?!!!"

"Well it was apparently federal, you have twenty days to answer not thirty, who knew."

"Why did you agree to this!"

"I donno, you signed it. Babe, I'm not awake yet, can we talk about this later?"

"I signed all the things you put in front of me, you did the deal, I expected you to know what the hell you were doing!"

I suddenly realized who this is, "Wait a minute isn't that Wess, the guy that's like Mafia or something."

And I was going to have to crawl up to San Fran and tell some Mafia guy I was really sorry that we'd taken millions of dollars-worth of websites, and could I somehow work something out on this judgement. And that's exactly what I had to do!

Since everything was in my name, it was my assets that were put up as collateral, and my ass getting hit. My husband had overpromised during a cocaine high and underdelivered on the come down, and now I have to make good on all the stupid things he's gotten us into. Some of his deals of course hit and it kept me excited, but now, nine out of ten would leave us in deep shit. I had lost respect.

I was working eighteen hours a day, pushing and pushing, and putting out fires on the back end, when I found myself wondering, *What is this whole rat race about?*

I had protected and fought for Larry Flynt like my life depended on it. But was he somehow right or more deserving? Hell no!

I am silently questioning my whole existence in this business, when one weekend I took a break and went with my mom to some kind of health expo. There was this psychic woman and she was going around the room giving messages, from "the other side," like a John Edwards kind of thing. She appeared to be really good. I was thinking, *I hope I get a message from someone.* She didn't pick us, but just for shits and giggles we decided to go to her workshop the next day. We had no idea what it was about, but the sign over the door read, "How to Become a Medium."

I thought, *Oh yeah, right. I'm not going to be doing that, but this should be interesting.*

Yet, something quite profound happened that day. Somehow, I ended up on stage telling everyone the names of their dead loved ones, what they used to do and messages for the future. I had no idea how I was doing this and didn't really believe it, but, I had tapped into a whole new world.

I go home that night and said to my husband, "I don't know what happened, but I can talk to dead people."

He looked at me like I had completely lost my mind, which admittedly, I probably had.

As I start telling him about relatives he has in spirit and different things they want to say to him, he went white as a ghost. "What the fuck are you doing? Stop it. How are you doing this? ARE YOU READING MY MIND?" He is totally freaking out and didn't like it at all.

Whether it was real or not, what really happened, to this day I cannot say, but I do know that this weekend changed my life.

Now, I'm looking at this sex business, like an outsider looking in, thinking, *What the hell am I doing here!*

And I'm listening to my husband, going on about "I'm going to sue this person, and they've got this and millions of dollars that I'm going to get......" All I hear is "Blah, blah, blah."

I'm thinking, *Oh my God! What horrible, negative energy. What am I doing with my life?*

I took a hard look at what I was doing and didn't like it. Not because it was the sex biz, like it was exploitation, it wasn't that at all. I rarely felt the girls were taken advantage of, in the soft magazine business anyway. Rather, it was all the backbiting and fighting. All that time with Larry Flynt and the people who hated him. The business end of it had become a cesspool of crap, everyone was suing everyone else. It wasn't fun anymore, it wasn't helping people or positive for anyone. Even some people I considered friends had turned on me just because they thought we had money and were looking to screw me over.

I changed. It wasn't instant, but over the following months, I just started feeling different. I just didn't want to be involved in this industry anymore.

Then finally, I asked my staff to pack up the entire photo library and put it in storage temporarily, until I figured out what to do with it. My husband just looked on, staring mouth open, while they loaded the photos into boxes.

I told my husband, "I don't know what I want to do yet, but something spiritual. If you want to run the business, go ahead, but I don't want to do it anymore. I want to do something more meaningful."

This was not the power mogul businesswoman, nor the breadwinner, he signed up for. "You wanna be a fucking sideshow psychic, or a spiritual guru or something?!!! You're going to give up a multi-million-dollar business!!! ARE YOU FUCKING KIDDING ME?!!!!!"

So, Jason took over best he could, managing our adult websites and continued putting us into bad deals and of course suing people.

Meanwhile, I started to write, travel and speak about this "Other World."

I started lecturing about intuition and psychic communication. Teaching workshops, meditation and energy healing and even communicating with animals!

My husband answered a phone call for me, holding the phone out from his ear in total disbelief, "Some woman's on the phone...says she wants you to talk to her CAT?!!!!!!!!!!!!!!!"

That about did it for him.

I was still questioning if it was real, and *Am I really doing this or is it just wishful thinking?* when I was asked to speak at a Mind, Body and Spirit convention. Over a thousand-people packed the room, and I was totally in my element, loving every minute of it. People lined up to meet me, in awe of what I was doing, validating that I was really helping them. I reveled this feeling, that I was giving back and being appreciated.

I wondered exactly what happened to me and why this sudden spiritual awakening? Had I been given some special "gift" *in spite* of my background. Or actually, was it *because* of my background. To relate to the average person and let them know that you don't have to be a monk sitting on a mountain your entire existence, to bring spirituality into your life.

I mean, it was still the same "me." I still cared about material things, sure. I just wanted to act in a more meaningful way.

My mother had been a good sport, helping out in the biz all these years, but I knew she really didn't like it and wanted to do something more legitimate. So together we decided to start a group of Elderly Assistant Living Homes. A real business to make money, but also one that gives you a feeling that you are giving back in the process.

My husband said, "It's a stupid waste of money and more 'Touchy feely weak shit' you're wasting your time on."

I'd gone from ball busting businesswoman, wheeling and dealing that turned him on, to soppy, spiritual, hippie chick that was a complete turn off to him.

Meanwhile, I'm looking at my husband, thinking *I have nothing in common with this person anymore.* Not that he had changed. I was the one who changed. I was now a completely different person and just didn't relate to him anymore.

Finally, I found a moment to have a serious discussion with him, "We are just so different now and we're leading totally different lives, we should just figure out how to split everything and get an amicable divorce."

There was no look of sadness or regret, rather his expression turned to stone, and he replied in a deeply menacing tone, "If you want a divorce, sign over all of the companies to me, all your properties, everything, otherwise you will never see your daughters again. And if you don't believe I have the power to do that with my FBI connections—try me! You better lawyer up bitch!"

Shivers ran through my very soul as I realized just what deep shit I was in. I tried to placate him, smooth things over and tell him we'd work it out, that we were fine. Perhaps marriage counseling? But beneath, I wondered how the hell I was going to get out of this marriage. There was absolutely no love lost at this point.

Over the next few months, on the surface, I put on a mask, pretending to be somewhat content in our relationship and stayed in a terrible marriage because the alternative sounded way worse. Underneath I was desperately looking for a way out.

All kinds of sneaky shit was going on. He started locking domain names, changing passwords, moving contracts, having communications with banks in Panama.... He was moving accounts, moving my deals to other countries, other lawyers and hiding things. I had built this million-dollar empire and it could all go away tomorrow.

I was away on a trip, staying in a hotel room and I had left my computer on the dresser, it was opened but turned off. About one o'clock in the morning, I'm in bed half asleep and my computer suddenly lights up and turns itself on. I thought it was strange but didn't think too much about it until I noticed that the mouse cursor was moving around on my screen. *WHAT THE HELL.* I jumped up and ran to my computer and could already see documents being opened and files being searched. I scrambled to it, trying to shut it down quickly somehow but couldn't and finally pulled the battery from the back. The screen went to black. *Was some hacker trying to get into my computer?!!! And how the hell did they do that?!!!* Jason probably knew how a hacker could do that, but I was slightly suspicious and thought I better not ask him.

A few days later I arrive home knowing that he left on a business trip just hours before me. I had a voice mail.

"Hi Babe, sorry I missed you and I'm not going to be there for Valentine's tomorrow, but I left you something on the kitchen counter. We'll celebrate in a couple of days when I get home. Love you."

There was a beautiful turquoise box from Tiffany's. I opened an incredibly sweet card and a most gorgeous and expensive pendant set.

Okay, something's not right here, I thought.

Just out of curiosity, I decided to check in his closet, see if anything was amiss.

Immediately to the right behind his bullet proof vests and cop uniforms, he had a fairly large safe where he kept jewelry and valuables, but more importantly his arsenal of guns. I figured I better check inside. But there to the right was a huge pile of books covering the front of the safe. As I pulled back a few books for closer inspection I found they were not leaning at the front of the safe, there was absolutely nothing behind them. The entire safe was gone! *Hum, strange,* I thought, *Something's going down.*

I decided to pop over to the office and make sure my most important contracts and documents were not touched. I had a smaller, two drawer filing cabinet where I kept the good stuff.

As I pulled back my closet door, to my shock and horror there was just a bare corner of wall. My entire filing cabinet GONE!!!

Shit was obviously about to go down.

We talked nice surface talk for a couple of days over the phone where both of us pretended nothing was wrong, while I desperately tried to get my website passes back.

"Honey I tried to get into the back end for our websites and my pass is not working. Did you change it?" I asked, trying not to throw up a red flag that I had him figured out.

"Oh, I think I had to change them, don't remember it off the top of my head, I'll text you later when I can look them up," he said very convincingly, "Oh and by the way I wrote a check on that investment account we never use. Please don't touch any funds in there."

Oh my God a divorce attorney retainer, I thought.

I was right.

A few days later he returned, and it was the big Show Down.

I'll spare you the overly dramatic details, but it ended with me on the floor with a bust nose and him running to the wall and violently smashing his head against it until his forehead exploded in half, blood squirting out everywhere. He didn't miss a beat but pulled out his cell phone and appeared to be talking to someone, "She's beating me, she's beating me, get off me, why are you hitting me," he cried, looking into the phone like he was recording himself.

I didn't realize, but this was a call he'd made to 911.

Unfortunately for him, on the police tapes you could also hear me in the background saying, "Why did you hit your head on the wall, no one's touching you. Who are you talking to? I'm at the other side of the room, what are you talking about? Are you Okay?"

The Sheriffs took him away in handcuffs, you could still hear him as they drove away, "You have no idea who I am! I outrank you! I'm going to have you fired! You can't do this! I know my rights…"

There was a full-blown investigation into how he had gotten so ingrained with Law Enforcement and his apparent layers upon layers of bullshit. They wanted to put me in a Victim's Protection Program, you know, change my identity, move the family to Arizona where they'd give me a new life as a waitress. No thank you.

My husband was finally out of my life. But he'd succeeded in locking me out of my hundreds of websites. Revenue streams were diverted, and all the cash flow was gone. I'd been asking the universe to get me out of this industry and here it was, answered.

Strangely enough a calm came over me. That I had my life back. I had this feeling that even if he'd taken everything, he couldn't take me. He couldn't take the core of me and I knew somehow, I'd be okay. In the midst of chaos, I knew I was at the center of my world; I'd created something out of nothing, and I could do it all over again if I had to.

I was flat broke and had pretty much lost everything......except maybe, just maybe, my sanity.

My entire empire was gone. Or was it? The real gold of course had always been the library, and that remained safely packed away in storage.

CHAPTER FORTY-FOUR

Smoking Hot

AS THREATENED, JASON contacted the Department of Children's Services, trying to convince them I was an unfit mother by smearing my reputation with every HBO love scene he could find, along with the most graphic detail he could reveal of my horrible "porn" company (the very company he was running) and worst of all in his eyes, my role as a spiritual "Voodoo cult leader." Luckily after a brief investigation they found me to be a good mother and his whole scheme backfired when they turned the investigation on him. After a year and a half of demands of Anger Management and failing psych tests they gave full custody to me. He tried to sue me for spousal support and any other way he could get to me, but eventually he left to another state and thankfully disappeared from our lives.

Life must go on, and through the aftermath, divorce clean up, I had no choice but to quickly figure out how to pull myself up by my bootstraps and make a basic living out of my new "spiritual" pursuits. Most importantly, I was happily single with my three beautiful daughters safe.

Fast forward to 2017: I'd reinvented myself and found my passion and my niche as a new-age motivational speaker. I'd published about ten books on mind-over-matter, following your intuition, natural healing and how to manifest your perfect life. My audience had flipped from ninety percent men to ninety percent women. I found my voice in empowering women and loved it!

I was travelling the world speaking at health and wellness conferences, teaching workshops and leading groups on expeditions to various spiritual hotspots around the world. Of course, it wasn't the income I was used to making, but it was enough, and more importantly, I felt fulfilled.

As a speaker, I still dressed like a sexy woman who liked to keep in shape and was proud of her appearance, a stark contrast to the spiritual hippie tie-dye they were used to. When I talked about learning from life experiences and moving on from situations like crappy relationships, I was the first to admit, I'd had my fair share and I was certainly no angel. I think my candid openness about our human frailties and my encouragement to have ambition, drive and manifest material things, was all in all, a unique prospective that other women admired.

I was after all, a forty-something-year-old, divorced woman with kids and a whole lot of life experience, recreating myself for the second half of my life, and women could relate to this. It seems, lots of women find themselves at their "prime," single and at a crossroads in their career. I loved helping women see their own self-worth, encouraging them to discover new purpose in their life.

In a short time, I had drawn a sizable following, but no one really knew what I used to do before, and I never offered it up. I mean if somehow something came up, I never denied it, but it's not like I said, "I used to do this… and then I became all Godly and spiritual" or anything.

Inside, it was still the same old me. I was still an entrepreneur at heart and was for sure, earning a living out of these pursuits. And the lure of Hollywood was still there, so, when I met a reality TV producer, I was all in for filming some of these spiritual adventures. Bringing new age, thought provoking subjects, to the masses, with an entertaining twist of sexy glamour was right up my alley.

My producer took it to a network who apparently agreed. They were so seriously interested in me, they started due diligence on me. And that's when they discovered a few things they weren't expecting… "What's this about Larry Flynt and some library of sexy model photos, is this the same person?"

My producer didn't know. I'd never bothered to mention my former life!

"I was left with egg on my face, Gail. I didn't know what to say."

I had to confess and tell him my whole involvement in the industry and the story of my library. From start to finish, relayed how I came to own the images, the phone biz, *Barely Legal*, the craze of the Internet… At the end of my long retelling of my life he was stunned.

"That's an incredible story. Now that's a TV show!!!"

He wasn't the first to encourage me to publicly tell my story. Months earlier my literary agent had suggested I might think about writing a book about *that* subject. And it was a yearning in me to tell it *my* way. You see, from time to time, my past would come up. Occasionally my clients would find little snippets of my background and they'd always put it together in a way worse light. Nude shower scenes from some less than stellar HBO movie I'd done were somehow mixed in with some vague knowledge of an involvement with Larry Flynt and something about websites and the usual conclusion was; "Poor innocent girl wound up being a porn star."

….. NO!!! I WAS NEVER A PORN STAR!!!! How could I explain, that I was not some poor girl forced by luring men to do anything? In fact, that the entire business was not at all what they perceived!

I decided it was a story that was dying to get out and be told. And so, I started the nostalgic task of writing these pages. In some ways it was therapeutic, and I chuckled as I recalled some of the crazy situations I'd been in.

…. Finally, I had nearly finished the book and with the idea that this would make a great TV series, I showed it to a friend in the movie biz. He loved it and took it to a very well know production company.

"THEY LOVED IT!" he called to announce with delight.

But a couple of weeks went by and I wondered why we hadn't heard anything. I called my friend. He thought it was strange too. He did some digging then he came back, "Listen there is some press coming out that they are worried about. Here, I'll send it over."

I read it.

"Why are they so worried? In Hollywood! Really! This is nothing. Like maybe it'll distract them for a week, but really, can't see the press are going to care much. I presume it will blow over in a week or so. Anyway, I guess we'll have to be patient for a few days."

But I was dead wrong. The press did care, in fact the press had a field day. Guess who was looking to do my sexy project?

Yeah ……. HARVEY WEINSTEIN'S COMPANY!!!. And the rest is history.

Meanwhile, back to the drawing board and back to my old contacts in Hollywood.

Having been excited about a TV series, based around my photo library, I had big plans to resurrect the library itself. Surely if my book had any success, there could well be a number of people interested in buying my library, which was still neatly tucked away in my old photo studio.

The business had changed quite a bit, but the library still held immense commercial value, especially with the futuristic synthespian rights we owned. However, it was my belief for a long time, that the real value would not be the commercial value, rather it would be for a private collector. No other collection of images comes close, and I was sure that to hold the largest library of this kind would be a great cue for someone.

My daughter Rachel was on the road to becoming a pretty famous artist. Very talented but being stunningly beautiful hadn't hurt her either. A woman from Playboy attended one of her art exhibitions and suggested that she shoot for centerfold. Rachel came to me, "What do you think about me posing for Playboy?"

"Absolutely!" I encouraged her, "Just make sure they mention you're an artist."

They did! And she became one of the very last girls to ever become a Playboy centerfold. Now almost every hot-blooded male celeb wanted Rachel to come to their private home and measure up their place for a custom piece. She was flying around on private jets and with men falling at her feet, her art was high in demand.

Most of her paintings were large ten-foot "installation" canvasses of modern art. In addition, she had become a contributing photographer for Playboy.com, shooting sexy pics of playmate friends. And she'd done an art exhibition, incorporating both sexy photos of herself and friends, embodied into large art pieces.

One night I'm watching one of these E Entertainment type shows and there is Rachel being interviewed. The host noted, "You're so beautiful, feminine and yet you have such a strong side and good business head!"

Rachel laughed, "I learned everything from my mother!"

What? She said WHAT? Rachel and I had never talked much about what I used to do, and I naively thought I'd kept most of it hidden. I'd never heard Rachel say anything like that, and there she was on TV, telling the entire world her mom was her idol businesswoman.

"Yeah, Mom, you were a mogul. You ran Larry Flynt's empire!" she boasted. I was shocked. She'd obviously paid much more attention than I thought.

So, with the possibility of a book and TV show, Rachel and I had already teamed up to take several of the sexy images from my library and incorporate them into art pieces with the aim to do a gallery showing and offer up, not only these art-photo pieces, but the entire library.

Anyway, moving on from the Harvey Weinstein debacle, I now have even better prospects lined up for my sexy project and the future looks bright and rosy.

It's almost Christmas but still warm here in Southern Cal and I'd been out to dinner with a friend, discussing the book. I'm now home on the ranch. As predicted, this night was a very wild "Santa Ana Winds" night, where the winds come howling through the canyon, something we Los Angelenos expect this time of year.

Whether it was the noise from the wind or whether I was just restless, I found myself awake in the middle of the night, up doing emails and making final tweaks to my book. I looked at my computer time display: 3.00AM, too early to really wake up. I decide I'd climb back into bed and try to get back to sleep. My daughter had snuck into bed with me earlier, due to the banging of the windows and the shaking of the house from the violent wind outside.

Snuggled back in bed, now half awake, half asleep, there was a loud booming bang that echoed throughout the canyon. *Wow another big tree limb or a barrel or something huge flew off and hit my house,* I presumed, envisioning the usual clean up in the morning after these kinds of winds. A second later there was a huge flash of light that lit up my entire room. Half asleep, I presumed it was a text on my cell phone across the room but couldn't be bothered to get up and check it. But a few seconds later I was startled completely awake by the loud ring of my house phone.

"GAIL!!!!!!" I instantly recognized this as my mother's screaming voice. She was calling from her house, a few hundred feet downhill from mine. This time my mother's panicked voice was a gut wrenching, terrified scream.

"FIRE!!!! LOOK OUT THE WINDOW! A HUGE FIRE! THE PYLON!!!!" she screeched frantically with no misunderstanding this was a dire situation. I looked towards the window and could instantly see the entire outside looked like daylight. Daylight with an orange glow. Oh, dear Lord, the bright orange glow was FIRE! And, right out of my front window, square in my view, on the hill facing us, I could see the high-voltage power grid tower was arcing electricity like a giant firework going off. Huge lightning forks, striking all over the hill, creating fire bombs. The base of the tower was covered in concentrated bright yellow flames, like an unnatural glowing fluorescent light bulb, so bright it was illuminating the sky for miles, like the end of a hot poker shoved in the ground. But the main source of the problem was arcs of electricity coming off the higher part of the tower, striking several times a second and igniting the dry bare patches of hill below. The resulting flames were running down the slope and jumping sideways, at high speed. The entire area was completely lit and bright. Even as I'm watching, the fire was spreading rapidly, racing out, across, and down towards us. I was stunned, paralyzed with fear as my grip released in shock and the phone dropped to the floor.

We had been through fires before, close ones, where the red glow of the fire could be seen coming over the crest of the north hills in the distance and they were extremely scary. But this was very different, this was already upon us and it was completely terrifying. A massive wall of fire, covering the entire front side of our ranch was now forming right in front of us. Not coming over the ridge, but right here and now. There was not even a second to stop and call 911, I knew there was less time than that to get out of the house. We needed to run for our lives and NOW. My heart leapt, adrenaline hit my veins and I was in full panic mode.

I screamed at the top of my lungs in complete terror at my daughter ripping back the bedding at the same time, "FIRE!!! GET OUT NOW. WE HAVE NO TIME TO GET ANYTHING, WE NEED TO GET OUT NOW!!!"

I frantically pulled on my jeans that were lying on the floor, slipping my toes in half my sneakers and grabbing at my T-shirt next to them. My daughter jumped up instantly, with a look of complete terror on her face. She had never before in her life seen me in such utter and complete distress. She flew out of bed and passed me, running out of the bedroom and down the stairs at top speed. I followed her running for the bedroom door, I grabbed my handbag, computer and phone, pulling them from the wall sockets in one fell sweep without stopping for a moment, to run at full sprint downstairs. My heart was pounding wildly and inside I was in complete terror.

I saw our Saint Bernard Ruthie running anxiously in and out of the living room French doors that had all been flung open by the wind. I ran straight to my daughter's bedroom screaming her name at full belt, as I ran down the hall, but she wasn't answering, she wasn't there. *OH MY GOD, WHERE DID SHE GO?* I panicked, my heart racing, I ran back into the living room, where there was no sign of my daughter. I was distraught, yelling my daughter's name, now in a frantic, horrified panic, before realizing she may be more organized than I thought, *She must be in the car already.* She was. No shoes, in T and underwear, she was already in the car in the driveway, exactly as instructed. I couldn't see my dog Ruthie now, but I had no time to get her anyway. The doors were open, and I knew Ruthie could run out and at this point all I could think of was to get my daughter and save my mom before the flames came over the top of her house. I needed to get to my mom and fast.

Outside the front door, I was hit by a blast of seventy-mile an hour, boiling hot wind, pushing me over, like a giant hairdryer on maximum heat. I could see my daughter inside the car in the drive but straight in front of the house was the power tower. The base of the tower was engulfed in glowing yellow flames, yet the upper part of the tower was still shooting out more forks of electricity over and over, hitting spots on the hill like lightning striking. Each hit looked like a match dropped on an oil bed, instantly exploding in what had to be twenty-foot flames, then jumping and running wildly down the hill. Fire was now engulfing the entire mountain and raging down at high speed, an impressive and horrifying sight. The heat all around us, was like being in the desert in one-hundred and thirty degrees while standing a few inches from an open fire and it burned my cheeks as I ran to my daughter in the car.

Now, no more than thirty seconds since my mom alerted me, the fire was rushing down the hill like cannon balls of flames. The heat was so intense because we were in the mouth of the fire and I knew my mother was even closer to the center. The whole area was daylight, like a huge spot light from both the brightness of the flames and the tower itself.

I could see the exit points off the ranch were quickly closing up, as this massive wall of fire raged towards us.

I needed to get my mother out, and I knew we only had seconds. As I got in the car, I prayed to God and whoever was listening to please get us out of here alive, yet I doubted very much it would be possible. I would have given us about a twenty percent chance of survival at that point. We needed a miracle. I was shaking and scared to death, but my muscles were running on pure adrenaline.

We are in a box canyon with the only exits onto the canyon road which was now completely on fire, behind us are miles and miles of tall hills. Our animals might be able to run into the hills behind us and have a better chance at survival, but our only way out was through a wall of flames coming down on top of us.

I drove down to my mom's house, no more than five-hundred feet from mine, where my mother was standing on her porch in her dressing gown.

I jumped out of the car screaming at her, "GET IN THE CAR!!! GET IN THE CAR!!!" She hesitated probably for a split second, but it felt like an eternity. I presumed she was probably thinking about whether she should get the animals. I was scared to leave the car and my daughter for even a second in case it would be overcome by flames, but I ran on the porch, jammed the door open for our cats to get out and literally pulled my mother away. She told me later that she had just given up, that she was certain at that point we had no chance at survival and we were all going to die.

But I wasn't giving up and I pulled at her, forcing her to run. By now we were in a complete fire storm, the intense wind blasting us, with not only ashes, but whole chunks of burning wood flying at us at high speed. Heads down, dodging the flying pieces, I felt a hot chunk of debris scrape the side of my face and stick to my hair, setting my hair on fire. More pieces were burning through my thin shirt. I was screaming to my mother but could barely be heard over the loud noise from the howling wind, crackling sparks and banging flying debris all around us. There was a pungent burning smell, but not of smoke, rather a smell of intense burning heat, like the smell of the white-hot flames of a blacksmith's furnace. In fact, smoke was probably hundreds of feet above us. We were at the core center of the furnace.

The horse corrals were immediately behind us, but our exit was closing in and I knew a minute to open the corral would be more time than we had. I couldn't risk turning back to the horses and perhaps my car with my daughter being overcome by flames. I reasoned that if the fire kept going down the road in the direction of the wind, the horses would be missed and safer where they were anyway. Either way, we were in a complete fire storm now and all I could think of was trying to get my mom and my daughter out alive. If I hesitated for a second, it could have been their lives. There was not a second to spare. My heart was racing wildly, and I was more terrified than I know I have ever been in my life, my thoughts solely on the survival of my family.

Mom jumped in the back of the car, I jumped in the driver's seat and we sped across the bridge to the gate.

The gate was now completely engulfed in flames, fire over each side and covering the mechanics completely but as the car hit the sensor pad, the gate started to slide open, amazingly the electric worked. An electric cable on fire drooped from the burning oak tree branch above, onto the hood of our car. The intense winds were blowing this wall of fire directly into our car and it felt like we were being roasted alive by a massive blow torch. It was as if we had entered a car wash but the brushes on the sides were our trees on fire and the spray of foam was a spray of burning ash. Then warning sensors started to light up on my car dash and I wondered how long the tires would stand the heat and if the car would still drive with no rubber. The gate was opening but it was too late, the road beyond the gate was just a ball of intense yellow flames like the middle of a furnace. The thousand feet of road that you can normally see, was the center of a cavern of flames. There was not even a tiny clear hole beyond and it looked like certain death.

I made a quick decision, backed up at full acceleration, screeching the tires and spun around. I hoped and prayed the north gate exit might be a better shot. As I drove back passed my mom's house, there was now a huge tree limb on fire completely covering the road making it impassable and I drove up over the grass and sprinklers, maneuvering our passage. Our tree line at the edge of the ranch was now on fire, whole trees engulfed and devoured by flames in a fraction of a second. Entire hundred-foot trees going off in flames like a flimsy piece of tissue paper as the fire-blazing wind torched our tree tops. The sensors on my car were lit with warnings lights and bells going off and I worried that the fire and heat had already burned holes in our tires and the car would simply give out on us any second. *Please let the car keep going,* I prayed in my head.

We are now in a complete fire storm, whole branches and huge chunks of burning trees and debris hitting the car windshield. I tried to make the turn to the north exit, but another massive tree down was blocking that road completely. I had to maneuver around, driving off road, through woods and finally able to get over the north bridge to the north side. Passing the studio building, I honked wildly to wake my worker who stayed in the back. "He must not have slept there last night, because no one could sleep through that," we all satisfied ourselves. We were wrong, he was there, and luckily, he would escape just a few seconds later.

We can now see the north exit in front of us. The fire is rapidly covering this side of the road but there is still a few feet of gap. The high voltage tower is still in full view and still throwing electric arcs setting fire to any remaining bare patches below it.

I barely ever take this exit and I didn't know if I had an electric gate opener for this particular gate. If not, there was no time to stop in the office, I was ready to ram it at full speed. Frantically pulling at my glove compartment, I felt the square gate clicker. I prayed to God that this was the correct one. As I hit the button, the gate metal cranked and started to pull back like a snail. OH MY GOD! THANK GOD! The gate slowly rolled back. But now the entire hill in front of us is also on fire. It's like a five-hundred-foot-high wall of flames coming right at us and the gate couldn't open fast enough. Then the only exit was to drive right into it.

"Maybe we're safer to go back and stay in the house?" my mother reasoned, terrified at the sight before us and seeing that this exit was closing in too. But I was already flooring the accelerator. This time at least, I could see safety on the other side.

A few horribly frightening seconds of scorching heat, we all held our breath and tensed for the worse and then we were through, beyond the fire and we could breathe.

The fire was moving fast on our tail up the road, headed north, but luckily the intense blow torch of wind and fire was directed south down the road and at this point just touching the side of our ranch. We prayed it would not cross the few hundred feet more, onto the buildings on our property and most heart wrenchingly, the stables.

Driving away and around a couple of bends, we could breathe a small breath. We had made it out alive and the bulk of the fire was behind us. However, our animals were still in there and we needed help to get them out. It was heartbreaking, but I also knew that a second to get them could have been death for all of us including any pets in the car. They could at least still run into the hills and maybe have a chance to outrun the fire. I tortured myself counting back the seconds and wondering if I could have gotten the animals out, but I knew that a few more seconds and we would not have been able to get out ourselves.

I was desperate to get up the road to the back side of our neighbor's house where we paused and honked and honked as we knew they had no way of knowing fire was upon them.

We needed to get help as soon as we could. There hadn't been an extra second to call 911 from the house and there was no cell service, so at this point we knew being the first on scene as it were, The Fire Department didn't even know yet. We needed to get to cell service fast.

As we drove up the hill, we were out of immediate danger, still the fire was on our tail, growing and spreading. Then as the canyon road makes a sharp right turn away from the fire, we could look back to see how massive it had become in just these few minutes. It was even now, probably hundreds of acres.

We prayed that the fire would stay to the west of our canyon, heading down the canyon in the direction of the wind and not cross onto our property. As we were looking back, a fork of fire, probably thousands of feet long, jumped eastward in the direction of our home and within a few seconds the whole southern mountain range lit up. We hoped to God that it wasn't our ranch, but it sure looked like it was.

A few minutes later we were frantically calling 911. But we knew no fire department could get near the center of the fire which was of course our home. We just prayed and prayed that by a miracle it had spared us and just somehow scorched the one end before continuing down the canyon. We prayed for our animals.

Finally, we arrived at Bear Divide, the Ranger Station, shaken and distraught, we were safe. Fire trucks were on their way. We begged every agency we could to try to get our animals out. No word came back. We tried ourselves to get back up through the burning roads, but the fire trucks wouldn't let us pass. The canyon continued to be consumed by the raging flames. There was no access back and all we could do was wait and pray.

This would turn out to be one of the largest and worst fires in California history. Other witnesses said it was jumping at a football field a second. In fact, minutes later, it had ravaged through the whole canyon and was on top of the fancy riding stables at the very bottom of the road, four miles away! All in all, it took out over fifteen thousand acres and hundreds of structures.

How lucky we were that my mother was woken by that same echoing big bang that we both heard, that presumably actually came from the power tower. How lucky we are that she decided to get up when she saw the flash of light that I saw. That she actually looked out of her window and saw the high voltage tower sparking electricity and saw the very moment the hill ignited, the very second the whole fire started. It was a complete miracle, as even a few seconds later it would for sure have been a whole other story.

The fire was still burning dangerously for days and firefighters couldn't even get in, as the entire area continued to burn out of control. All we could do was hope and pray. Pray for the animals that were still there and that our homes and business were still standing. We were holed up in a hotel for days, not knowing and feeling helpless and distraught.

It was three days later when anyone was able to get close. As we drove up the burned-out canyon, still smoking with odd patches of flames, it was a scary road of devastating destruction. An eerie reminder of that night of terror, running for our lives, that would haunt our thoughts, playing havoc in our memories for years to come.

Still I was hopeful that everything on our ranch had somehow been spared but I tried to brace myself for the possible outcome.

Nothing could have prepared me for what I saw.

COMPLETE DEVASTATION.

My home of twenty-five years burned to the ground and unrecognizable, everything I owned gone. My stables devastated, and worst of all, our two ponies perished. Our chickens, rabbits, birds, turtle… gone. And our dog Ruthie, missing. Words cannot express the feeling of loss. I stood frozen and disoriented, shaking and writhed with disbelief; and at the same time, guilt, regret and complete horror and sadness came over me simultaneously. I would forever torture myself reliving and counting those last seconds, wondering if I could have, should have, done something different.

The images of my beloved pets those last few moments with burning debris everywhere and now the heart wrenching scene that tormented me. I wanted to tell them with all my heart how sorry I was that I had let them down. My heart sunk so low, all the air left my lungs and I couldn't catch my breath again. Tears ran down my face, and yet I stood there speechless. I couldn't mutter a word. It was as if I didn't quite believe it. We had been through fires before and had always come through, I was certain we would be unharmed, but here it lay in front of me, the horrible smoldering sight. I didn't believe it. I couldn't comprehend it.

All around for miles was just ash and smoking dirt. Nothing was left to recognize as anything. The heat had been so intense, even the metal was melted to the ground. Not a scrap of anything had survived. My two-story house was now just a few inches of smoking dust. Confirmation that had we stayed a moment longer, had my mother not been looking out of the window at that very moment, had I slept an extra minute, we would have been inside that raging furnace.

And now it was clear, the unforgiving rampage in this fire's path. My office, a burned pile of ashes. My guest house just a stone chimney remaining. The bridge we had escaped over, now just a hole with some molten metal, a reminder of just how close we had come.

And my three-story studio…. completely gone, burned to the ground. The studio that housed my photo library all these years.

OH MY GOD NOOOOOOOO!!!

THE ENTIRE PHOTO LIBRARY!!!

Over one million original chromes! Plus, all the model releases. Plus, all the hard drives containing digitized versions of these images and all the digital files. Not only the originals but all the copies, the only backups in existence…ALL GONE. The video masters, the audio tapes, the magazine plates… all of it! ALL GONE!

Photos I had bought out from the era of Marilyn Chambers, the sixties and seventies. Magazine layouts I had produced through the eighties and nineties and through the creation of the Internet…. **ALL GONE!**

THE ENTIRE PHOTO LIBRARY HAD GONE UP IN SMOKE!!!!

Years of history that could never be replaced… All up in smoke!

A few burned out remnants that could be made out as bits of 35mm photo chromes and some odd shards of burned paper that could be identified as model releases, or copyright filings, were all that was left among the ashes. The largest library of this kind, in the world, and all that remained was a few inches of ash.

Now just a memory, a story…

It was now over.

This time, I had truly been left with absolutely nothing.

And yet I was so grateful. My mom, my daughter and I had survived, despite the incredible odds against us. I realized at that moment, that the most important thing in life is our family, our loved ones. This fire was not the hardest thing anyone has ever been through. I have friends who have lost loved ones or who are dealing with health crises, and I knew at that moment, I was lucky. The fire had taken away all my possession, all my business, and yet I was still okay and that made me feel strong. To know that even without anything, I'd still be okay.

It was not going to be easy, but I knew I had three amazing daughters, and an incredible mother and I knew that once again, we would pull it together.

We would rise like a phoenix from the ashes because, well… that's what strong women do!

Acknowledgments

WITH DEEP APPRECIATION, I thank the following people:

Joel Gotler, one of the best agents in the business, for believing in me as a writer and encouraging me to come out of hiding and to write this book. And his East coast counterpart Murray Weiss for his expert direction and determination to get the right publisher.

My long-time friend and Hollywood Manager Mike (Greenie) Greenfield for his support throughout my career and his enthusiasm and connections to get this book to the right people. (Yes, he's in the book).

My dear friend and attorney Peter Dekom who encouraged me years ago to write this book and for his continued advice.

The brilliant writer Sean-David Morton, who taught me much along the way and contributed his wit and humor.

Alexis Gargagliano, who's pointers helped me stream-line my manuscript which was way too long.

Leonard Rosenbaum and his OCD book review.

Michael Levine my friend and publicist for his cutting-edge vision and wealth of experience.

And most importantly my family; my mom and my girls who believe in me and support me through my crazy adventures. For it would not be possible for me to write without their beautiful and loving acceptance. That being said, my mom hasn't read it yet so I'm cringing at the thought, and I don't know what my older daughters will think. My youngest isn't allowed to read it until her 18th birthday!

About the Author

WELL, IF YOU got this far you know me pretty-well already!

We are rebuilding the ranch after the fire and looking forward to returning to our beautiful home. I am close with my three beautiful daughters, who are each successful in their own right and the youngest one still lives with me.

I am friends with most of my Ex's and occasionally talk to my two ex-husbands, although they may not speak to me again after reading this. I am a hopeless romantic still waiting for Mr. Right to sweep me off my feet.

Although this book may change the way people view me, I am happy that all sides of me have been revealed.

It's been fun reminiscing about this crazy time in my life, a time I thought was long gone. I am now excited to move onto the next chapter.

My life experience may have been a little different from most, however I believe this has helped shape me. I hope to continue as a speaker, teaching workshops with a passion to empower people to believe in themselves.

www.GailThackray.com
www.RunningWithWolvesBook.com

16278276R00179

Printed in Great Britain
by Amazon